Rural India and Peasantry in Hindi Stories

Rural India and Peasantry in Hindi Stories

Narratives After Premchand

VANASHREE

OXFORD
UNIVERSITY PRESS

Great Clarendon Street, Oxford, OX2 6DP,
United Kingdom

Oxford University Press is a department of the University of Oxford.
It furthers the University's objective of excellence in research, scholarship,
and education by publishing worldwide. Oxford is a registered trade mark of
Oxford University Press in the UK and in certain other countries

© Vanashree 2023

The moral rights of the author have been asserted

First Edition published in 2023

All rights reserved. No part of this publication may be reproduced, stored in
a retrieval system, or transmitted, in any form or by any means, without the
prior permission in writing of Oxford University Press, or as expressly permitted
by law, by licence or under terms agreed with the appropriate reprographics
rights organization. Enquiries concerning reproduction outside the scope of the
above should be sent to the Rights Department, Oxford University Press, at the
address above

You must not circulate this work in any other form
and you must impose this same condition on any acquirer

Published in the United States of America by Oxford University Press
198 Madison Avenue, New York, NY 10016, United States of America

British Library Cataloguing in Publication Data

Data available

Library of Congress Control Number: 2022913614

ISBN 978–0–19–287157–2

DOI: 10.1093/oso/9780192871572.001.0001

Links to third party websites are provided by Oxford in good faith and
for information only. Oxford disclaims any responsibility for the materials
contained in any third party website referenced in this work.

Contents

Introduction: Rural India and Peasantry in Stories 1
   The Focus of this Study on Narratives in Hindi 3
   Rural Economic Conditions: Era of Premchand and the Rise of Hindi   4
   India's Freedom Synchronized with the Freedom of Peasantry 6
   Post-Independence Rural India and the Programmes Espoused
      by the State 7
   The Impact of Green Revolution: Agriculture Embodied
      Chaos of India in the Throes of Development 9
   Fasal Bima Yojana 2016 (Prime Minister Crops Insurance Plan) 10
   Indebtedness and the Financial Assistance Programmes 10
   Gram Swaraj: A Farce 11
   Agrarian Society in Deep Distress 13
   Why Only Short Story 21
   A Note on Translation of Excerpts from Hindi into English 22

1. Village India: Difficult Stories 27
   'There Cannot Be Good Stories of Peasantry; There Are Only
      Difficult Stories' 28
   From Premchand to Shrilal Shukla: Colonialism to
      Elite Nationalisms 29
   Winter's Night ('Poos ki Raat') Is Severe 30
   Usury Renders Them Refugees in Their Own Land 32
   Tortuous Snare of Moneylending: Private Loaners and
      State Assistance Programs 33
   Panchayats to Rural Banks: Agencies of Rural Welfare 33
   Doublethink in the Welfare State: Experts and Intermediaries 35
   Deal Done! An Ailing Buffalo with Three Teats 37
   Poor Peasants, Targets of Indignity of Vasectomy 38
   Indirect Violence: Land Ceiling Act 39
   Rural Population, Streaming to Distant Lands 39
   Clearing of Forests Have Cleared Even Vultures and Bats,
      Neel Gai, or Even the Crowd of Deer 40
   The Village, a Site of Crimes, No Police Patrolling 41
   The Caste of Power Matters 42

Toddy Sinks Hori into Unthinking Stupor, Prolefeed Lends Illusion	43
Dreary, Drudging Village, but There Is Surfeit of Bright Images to Keep the Blues Away	44

2. Land Grab: The Dispossessed in the Spectacles of Jugaad — 51

Faustian Bargain: 'Bhudan'	53
They 'Hold Your Nose from Behind'	54
Resistance to Indigo Planting: 'Chest Stained with Blood'	55
The Grim Outcome of Development	57
Chakbandi (Land Ceiling): Benami Holdings and Profiteering in Dikshit's 'Darwaje vala Khet' (Farm at the Door)	59
Spectacles of Jugaad: Surplus Lands in the Phony Names, Divorced, but Not Divorced Wives, Temple, Cats and Dogs	61
Manipulating Provisions of Law	61
The Aggrieved and the Sahib; Sahib Has No Patience for Nonsense	63
The Destiny of Marked Letter: They Reach Nowhere	64

3. Small Farmers of Cane and Paddy: Post-Harvest Delays and Non-Payment — 70

Difficult Relationship with the State: The Bowl of Sugarcane Farming	71
Maiku's Travails of Wait: Such a Long Journey!	72
The Set-up Is Staged: Heckling and Manhandling	73
Flouting of Moral Economy: Death by Starving or Cardiac Arrest	76
The Village Administration and the Profiteers: Hassles of Long Wait	77
Middlemen, Grocers, and Dealers Slide Ahead of the Farmers	78
Difficult to Seek Hearing: Sahib Speaks English	79

4. Women Peasants in Triple Jeopardy: Conmen as Philanthropists — 83

Women and the Village Administration	84
Land Remains a Covert but Contentious Issue	85
Saguna's Derangement and Death	87
Treacherous Plan to Usurp the Land	88
Saguna's Plot of Two Bighas Is the Target	89
The Stronghold of a Race of Parasites: The Handler-Manipulator	90
Land Declared Benami: No Scope for Damage Control	92
The Development: Reality Check	93
Human Trafficking and Murders: Underbelly of Rural life in 'Kasaibada'	94
Women Complainant: No FIR at the Police Station, but Sexual Expletives	96

Special Connect with the Police: Villages, the Site of Roguery, Addiction, Arrack	98
Illiteracy of Womenfolk: The Literate Offenders Defend Their Crime	100
New Class of Rich: 'Progenies of Parasitism'	100

5. Why Do Rural Poor Continue to Remain Poor and Uneducated? — 105

Wrongs, since the Foundation of New India after Independence	107
Dearth of Adequate Number of Schools: Village School in Debris	110
Caste Identity, Branding, and Expletives	112
Casual Cruelty to Inhuman Punishment: 'Can Studies Make a Crow Sprout the Peacock's Wings?'	113
Pairavi, Jugaad: The Crafty Deal to Manipulate School Inspection	115
Trying Times Force Us to Call 'a Donkey Our Father'	116
Post-Mandal Storm: Forged Upper-Caste Solidarity	119
Male Teachers: Lower Female Attendance in Rural India	119
Status Quo Challenged that Calls for some Shadayantra (Conspiracy)	120
Fault Lines in the Rural System of Pedagogy	122

6. Rural Migration: Dismantling Rural Resources — 127

The Presence of Migrant Subculture in the Cities	128
Peasants, Non-cultivators Associated with Farming, Buckled under the Pressure	129
Straddling Country and the City: Mansaram's Craft and Labour is Not Wanted	130
Times Have Changed the Village and the Values	132
For *Pardes* (Foreign Land): The Tough Toiling, Precarious World of Migrant Labourers	133
Harassment at the Hands of Employers or Police or Anti-social Elements	136
Drift into Criminal Route: 'The Boats Capsize, Where? Nobody Knows!'	136
Weavers Made to Abandon Their Work	137
Lives Hostage to Anonymity, Could Have Sinister Ends	139

7. When Hunger Hits the Rural Poor, Aged, and Disabled: The Meal of Mice and Dead Cow — 143

Premchand's 'Kafan': The Indignity of Hunger; the Joys of a Good Feast	143
Disabled in Rural India: No Friendly Infrastructure	145
Hunger and an Injured, Disabled Body	146
The Ritual of Punishment	148

Starving in Parched Fields: Jayakaran's Ordeal	149
The Caste Tensions Polarized the Upper Caste, The RED Flag Instigated but Failed to Help	149
Mango Kernel and Field Rats	150
The Famine Relief and the Intermediaries: The Red Card Was Withheld	151
Manoeuvring: Prem Kumar Mani 'Jugaad'	153

8. Farmers in Death Row: Farming—Risky, Sisyphean; Usury—Back Breaking — 157

Peasants Not Attuned to Alternative Modes of Subsistence	158
Drought, Debt, Daughter: 'Pret Chhaya'	160
Farming on Lease, Vagaries of Weather, and Predators of Drought: 'Prakop'	163
Drowned in Suffering, None Could Understand	165
Peasant's Death Is a Commodity: Police Extortion	165
Wrath of God and Ludicrous Relief: 'Tractor and Suhaga'	166
'Mukti': The Promise of Quick Money	169

9. Despoiled Environment: In the Politics of Integrated Development, Money Grows on Trees — 178

Nepotism, Bribery, Complicity in Corruption, Cut/Commission	179
The Rise of Swami/Guru	181
Village, a True Model of Communal Amity or Business Interest!	182
Discourse of Progress Overawe the Common People	183
Appropriation of Land, Deforestation	184
Trees Are Withered Skeletons: When Corruption Infects the Sovereign Segment of a Society, Every Individual Becomes a Predator	186
The Destiny of an Ancient Forest: Instead of the Trees, Trucks Line Up: Logging, Stealing, and Auctioning	187
Corruption and the Politics and Economics of Development	188
The 'Finished' Job of Transporting the Stolen Goods	189
The Sinister Sound and Sights of Logging	189
The Seed Capital and More Network	190
The Land Utilization Act and the Project: Slaughter Trees	191
State's Ownership of Forest	193
What Are the Implications of Despoiled Environment?	193
Slow Violence: Calamities That Are Slow but Long Lasting	194

References	199
Index	207

Introduction
Rural India and Peasantry in Stories

Let us be down to Earth
Trees that want to touch the sky must extend roots into the earth

The stories[1] of rural India written in Hindi[2] yield a storehouse of knowledge that upholds their tensile strength, even in the subsequent times. While writing novels and stories has evidently gained major impetus in the democratic fabric of India, many such rural narratives dealing with peasantry[3] and rural existence in vernacular have had a history of being stacked together in the category of 'regional'.[4] A much larger area of human experience therefore remains marginalized for not being written in the language of the western world and for addressing local indigenous concerns. The changing ways of life have further distanced the urban-educated class from farming and harvesting culture; terms like *rabi*, *kharif*, rain-fed, rural indebtedness, fractured landholdings, scarcity of seeds, procurement price, etc. sound other-worldly to the average 'modern' (educated, urban) Indian. Arguably, farming is much more complex[5] than any industry. In any industry or manufacturing body, the damage can be controlled or the risk is subject to mitigation, but not in farming. Fighting the yearly battle with crops, while the prices are likely to be unstable and volatile, indebtedness, input credit and electricity exorbitantly expensive, dealing with extreme weather, fatal illness of a near one, lack of adequate medical care call for real fortitude and testify why and how poverty has become a distinct identity of rural existence, specifically for small,[6] middle-level, and landless peasants.

Walter Benjamin's comparison of information with storytelling lets us understand what is at the heart of this study. 'The value of information does not survive the moment in which it was new. It lives only at that moment; it has to surrender to it completely and explain itself to it without losing any time. A story is different. It does not expend itself. It preserves and concentrates its strength and is capable of releasing it even after a long time'.[7] Indeed, the newspaper surveys, academic discourses, research surveys, and the state-sponsored policy programmes paid due attention to the gradually dismantling village society and ongoing agrarian crisis. It can be argued however that visiting this world in fictional idiom lends an authentic vision of how in spite of India's emancipation from the colonial rule and the foundation of Indian democracy, a farmer's routine labour and struggle for a good yield remain implicated in an intricate array of messy complications and contingencies. Undoubtedly, the story layout brings to the fore the diverse circumstances and subterranean issues—even the most elusive ones—that seek solution.

Villages have always been the basic units of administration in India since the ancient times. For centuries the rural world has produced grain and fostered the culture of our land. James C. Scott (2010, 2–3), a scholar of political science and an avid researcher in the field of South Asian peasantry, considers agriculture to be the core of the political and puts it succinctly, 'since peasants were the most numerous class in world history, it seems to me that one could have a worthy life studying the peasantry. If development is about anything, it ought to be about peasant livelihoods and the improvement of peasant lives more generally'.[8] His own approach to knowledge strongly endorses the study of stories for greater understanding of human sciences and this perspective is manifest in his talks and writings that demonstrate genuine interest in the fictional narratives and oral stories of peasantry. The engagement of the present work with a series of rural stories concurs with Scott's (2–3) belief that literary narratives may be dealing with historical event but they work through characters either belonging to the periphery of the society, or in diverse contexts of rural existence, even anonymous, or those who we meet face to face, we impulsively participate in their routine lives as repository of the local indigenous brass tacks, grounded in ethnographic experiences—localized truths, carrying orally transmitted cultures—and their crisis. In rendering smallest details of soil contour, crop, and vegetation, they retain our interest in the topography, and record of life almost as reliable as a sociological survey. Exploring obscure, non-canonical literary narratives in Hindi, those who have not received the much-deserved attention, offer this study diverse resources and rich possibilities for analysis of essential modes of expression in a period of Indian history, of a very large part of India.

The Focus of this Study on Narratives in Hindi

India, an ancient civilization of great magnitude, is marked by not only varied languages but also terrains—plains, plateaus, hills, coastal areas, deserts—varied weather conditions, agricultural practices, crops, and density of population. The linguistic differences are marked by cultural differences and adherence to different artistic traditions. These traditions, say in Punjabi and Bengali languages, are as far removed as their geographical locations. They tend not to collate and comingle. My selection of the Hindi stories is based on one larger and more marked literary tradition in the peasant writings.

Hindi is the third most spoken language in the world with about 615 million speakers after English and Mandarin. The Hindi Heartland covers a number of states and a large population of about two hundred and forty million. A large part of UP and Bihar and the regions in vicinity, also known as the Hindi Heartland, has been the principal engagement of Premchand. This study, *Rural India and Peasantry in Hindi Stories: Narratives After Premchand,*[9] resonates with a vast expanse of lands and multitudes of people whose historical and political problems could not be ameliorated even after our country acquired freedom from the colonial rule. The stories of UP and Bihar not only inherit a strong tradition of peasant narratives but also offer serious reflection on a range of crises the rural populace has experienced since the early decades of independent India through the period of liberalization and in recent decades. While in India, different states have varied parameters of growth and development, as parallel regions, these two states form a continuum of agrarian culture. They have shared histories, politics, demography, cultural mores, agricultural landscape, and most importantly, farm produce.

Rural Economic Conditions: Era of Premchand and the Rise of Hindi

The early decades of twentieth-century Indian history abound in the narratives of distressed condition of Indian farmers in the colonial rule. Claude Markovits' study on Gandhi finds that the period from 1920 to 1947 in the Indian countryside was marked by a rampant agrarian crisis aggravated from 1926 onwards by a steep drop in the prices of agricultural produce (2006, 141). Cultivation, now costlier, demanded greater investment in sowing and planting, which a farmer managed by raising money at interest, but the subsequent harvesting failed to give him the return desperately needed. Besides, the onset of global depression worsened the condition of small farmers. In the economic interest of the colonial rule, farmers had to pay increased rent for the cultivation of lands and were coerced into opting for cash crops (jute, indigo, opium, and cotton)[10] required for the growing demand of British industries for raw materials. It was also the time of early industrialization in India, beginning with sugar and textile mills owned by the British. For many small farmers, the crisis was so difficult that they gave up cultivation and sought factory jobs.[11] Although the crisis affected all strata of peasantry, Radhakamal Mukherjee, a champion of Asian communism, observed in 1933 that the economic position of the small peasants had further weakened, while the contrast between the increasing class of rent receivers and the toiling agricultural serfs indicated a critical stage in the agricultural history of India.[12] The system of regulations sanctioned by the colonial governance authorized the elite landlords to act as coercive revenue collectors, empowered by their retinue and the police to earn shortcut profit. The contingencies attached to the activities of farming always existed and were miscellaneous. Prayag, a peasant, in Premchand's novel, *Karmabhoomi* (The Land Where One Works), set in the UP of 1930s, narrates: 'Brother! never take up cultivation which is nothing but a great botheration. Whether your field yields anything or not, you must meet the rental demand of the landlord. It is flood now and drought later. One misfortune or the other always chases you. If your bullock dies, or your harvest catches fire, then everything is lost' (2006, 153). In the ensuing new land settlement, Scott saw the introduction of western-style capitalism in Indian agriculture. The villagers lost land rights and usufruct rights, becoming tenants or agrarian wage labourers. In addition, produce was brought within the ambit of international market (61–62). Premchand (1962, 483) writes, 'Who does not know that the farmers of India are drowned in debt, right from sowing seeds to borrowing bulls, wedding of daughters, the subsistence of peasantry means living with the burden of ever-increasing loan, suffering starvation, illness, ignorance, misery and death'. In another novel, *Premashram* (The Abode of Love), a peasant relates his woe: 'Perhaps in no other province the peasants are so troubled and in no other province the landlords can act so arbitrarily. This situation has remained the same for the entire 150 years of British rule. These unfortunate people regularly face the tyranny of the police, the landlord, the moneylender, in brief, of every official' (Premchand, 403). *Godan* centres on the brave but silent struggle of two peasants, Hori and his wife, Dhania, against the extortion by the moneylenders in the colonial order. Hori narrates his helplessness to Bhola. In spite of paying double the amount of loan, the interest still hangs over his head:

> My grain is all weighed out at the village barn, the master took his share and the money lender his. Leaving me just ten ser (kilos). I carried off the straw, and hid it during the night, or not a blade would have been left for me. Of course, there's only one zamindar, but there are three different moneylenders. I have not yet paid off the interest to any one of them, and there is still half the rent for the zamindar also, but nothing helps. (36)

Such extremities were almost growing rampant, in the 1930s. The uninhibited flouting of 'moral economy',[13] of the peasantry in the new configuration embodied in Scott's observations, the standard colonial practice to bolster the rural rich, the allotment of blatantly large powers to the landlords over the peasants, and the introduction of private property, high revenue demands, and often forcible auction of cash crops, which reduced many small farmers through administrative decrees to tenants-at-will (2–10).

India's Freedom Synchronized with the Freedom of Peasantry

The impact of various agricultural transformations on the peasant and how these moves caused the disruption of self-contained rural resources were astutely perceived in the writings of Premchand. He preferred to engage in the delineation of social and economic structures and processes, especially, rural poverty and agrarian economy, rather than narrating event centred history dominated by linear political narrative. The escalating monetary pressure on the peasant spurred the emergence of a new clan of moneylenders eyeing the helplessness of peasants with greed. During the publication of *Godan* (1936), peasantry's unrest gained momentum, spreading across the northern and eastern UP and the neighbouring rural regions of Bihar. The persecution of peasantry had agitated Indian politics for freedom, and the reformation of historically exploited peasants became one of the prime objectives of the nationalist movement. India's freedom at this juncture was officially synchronized with the freedom of peasantry. Reflections on the peasant question in European and Indian cultural histories of the 1920s to the 1940s reveal a visible difference between them. While European modernism prompted in the literature of industrialization, a view of the peasant as a 'historical residue or an anachronism, in sharp contrast, South Asian writers and thinkers saw invested in the figure of an earthy peasant an alternative to western capitalism' (Joshi, 102). Gandhi's keen involvement with the mass unrest of peasantry in Champaran[14] and Kheda infused a surge of creative energy in the realms of social activism, politics, and literature. Ganesh Shankar Vidyarthi, Acharya Narendra Dev, Purushottam Das Tandon, Pt. Madan Mohan Malaviya, Sampoornanand, Swami Sahajanand Sarasvati, Radhakamal Mukherjee, Balkrishna Bhatta, and Premchand forcefully addressed on several forums, the political reasons behind the impoverishment of peasants. Premchand's journalistic analysis of the worsening rural economy ascertained that the subalternity of Indian rural population was entangled in indigenous anthropological, sociological, and, to some extent, global causes, but the crisis that the agrarian rural world faced was exacerbated by local and colonial interests.

Even before the Avadh movement[15] of peasants in 1920–22 made news, the analysis of rural economic condition frequently featuring in Hindi magazines marked the emergence of popular interest in the freedom of Indian peasantry. Orsini (309) notes that the journalistic writing[16] of 1920s and 1930s saw the misery of indebted peasants as almost akin to the state of refugees in their own lands (311–14). Writers, poets, scholars, and patrons of the arts stood behind the publication of magazines in Hindi such as *Saraswati, Vishal Bharat, Samalochak, Hansa, Yuvak, Vijayai Bharat Mitra, Nrisingha, Pratap, Saroj, Senapati, Bharat*, and *Abhyudaya*, all of which with missionary zeal, involved common people in debates on literature, art, philosophy, and politics and specifically displayed profound concern for the peasant. Sumitranandan Pant's collection of poems invested the spirit of mother India in the rural world.[17] Emancipation of Indian kisan was the foremost topic which engaged the then newly flourishing trends in Hindi and vernacular magazines. The collective surge of emotions for the oppressed peasantry was manifest in postulating in the figure of 'an earthy peasant an alternative to western capitalism' and 'peasant as the real nation' (Orsini, 311–41). Premchand's works articulated that the writers have a mission to envisage revolutionary changes and they must perform a committed role in nurturing the literary and artistic trends to bring awakening in the society, inspire sincere involvement with the real problems of the common people.

Post-Independence Rural India and the Programmes Espoused by the State

In the economic field, when the post-colonial, independent India was being geared for new reconstruction, the villages of the country were left out, which seriously weakened the social, economic, and ecological basis of peasant agriculture. Amita Baviskar (1995) finds Gandhian principles totally ignored in the economic field with the inauguration of the Second Five-Year Plan[18] in 1956, when the bulk of state development funding focused on heavy industry. Only 22 percent of state budget was allocated to agriculture despite the fact that 75 percent of the population was engaged in agriculture and only 11 percent of the population in industry. This policy was dictated by the assumption that the recurring expenditure could be financed in part by the surplus generated by agriculture (200). The economists distant from agriculture further complicated the issues of resolving agrarian crisis, for the daily lives of peasantry: precariously surviving labourers, tenants, artisans, and small- and middle-level farmers were only vaguely known to them. The procedures of democracy and capitalism congenially continued with the already established discriminatory norms because they suited the interests of the aspirational business class and political elite at all levels. The government's projects were dedicated to the development of metro cities on the model of world-class cities, while in bizarre contrast, the villages of UP and Bihar remained incongruously deprived of the basic amenities.

The other agrarian development programmes announced as the doctrines of Sarvodaya made to dissolve disparity ironically served as the impetus to promote the selfish interests of the privileged. Their implementation in the charge of bureaucrats, facilitators, and handlers somehow let down the disadvantaged. Several narratives have highlighted the discrepancies between the state-driven programmes and actuality. Bhudan[19] (Land Gift) initiated as a development project meant to mitigate the glaring inequality by fair distribution of the surplus land of the big landowners and create opportunities for self-reliance was schematized in a way that it helped the landowners and mediators and caused grievous injustice to the small peasants and labourers of UP and Bihar. Kunwar Jayanti Prasad, one of the characters in Shrilal Shukla's Bisrampur *ka Sant*[20] (1978), ends his life, but before that admits to have played a major role in blemishing a sacred movement like Bhudan. Being in the Administrative Service, Shrilal Shukla could see through the dynamics at work which contributed to the miserable distortion and failure of both Bhudan and Chakbandi (Land Ceiling Act).[21] He discloses the bare facts: 'The landowners were made the presidents of cooperative farming and continued to hold on to the same for many years. They gave their surplus lands as gifts to poor peasants by taking their thumb prints. At the hour of harvest nonetheless, they forcibly re-claimed the gifted land. This is enough to understand that in the Hindi belts of UP and Bihar land reformation has not really occurred' (2005, 198). Subsequently, weaker and uneducated cultivators and small farmers, who had been tenants since generations, incurred huge losses. The constitution of the Land Ceiling Act, a component of the First Five-Year Plan, was initially hailed as a promising reform movement meant to reduce the huge disparity between the income of large landowners and that of the small or landless peasants and the glaring inequalities in land ownership. Its goal was to develop a cooperative rural economy and expand self-employment in owned land as distinguished from subletting and tenant cultivations. But it soon became the instrument of surreptitiously displacing the small landowners and tenants. The problems of transferring ownership rights from the actual cultivators of the land, the tenants, the sub-tenants, and sharecroppers remained complicated and unresolved. Ironically, the act was treated as malleable and was randomly used in the individual interest giving incentive to the influential to claim even those lands which were deemed as public in the agrarian society. Several such spaces were turned into privately owned properties, and in this situation, the lives of the poor cultivators had grown more difficult than the earlier times.

The Impact of Green Revolution: Agriculture Embodied Chaos of India in the Throes of Development

Policymakers advanced the Green Revolution (1960s), promoting imported seeds, chemical fertilizers, pesticides, herbicides, and water from expensive foreign-funded irrigation projects. With the passage of time, although wheat and rice crops in some regions were reportedly aided, pulses, an affordable source of protein for the poor, were severely damaged. It was increasingly evident that the Green technology also caused loss of biodiversity. It is reported that before applying its measures, there were 3000 varieties of rice growing in India, but afterwards only 10 varieties remained. Research findings by Archana Shrivastava (2010, 30–35) argue that instead of proving helpful, they wrought serious damage upon the soil. Availability of pulses per head during the period of 1981–85 was 19 kilograms per year, which decreased to just 12 kilograms per head, per year in 2004–2007. Those familiar with the Indian agriculture know that the price of pulses was most visibly impacted with inflation. They became unaffordable to the poor. In the regions of UP, Bihar, and Chhattisgarh, the poor consume a cheap substitute for pulses, khesari dal, which is known to pose serious health risks, like rheumatic ailments. Besides, the pesticides mingling with the soil pollute water and rivers and have caused damage to health in rural India. Its adverse impacts are also known on environment in the form of depleting the soil of the necessary ingredients that promote horticultural produce other than causing land degradation and increasing greenhouse gas emission. Land degradation and soil nutrient depletion have forced farmers to clear up formerly forested areas to keep up with the production. Chemicals depleted the natural fertilizer of soil. Subsequently in the later years, the soil grew pest resistant and needed more supplies of the pesticides.

Fasal Bima Yojana 2016 (Prime Minister Crops Insurance Plan)

The government's initiatives such as the Pradhan Mantri Fasal Bima Yojana (Prime Minister Crops Insurance Plan, 2016) to alleviate the losses of the farmers due to uncertainties of weather, until lately, were not showing results due to poor implementation. To receive the compensation, the stipulated criteria were to be met, which is very often caught up in muddled up norms and directions pre-empting it from reaching the really aggrieved or deserving. The individuals in charge or officials at the district level and the local village level were failing in making fair judgement in identifying the needy. Besides, delayed assessment of loss and settlement of claims by insurers has led farmers to lose faith in such schemes. In the regions beset by flood or famine, the promises of relief remained on paper for a long time; by the time the relief reached the farmer, it would generally be late. We hear, in quite a few cases, the frustration of long wait led to suicide.

Indebtedness and the Financial Assistance Programmes

Relying for subsistence on farming alone puts a farmer in a state of insecurity and indebtedness, inevitably spurred by miscellaneous reasons: rising inflation, investment required for a successful crop, fatal illness of someone in the family demanding adequate treatment in the city hospitals, educating children, wedding or some rituals and celebration, death of a near or dear one, or of cattle. Issues such as unpredictable weather, erratic or unseasonal rainfall, hailstorm, rising temperatures due to climate change, wilting crop threatening to relentlessly deplete whatever could have been enough for subsistence bring deep disquiet. Smallholders and marginal farmers are the worst hit; if the crops turn out bad, it only adds up to the mounting debt—everything gets stalled, that made subsistence even for the moderately poor more difficult. Besides, the sale of their harvest dictated by agencies beyond their control tends to be highly unpredictable. The fall out of which has been the flourishing business of assistance programmes such as Gramin Banks (Rural Bank). It was realized rather too late that the micro-finance scheme of the Gramin Bank, though projected initially in the rural world as emancipator—almost as a deity of poverty eradication—brought larger rural communities into debt from which they could not escape. Their methods of extortion ensured that in the free India, the procedures of democracy and capitalism congenially continued with the already established discriminatory norms. The complicated procedures of welfare programmes for the poor in the rural society in six decades ironically encouraged the hectic activities of unscrupulous intermediaries—fixers and brokers, both official and unofficial bureaucrats. They flourished as participants of the reforms and welfare programmes, while many among rural population deteriorated from being middle poor to the lowest rung of society.

Gram Swaraj: A Farce

Gandhi (1962, 71) toured all over India to impart a vision of Gram Panchayat, an institution which was to undertake the responsibility of upholding political and economic democracy at the grassroot level, equality of all human beings, their right to participate in social and political transformation, and the right to development, to live in dignity. In 1959, on Gandhi Jayanti, his vision of Panchayat (Village Council) came into being. The immense hope it generated however turned short lived, very soon Panchayats drifted away from their goal and let down the rural middle poor and very poor. Though the desperately failing system received new grafting[22] to stimulate the triad of the Panchayat system into purposive action, it pursued work with the same old methods. The administration remained colonial in spirit. Mistrust of the ordinary rural populace was the basis of colonial administrative infrastructure, and in the style of governance, the same trend operated. Those who held office as village functionaries thought of themselves as rulers rather than public servants meant to serve the village society. A tendency was setting in of identifying rustic mentality with lies, distortion, frauds, and endless civil and criminal suits. It has been difficult for a poor petitioner to hope for justice in the Nyaya Panchayat. The backward layer suffered from injustice, ignorance, and non-information. Panchayat deemed the property of wealthy landowners who possessed political clout, employed musclemen to physically and or materially harm justice-seekers, having contacts in bureaucracy and police at the higher level. Since the landowners invest in the Panchayat elections,[23] they are granted access to marketing milk products and poultry. The general practice has been to authorize the educated and cleverer biggies with the legitimate right to act as the intermediary and spokesperson between the state and the needy. One very significant factor has been the caste and class affiliations playing a dominant role in the functions of Panchayats and our electoral system further aggravated it. All across UP and Bihar, Panchayats are known as inexorably wedged in the larger network of systems: district political parties, leaders, and officials seeking the electoral support of village heavyweights to sustain their hold on the larger populace. In the 1970s and 1980s, as the bureaucracy at all levels was growing increasingly dominant, the people's voice remained feeble and often stifled.

Panchayats remained irredeemable because of their customary habit of pilfering from the funds allotted for the welfare schemes of the village. MNREGA (Mahatma Gandhi National Rural Employment Guarantee Act, 2005) is the recent example of crores of funds siphoned in the transaction. What is conspicuously lamentable is that they failed to exercise their power to monitor and ameliorate the lamentable neglect of the rural education system. Most critically, the visible indifference of Panchayats to medical care services could be considered a culpable wrong. Due to this, minor ailments or bruises caused by injury grow severe for not being diagnosed and treated early and have led to numerous cases of disability in the villages. One gets to know how malnutrition or hunger, lack of hygiene, and unclean drinking water have caused avoidable deaths in our countryside.

Agrarian Society in Deep Distress

The lethargic pace of progress has thrust the Indian rural existence on the brink of margin. Crop growing, the principal occupation of rural life in the last seven decades, has not been without anxieties. The manner in which the village societies and agricultural issues were dealt with at the block, district, state, and national levels could most suitably be described as 'governmentality'.[24] Foucault's notion of the dispersed practices of the government lets us understand the operations of the Indian state historically functioning as a 'bundle of everyday institutions and forms of rules, devices, and technologies' invisible to the common semiliterate or illiterate observer, assembled into an arrangement having neither unity nor the functionality often ascribed to them. A conversation of a visitor with a peasant in *Katha me Kisan*[25] shows that today even the relatively rich and middle-level farmers describe with self-deprecating irony that attempting to farm paddy, sugarcane, groundnut or vegetables or cotton by deploying organic methods or technologies, and ethical payment to the farm workers remain in shambles and bring about frustration:

> Yes, you're right. There were brokers earlier too. But we possessed more resilience then—the strength to live and they did not have hold on things—as they've now. Previously, we used to borrow loan from them, and grow our crop. We borrow now also, and even dabble with the bank loans too. But cannot grow our own crops. Now we've to plant seeds that the government sends to the market. Our harvest and our seeds are of no value in the market. Look at this cotton blossoming! … peeping though the fruits! Earlier our ancestors would dance watching them and prepare their oxen for a round to the market. But now this scene doesn't arouse any excitement. 'Stuff the cotton of this year into the mandis by Diwali, you'll receive the payment by Holi'. That too less than what was received previously. The government of the state announces, 'increase the harvest'; when harvest is bumper, the rate drops. In the end, the defeated farmer instead of dying every day chooses to die one day.

Indeed, the life or future of 600 million people engaged in farming remains vulnerable. Fighting the yearly battle with crops while the prices are likely to be unstable and volatile, input credit and electricity, exorbitantly expensive, call for real fortitude. While the income from agriculture is shrinking, the pressures of the consumerist society are impacting the small- and middle-level farmers and their families and many have chosen to quit farming and migrate to survive. P. Sainath[26] substantively backed by his empirical research and fieldwork indicts the bad economic policies since 1991—liberalization that accelerated the gradual process of the collapse of agriculture in India. One gets to know how the scenario of 2011 and thereafter 2016 demonetization destroyed the agricultural scenario and hastened the migration further. India's growth story is judged by the clamorous, flourishing world of MNCs, flyovers, patents, free market, culture, internet, GDP growth, and rising exports of global recognition. The mechanics of which multiplied the number of very wealthy while the poverty rate in the rural regions exacerbated.[27] The subsequent eight chapters in discussing more than thirty representative stories of UP and Bihar after Premchand unfold the brass tacks of rural existence specifically of small peasantry in the post-independent India.

In Chapter 1, 'Village India: Difficult Stories', Shrilal Shukla's several stories in overtly comic and satiric narratives serve as laconic but intensive sequel to *Raag Darbari* (1968, 2013), taking us to a tour of many facets of village life that make us review our long cherished romantic notions of the beauty, vitality, and simplicity of the idyllic country life. The opening two stories let us into the murky realities of the post-independence rural India: water-logged dirt tracks, damaged irrigation facilities, dysfunctional medical care, ignorance, poverty, pilfering, intermittent land disputes, violence, and unending criminal litigations. In the subsequent longer story, 'Hori aur *1984*' (Hori and *1984*), Hori, the iconic small peasant of the contemporary times, is trapped in the Orwellian *1984*, the world of 'double-speak', immense mess and chaos. Images of Premchanda's Hori impinging on the consciousness of Shukla's Hori subsisting in the Orwellian world are sharp reminder of the fact that the colonial times and also the times after India evolved into an advanced liberal democracy were not only marked by tolerance of high levels of inequality but also poverty pervasive in the rural world is accepted as natural norm. Premchand portrayed the bruised and insulted psyche of the rural poor unashamedly exploited by the moneylenders and the rural elite in *Godan*. Coveting hefty interest had to be the *dharma* of a usurer that disallows any sentiment towards the borrower other than the matter of profit. In the world of 1984, Hori's community is grievously troubled by a more updated and smarter system of money lending. The labouring class of Hori cannot forget the moments of 1970s—when it was subjected to a new form of torture—forced vasectomy, performed by the state-sponsored biopower (Emergency).

In Chapter 2, 'Land Grab: The Dispossessed in the Spectacles of Jugaad', several narratives invoke the varied times since the 1950s. The deeply delved history of peasant community lets us know how the land reforms like *Bhudan, Chakbandi* (Land Ceiling Act), and projects like building dams and canals meant to liberate the small farmers from many pressures, by helping them to become self-reliant and increase the produce, affected them adversely. The analysis of the stories of varied lengths and contexts reveals the narrators' ability to distil an emotional and psychological state into images. The evocatively described scenarios where the local representatives, arrangers, officers of the programmes either play tricks with the uneducated tenants, labourers, and small peasants or remain aloof from their grievances. The opening story relates how *Bhudan* movement raised the hope of every downtrodden rural population in the magic that the spirit of freedom of India could bring about, but it turned into disappointment. The opening story subsumes an iconic folk tale which conjures the do or die spirit with which in the nineteenth century a farmer defends his land from the indigo planters. In spite of the Angrej Sahib's murderous rage and coercive physical violence upon a peasant, forcing the latter to surrender his field, the bleeding but unyielding peasant remains invincible. The successive stories based on varied time lines reveal the strife of peasants forever dispossessed of their lands in the wake of the state's Five-Year Plan. Development and Land Ceiling programmes generally helped the privileged and the profiteers and gave impetus to gross flouting of moral economy, endless litigations, and criminal cases. What could also be of concern, so very tellingly foregrounded, is the brutal insult and aloof arrogance meted out to the petitioners lower in assets and in caste by the government officials.

In Chapter 3, 'Small Farmers of Cane and Paddy: Post-Harvest Delays and Non-Payment', the consciousness narrative in the two stories lets us see the insecurities threatening the farmers who have to take several steps for the cultivation of cane and paddy. Their problems do not come to end with sowing, fertilizing, planting and harvesting, braving drought or inundation, but the ordeal grows multiple times in dealing with marketing the produce and receiving the due payment. The world of actual transaction with the local arrangers and the state-appointed employees can bring about extreme hardship and sometimes death. Those who work as the functionaries in the transaction of cane or paddy, with the covert approval of their bosses in hierarchy and in solidarity with them, dittoed the colonial system, favouring the bribe givers, assuming that it was their obligation to harass and discipline the poor peasants. Empowered by the system, they grant themselves the freedom to unleash their malevolence on the peasants who catch up long distances, exhausted, starved, waiting for the deal done. An ordinary small farmer is snubbed and manhandled, his voice remains stifled. One who musters the courage, demands justice at the higher level would invariably be ineffective due to the intimidating gap between the peasant and the Sahib, and due to the smarter local machinery, that nonetheless remains invincible.

Chapter 4, 'Women Peasants in Triple Jeopardy: Conmen as Philanthropists', finds that the notion, 'India is progressing', is like a truism, as much true as false, more conspicuously, with regard to the condition of rural women specifically those who are in peasantry. While the urban women are ascertaining their rights in every sphere of existence, the same is not the case with rural women. It is not that they submit to injustice, but the stakes against them are too convoluted and difficult to combat even though, in the recent decades, seats have come to be reserved for elected women members of the Panchayat committee. The stories, Madan Mohan's 'Jahrili Bijliyon ke Beech' (In the Midst of Poisonous Lights) and Shivmurti's 'Kasaibada' (The Bucher House), unfold an inclusive spectrum of cultural and political information about the evolving rural scenario in the democratic India of our times. In their two respective characters, Saguna and Shanichari, one finds represented the struggle of village women under the circumstances where, for being a widow or due to an absent husband, with meagre means of subsistence or frail health, they are rendered vulnerable to exploitation. The world they confront is a dissolute arena of roguery, violence, selfishness, sloth, cunning, affectations, superstition, and cowardice. Their lives represent that the rural women are the worst casualty in matters of caste clashes, sexual assaults, human trafficking, land disputes, and land profiteering. The stories reveal that the notions conjuring villages as romantic or revolutionary, both are redundant even in the recent times. Women in peasantry comprise nearly 16 percent of India's female population. What is of conspicuous concern in the two stories is that in a dominantly male-centric rural mores, there is almost no space for women who do not have a male support system. Their oppression grows more complicated—due to poverty, illiteracy, and exploitation—both sexual and monetary. What is remarkable about the stories is that they portray the incredible violence perpetrated upon the souls of the women which goes unpunished and unchecked, as if it were absolutely ordinary and 'normal'. We feel the tension behind all that is not said and fill in the gaps. At times the narrative voice is disengaged, the tone uninflected, the style economical, understated—the writers nonetheless understand not only evil but also the extravagance of tricks with which evil presents itself as good. One feels that they cut right to the heart of the matter, to the essential rottenness of the world.

Chapter 5, 'Why Do Rural Poor Continue to Remain Poor and Uneducated?', relates the experiential facts of schooling in the remote villages of Bihar. The long narrative of 'Shadayantra' (Conspiracy) in a series of comic-pathetic episodes invokes the scenario of a government school in Bihar in the decades of 1970s to 1990s, where *Pairavi* (recommendation) is the key to the appointment of the teachers and probes the factors causing failure of education in rural India in spite of the apparently well-meaning schemes of the government. The reader confronted with the infrastructural deficiencies in this primary cum middle-level school can figure out the utter negligence with which education is treated in most rural schools. This is only one government school, situated among three villages which lacks a proper building, toilet facilities, and arrangement of conveyance or roads to school. The teachers' habitual use of expletives or caste names—as the ways of addressing the students, violent thrashing of boys, subjecting of girls to explicit sexual gestures and innuendoes—all point out the reasons why the rural boys and girls if at all seek admission, drop out or are discouraged from attending the school. The teacher–student ratio generally crosses limits of absurdity, teachers' absenteeism managed by lies and fraudulent registers is not specific to one or two schools but to many schools in the villages of India. The system grows unredeemable because of the inept implementation of reforms, crafty management of audit and siphoning of funds by those in charge. The village administration or the parents at large do not show any concern. Besides, the periodic visit by the inspector of schools is easy to manipulate. The intersecting shorter stories in the chapter also plead for the measures for redressal. While Shrilal Shukla's *Raag Darbari* draws the picture of inept rural education at the higher level with a poker-faced irreverence, the short narratives here however focus on identifying the shortcomings and force us to ponder on the need to rectify the deep structures rotting beneath.

The stories discussed in Chapter 6, 'Rural Migration: Dismantling Rural Resources', investigate the repercussion of mass migration of rural India, the social changes, the wreckage it leaves behind. When young people migrate, the closest bonds break and a way of life ebbs away. The foremost realization spurring the need to earn money and seek employment in the distant pastures is that the rural resources or farming alone cannot provide for a large family. Several fictional narratives since the time of Premchand reveal the moving tales of lives away from one's nearest family members, year-round. It could involve living hazardously, beyond the margins of subsistence and exposure to the threats of disease and death. Migration to the cities in the last quarter of the twentieth century has occurred at a conspicuously faster pace. Weddings of daughters, debts, vagaries of weather, fast disappearance of indigenously running workshops that were traditionally aligned with farming, drive the rural existence to the brink of full-blown crisis. In the last four or five decades, the traditional village structures and arrangements maintaining the rural society have gradually become dysfunctional. The advent of the computerized age has also given rise to a feeling of worthlessness in the village youth. Agriculture, once a pivot of rural life, no longer promises a decent living. The stories poignantly describe the distress-driven migration of the rural people to bigger cities or even to the Gulf countries. Lakhs of workers from the rural India have been toiling in the cities to earn their living. The larger urban population hardly registered their presence or cared about the migrant populace, even though they were very much around, until the break out of COVID-19.

In Chapter 7, 'When Hunger Hits the Rural Poor, Aged, and Disabled: The Meal of Mice and Dead Cow', the two stories quintessentially relate the rural conditions when either drought or adverse weather generate great difficulty in dealing with hunger. The grind in the fields and the inadequate hygiene and healthcare several times take its toll on the poor rural people severely affecting means of earning and surviving. Even a middle poor is likely to slip into grave food crisis in difficult times of famine or floods, when all means to earn and to avail food are blocked. It has been an unacknowledged reality that in the rural parts of UP and Bihar, amongst poor, there is a visible number of disabled, aged, accident victims, or afflicted with severe health issues. The first narrative, 'Bhookh' (Hunger) renders the humiliating struggle of a disabled *Dalit* farm labourer for food for his family during the times of incessant heavy rains. In desperation, he had no other option but to cook the flesh of a dead cow for which he was brutally thrashed for violating a religious norm. In the following, of the same title, 'Bhookh', the head of a family, an aged wobbling old peasant, a *Dalit*, who in normal times earns some daily wages, in the times of drought has no employment and no money to buy food. For weeks, his four grandchildren, a widowed daughter-in-law who was also disabled due to acute arthritis, struggle with hunger. In spite of enough storage of food as a result of government relief aid, the cooperative shopkeeper withholds the red card of his family. After a long struggle, when left with nothing, one evening, they consumed rotten meat and that night they vomited and died. The news spiced with rumours that the entire family was wiped off, prompted the frequent visits of the leaders from different political parties. The death of the entire family was declared as 'not because of hunger but food poisoning'.

Chapter 8, 'Farmers in Death Row: Farming—Risky, Sisyphean; Usury—Back Breaking' raises one of the most disturbing issues that has made an ordinary citizen of India get to know that a segment of humanity has suffered enormously. Drawing their themes from diverse sources and contexts, the stories force us to enter into a very relatable world of men and women and perceive the entire spectrum of emotional vicissitudes, the trauma driving peasants to take extreme action when everything gets stalled, or life is not worth living. Few of us can measure the labour, strength, stamina, and willpower involved in the farming life. The village life is a difficult ordeal, most well-off city-dwellers could not imagine. The income from agriculture is shrinking, the pressures of inflation in a consumerist society are taking a toll on the small- and middle-level farmers and their families; the vagaries of Indian climate condition do not always allow the crops to flourish as expected. To coax their single crop out of the ground, they need to take credit to procure inputs like seed and fertilizer, sometimes even water. Every attempt to rectify the failing crop off and on fails. If the crops turn out bad, it only adds up to mounting debt. The stark fact cannot be countered that agriculture is a loss-making enterprise which does not even bring enough to eat, let alone any surplus. Not that the farmers were not ending their lives earlier as well, but that it has visibly catalysed in the recent decades is a sure indicator of a greater structural drawback that is allowed to remain entrenched in Indian agriculture, particularly over the last three decades. Relying on farming however does not enable a farmer to fill his stomach or carry the burden of the family successfully. Even then he is unable to quit farming. Let us accept that no segment of India has been as long battered by adversities as the peasantry, several times with no option but standing in the death row.

Chapter 9, 'Despoiled Environment: In the Politics of Integrated Development, Money Grows on Trees', explores with shrewd insight, the historical and structural conditions of a rural township, in 'Umraonagar me Kuchch Din' (Several Days in Umraonagar) in the collection, *Jahalat ke Pachchas Saal (Fifty Years of Stupidity)* and draws the chaos of plans and programmes of development. The relentless logging in the forest village, Umraonagar, known for its adjoining dense forests, at alarming rate, reveals the double game behind the show of growth story. The long, meandering narrative, in vignettes, traverses through various local histories of the village, making the reader aware of the shaping cultural and political configurations in the post-independence rural India of 1970s and 1980s. The story subtly ferrets out the fault lines in the claims made by the champions of development who are out to push the village to a different level, described as rural–urban. Most significantly, the narrative attains a semblance of history in recording the insidious techniques with which the contractors, forest officials, development agents, specialists (local and the city-bred), and stakeholders in connivance, employ their might and skill to deprive the centuries-old forest village of all its resources. We are confronted with the images of the now denuded, wounded forest; most wildlife disappeared, rivers and waterways polluted, beyond recognition, the dust raised by the buses hanging in the air, and ramshackle trucks carrying the slaughtered timbre engulfing all life around in the air, on the ground. And it still does not seem to matter to most. The story drives home what the environment historian, Donald Worster posits: 'the cause of ecological crisis is not a result of "how the ecosystem works but rather because of how our ethical system functions".

Why Only Short Story

I think a few words need to be said on my choice of short stories for this study. It has been mentioned that this project covers more than thirty short stories. In the course of my analysis, however, several novels have been alluded to, drawing their analogous engagement with certain situations that the stories convey. The loose and sprawling fictional work (Novel) explores its subject-matter lengthwise or horizontally giving more importance to expression rather than in-depth exploration. The short stories have a tensile strength and examine the subject-matter depth-wise or vertically. Studies focusing *exclusively* on short stories that deal with the multiple facets of agrarian crisis and rural India are rare. In shorter works, the writer's focus is sharper and exploration is deeper. The short stories are compact with varied emotions and sentiments and therefore defy longer expressions and demand focused, deeper probing for a realistic conveyance.

These stories written by the writers who belong to folk culture ferret out the concealed portions—the backyard of agrarian lives and a much more nuanced and complex universe of agrarian lives emerges that a variety of novels cannot offer. Besides, while novels dealing with agrarian crisis have already been dealt with in the academia, short stories—especially many of those discussed in this book—remain academically under-represented. They are trapped, as it were, somewhere between the pedagogic and the performative. Hence, my project is also a recuperative one. Of course, there are many such short stories, published in prominent or obscure niches, but the many stories chosen by me appear to be *representative*, in many ways, more significantly in terms of the timeline—the historical context, they represent. They represent the themes this work deals with, in the most direct and pertinent way. Hence, rather than choosing more such stories randomly, I have focused on the most significant and relevant short fiction representing the central struggles of the Indian rural world in the Hindi-speaking regions.

A Note on Translation of Excerpts from Hindi into English

The prose, I engaged with in Hindi, involved me in varied fields of rural experiences, inhering multiple linguistic-cultural layering, alive in all their visceral power. As a translator of the excerpts into English, I felt challenged, even though I have been an insider and an outsider. It has been a commitment to be truthful to the local patois, transmitting the ambience of varying contemporary folk idiolects, which resisted homogenising, belonging to the vast rural heartlands of UP and Bihar. An experience of transferring what I experienced, reading the text has been an advantage too. It was like a transmission of Indian spirit of the text into English. There were times when the corresponding English term lacked the resonance of the idiomatic Hindi. There were moments when the syntax grammar and vocabulary of English looked like they might come to a complete standstill and also the moments when the transcribed passage absorbed a new stimulus. Carrying out this work, I am reminded of Bakhtin (1981, 293) who puts it: 'Each word tastes of the contexts in which it has lived its socially charged life'. That word ingrains—the memory of their past context and being—in that social interaction. In the process of reading, finding, I felt involved in a creative bonding—the connection forged had been almost mystic. It dissolved boundaries of the self. I find myself altered by this bonding with the words, stories—the landscape they conjure and—the people who inhabit them.

Notes

1. All excerpts drawn from the stories are translated into English by me.
2. Suraj Palival in 'Gram Katha Likhna Aaj Chunouti Hai' (The Challenges of Writing Rural Stories Today) writes that rural stories have come to a standstill; the reason is the fast-transforming realities of the rural existence since the onset of liberalization (188–95).
3. Marc Edelman, a Professor of Anthropology (medelman@hunter.cuny.edu.), in the paper dealing with the 'Rights of Peasants and Other People Working in Rural Areas', Geneva, 15–19 July 2013, offers an inclusive definition of peasantry. Social scientific definitions of 'peasant' generally recognize both—that the category is extremely heterogeneous and that individuals and groups in the category

typically engage in multiple forms of livelihood—including agriculture, wage labour, pastoralism, and livestock production, artisanal production, fishing and hunting, gathering of plant or mineral resources, petty commerce, and a variety of other skilled and unskilled occupations. A peasant is a man or a woman of the land, who has a direct and special relationship with the land and nature through the production of food and/or other agricultural products. Peasants work the land themselves, relying above all on family labour and other small-scale forms of organizing labour. Peasants are traditionally embedded in their local communities and they take care of local landscapes and of agro-ecological systems. The term peasant can apply to any person engaged in agriculture, cattle-raising, pastoralism, handicrafts related to agriculture, or a related occupation in a rural area. This includes Indigenous people working on the land.

4. The narratives of rural India render larger human experiences and yet remain marginalized, labelled as regional despite the fact that their concerns have been national. Satyakam in 'Aanchalikata ke Bahane' (In the Pretext of Regional, 147–51) expresses with deep regret the neglected state of literature in vernacular. Rural narratives remain unnoticed just because they are not written in English. The dominance of elite English educated in the literary world and the obsession of native intellectuals with English literature undermine the significance of writings in Hindi.

5. Narendranath, Gorrepati's narrative on the enormous challenges of farming has been an eye opener and is a major motivator in writing this book.

6. Historically, India's rural poor have been difficult to pin down in terms of stable categories. The small- and middle-level farmers have meagre assets. If the crops turn out bad, it only adds up to mounting debt.

7. Maria Popova cites Walter Benjamin's assertion that we are overwhelmed with heaps of disjointed information that is devoid of the sense making context. It is only deftly told story that reveals what information cannot. Information should better not be mistaken for truth (415).

8. 'Agriculture as Politics: Theory Talk' (18 May 2010) mentions that to a question: 'How did you arrive at where you are currently in your findings?' Scott C. James, a political scientist, known for his pursuit of serious research in the field of agrarian life, agrarian economics, and south Asian peasantry, assertively replied that when he was working on *The Moral Economy of the Peasant*, he read all the peasant novels, all histories; in short, as much as he could stuff from outside of political science. He also argues that the works that have been most influential historically comprise the index or bibliography that testify to the author's wide reading outside the normal range of standard, mainstream work. Foucault argues that we should analyse literary texts as part of a larger discursive formation rather than assuming that literature has a separate and privileged status in relation to other texts (1978–1993). Morton's (141) reading of Spivak endorses the role of literature as providing the readers the cultural and material spaces in which the

subaltern segments communicate and this is what renders the division between the experience of literary and cultural texts and the economic texts questionable.

9. Munshi Premchand resigned from his government job in 1921 after attending a public meeting addressed by Gandhiji who appealed people to join non-cooperation movement and contribute to the freedom struggle. As a writer-activist, his analysis of Indian peasantry in the early decades of twentieth century offers perceptive analysis of agricultural society in rural India.

10. The cultivation of indigo and poppy at the behest of colonial state was an unprofitable undertaking for the peasants in the Gangetic Valley. Amitav Ghosh's *The Sea of Poppies*, based on a thorough examination of the Reports of the Royal Commission on Opium, contemporary ethnographic materials, and the District Settlement Records, elaborates the coercive methods applied by the colonial Sahibs for planting opium.

11. In Premchand's *Godan*, Hori's son, Gobar, is compelled to leave the village to work in a sugar mill in Calcutta. The old Hindi cinema, *Do Bigha Zamin*, depicts the plight of small farmers forced to earn by rikshaw pulling in the city.

12. P. C. Joshi quotes from Radhakamal Mukharjee's *Land Problems of India* (1933) in *Economic and Political Weekly*, 16 August 1986, 1455–69.

13. Shashi Bhushan Upadhyay's 'Premchand and the Moral Economy of Peasantry in Colonial India' (2010, 1–34) examines in Premchand's works a profound concern with moral economy. In *Godan*, the near-total breakdown of moral economy manifests in complete absence of reciprocity between the landlord and the peasant. James C. Scott's (1976) studies based on his fact-finding mission in South East Asian peasantry enabled him to further expand E.P. Thompson's idea of moral economy, as a strategy to ameliorate the condition of peasantry since economic and moral concerns increasingly seemed to drift apart. It was also known as the subsistence ethics of peasantry, as an ideology of survival and reciprocity in the peasant societies in pre-capitalist mores, particularly during times of adversity and food scarcity (2). Scott implies that the local social arrangements in the villages are customarily structured so as to respect the subsistence needs of the rural poor. Thompson noted that the peasants' communities are aroused to protest and rebel when the terms of the local subsistence ethics are breached by local elites, state authorities, or market forces. He saw market as the site for exercising moral economy where the regulation was sought to be applied, adhering to the conventional notions of rights and wrongs (237–60).

14. Gandhi returned to India from South Africa in 1915 and saw the grievances of the peasants in northern India oppressed by indigo planters. The farmers were being bullied into planting indigo in their fields without any payment. In Champaran, Bihar, in the leadership of Gandhi, mass uprisings of peasants mobilized in 1917 to protest against injustice. It was called Satyagraha, a non-violent revolt.

15. Awadh peasant movement was against the landlords and Talukdar, who insinuated by the Colonial bosses demanded much higher rents from the

peasants. Peasants were made to perform *begar* which meant compulsory work at the landlord's farm without any payment.
16. Orsini's research finds that the special issue, 'Kisaan' (The Peasant), in the magazine *Abhyuday*, 30 November 1931, demonstrated a popular concern to which most magazines in Hindi (published in Calcutta, Banaras, Patna, and Darbhanga) subscribed. Shambhunath in 'Hindi Navjagaran ka Kisan Prashna' (Peasant Question in the Reawakening of Hindi) tellingly illustrates how the dominant concern for the freedom of peasantry from oppression energized the publication of Hindi magazines and expanded their sphere of readership. The contemporary Urdu writing, however, remained distanced from rural experience.
17. Pant '*Bharatmata Gramvasini*' (1939) sees the spirit of Bharat Mata (mother India) residing in villages and demonstrates the urge to see our rural world to prosper. It is borne of the compassion for the suffering peasantry: 'Trapped in totems and taboos, is this the home of an architect of life? ... Saturated with overwhelming ignorance and helplessness/ broils in homes, in fields.'
18. All the four Five-Year Plans of the Indian state apparently committed to improving the state of rural India in terms of agriculture proved unsuccessful. Considerable emphasis was laid upon the land reforms as it was recognized that three-fourths of population dependent on agriculture and 49 percent of national incomes comes from this sector.
19. The *Bhudan* movement initiated by Vinoba sought inspiration from Gandhian idea of Sarvodaya. Its principal aim was to raise the lives of deprived and landless. Supported by the state, it attempted to persuade wealthy landowners to voluntarily give a percentage of their land to land. It could not be effective in UP and Bihar and turned out to be a failure.
20. I have drawn this matter from Shukla's novel, *Bisrampur ka Sant*.
21. The Land Ceiling Act or '*Chakbandi*' was a core part of land reformation in India intended to meet the land needs of the landless in rural areas. It was also intended to reduce the glaring inequalities in land ownership, with the goal of developing a cooperative rural economy and expanding self-employment in owned land as distinguished from subletting and tenant cultivations. By 1961–62, *Chakbandi* (Land Ceiling Act) had been passed in all the states and it however became one of the controversial measures of land reforms in India. The nature of its execution varied from state to state. The ceiling on existing holdings randomly varied from 20 to 125 acres. The act however did not benefit sub-tenants and sharecroppers, as these people did not have occupancy rights on the land they cultivated. Intermediaries were abolished, but the rent-receiving class continued to exist.
22. Pinto's findings unfold that Panchayat is a caricature of what we describe as governance. See *Indian Political Science Association* (Stable URL: 855614, 138–39. http://www.jstor.com/stable/41). The Amendment Act of 1992 contains provision for devolution of powers and responsibilities to the panchayats both for the preparation of economic development plans and social justice, as well as for

26 INTRODUCTION

     implementation in relation to twenty-two subjects listed in the eleventh schedule of the Constitution.
23. During Panchayat elections, the generally deprived villagers are wooed by the candidates with the feast of country liquor (arrack) and chicken. Trucks of liquor were seized during such occasions. Several deaths also took place due to spurious liquor.
24. Parth Chatterji in *Omnibus: Impossible India* (253) and Barbara Harriss-White in *India Working* draw upon Foucault's notion of the dispersed practices of the government as 'governmentality' to understand the operations of the Indian state functioning as a 'bundle of everyday institutions and forms of rules, devices and technologies invisible to the common observer assembled into an apparatus having neither unity nor the functionality often ascribed to them' (1). Bruce Curtis explains this further in 'Foucault on Governmentality and Population: The Impossible Discovery' (505–33).
25. I have quoted from Amit Manoj's conversation with a peasant in his Bhumika (A short Introduction) to *Katha me Kisan*, Part I.
26. Suman Guha Mozumdar reports on Sainath's lecture in New York, *Rediff*, October 2006, 15:52 IST.
27. Yogima Seth Sharma in 'India Has 100 Million More Poor' mentions the report of C. Rangarajan Committee which finds that rural poor percentage in rural areas was 30.95 as compared to the previous 25.7.

1
Village India: Difficult Stories

Some are more equal than others.

—Orwell

Premchand's stories of rural life created a vast readership in the Hindi belt and were read as a movement for the many-sided reformation in the economic and social structure of village life. The concerted efforts his spirited contemporaries made in the direction raised the hope of restoring health and happiness in the rural world of free India. In the subsequently independent democratic India, all across the schools and colleges of the Hindi belt, the songs of Maithili Sharan Gupta's[1] (2018) 'Aha *Gramya* Jeevan!' (Aha Village Life!) were cited as the illustration of the simplicity and diligence of the rural world steered towards building a great nation. The survivor characters of Phanishwar Nath Renu's[2] (2021) popular novel, *Maila Aanchal* (Soiled Border) raised hopes in the promises of new democratic India in the regions of Uttar Pradesh and Bihar. Shrilal Shukla's (2004, 1–423) rural narratives,[3] in the collection *Jahalat ke Pachas Saal* (Fifty Years of Stupidity): 'Swarna Varsha' (Golden Rains), 'Pahali Chook' (First Mistake), 'Hori aur *1984*'[4] ('Hori and *1984*') however embody the brass tacks of Indian peasantry showing how within a few decades of the independence of India, the enthusiasm for the upliftment of our villages as an integral aspect of our new nationhood began dying down. 'Hori aur *1984*' engages the interest of this chapter more specifically, for invoking Premchand's Hori as an iconic figure of small peasantry in India. Images of Premchand's Hori of 1930s, impinging on the consciousness of Shukla's Hori subsisting in the Orwellian world of 1984, are sharp reminder of the fact that the colonial times and also the times after India evolved into an advanced liberal democracy were not only marked by tolerance of high levels of inequality, the rural world perennially in the grip of poverty and struggle for survival is accepted as natural and normal.

Being a part of the Indian Administrative Service in UP, for more than three decades, Shrilal Shukla could make sense as an insider that the ordinary villagers were looked upon in the public domain, not listened to at the block, district, state and national levels. He knew why the Public Distribution System failed; why relief failed to reach on time; why many deserving individuals were denied below poverty line (BPL) cards; why subsidies did not deliver; why most policies and programs remained on paper and never materialized or, if materialized, proved inadequate; and why complicated, lengthy development projects involving heavy expenditure of state funds, too complex to audit, were coveted because they allowed underhand means of making money and manipulating massive diversion of government funds.[5]

'There Cannot Be Good Stories of Peasantry; There Are Only Difficult Stories'

The artificial construction of village life in literature and cinema—young rustic men and women, seesawing in lentil fields, singing, dancing, and romancing while harvesting—urged Shukla to write the experiential facts of village life. 'Swarna Varsha' relates the visit of a poet enamoured of a poetic-romantic view of the village in the rainy season. His confrontation with stinking open drains, lack of drinking water, and unavailability of rural health care disillusions him:

> for the sick, there is some kind of room known as hospital; the compounder lived four kilometres away; he wouldn't come in spite of the urgent need. He was dismissed for stealing medicines. There are no roads; for thieves—the village is an ideal site; the police station—too far off. The walls of hovels half collapsed, those that are whole, are porous, easy to break in, having soaked too much humidity...[6] (Shukla, 11–15)

Another episode during this visit makes him lose faith in all the platitudes about idyllic serenity of rural life:

The mess created by incessant rains incites bloody battles between the rival groups. The day-long binding of boundaries to stop the gushing water after the heavy downpour led to twenty criminal cases. To evacuate the inundated water from one field through the other caused fifteen more criminal cases. To unblock water from one's drain through the other's roof led to twenty criminal cases. The times of ploughing fields arrive; now the village biggies equipped with the musclemen are out to dispossess the weak. (Shukla, 13)

Unchecked serial violence remains an endemic feature of the rural regions that on several occasions costs many lives. The motives most often are caste prejudice, or land dispute among close relatives or tenants. In 'Pahali Chook', an unnamed urban-educated young man who confuses 'bajra' (millet) for the name of a person is inspired by the romantic depictions of farming life in cinema: 'famous heroes ploughed fields, singing; the heroines, carried rotis in the basket in the midst of fecund greenery' (125).[7] The real experiences of farm life, however, make him realize the struggles involved in buying seeds or pesticides or an efficient plough, or rushing to the town for each purchase since nothing standard is available in the village. More frustrating has been seeking 'sanction from the Chief Engineer for setting a pipe in the river canal, or dealing with the absence of the dealer, or complaining against the corrupt employee of the agriculture department' (127). The young man's account reveals how frivolously the Indian peasantry has been treated by those dealing with agriculture. Giving up finally, the urban youth realizes that, 'there cannot be good stories of peasantry; there are only difficult stories' (127).

From Premchand to Shrilal Shukla: Colonialism to Elite Nationalisms

Hori, the protagonist of Premchand's (1936) elegiac narrative, *Godan* reappears in 'Hori aur *1984*'. In his narrative, Shrilal Shukla records several decades of oppression of Indian peasantry and we are drawn to the immense messiness and chaos afflicting rural India of Uttar Pradesh and Bihar in the post-independent India. Hori's random musings and dialogic monologues in 'Hori aur *1984*' connect the reader with the estranged and derelict small farmers[8] of all castes, trapped in the Orwellian world of 1984, driving home the uneasy implications of the silences and gaps between Premchand's Hori of the 1930s and Hori of the contemporary world of *1984*. Hori's wife Dhaniya, who played a major role in the life of her husband in Godan, is absent in the story of Hori aur *1984*. In many cases, in the households of the very poor, women are the most deprived, suffering drudgery, malnutrition, and disease. The creepy silence and loneliness in Hori's life makes one conscious of what Sam Hicky and Sara Bracking point out that 'even groups that include the poor are likely to exclude the poorest either at entry or over time' (2005, 856). It has been observed that people suffering extreme hardship are generally expelled from the social context.

Shukla's Hori of 1984 drives the reader into the dark zone of democratic India: 1950s to 1990s—a period marked by the transition from colonialism to elite nationalism and forces us to acknowledge that the rural world remained untouched by the movements conducted and espoused by the political class of the democratic state: every sphere of progress was denied to the rural India. In the Orwellian frame of reference, 'Hori aur *1984*' delivers more complex implications of the callous indifference that India's small farmers and landless labourers suffered in the post-independent India. A small farmer no longer encounters, as in the colonial times, exploitation in the guise of local controllers, such as a wicked zamindar,[9] a heartless usurer, a calculating village accountant, a greedy Brahman priest, or the scheming colonial bosses. Suffering massive indebtedness, the peasant finds himself surrounded by the invisible or vaguely visible agencies of control: assistance programs, policies, and regulations, as well as an increasingly crafty political economy, all of which have helped either established wealthy landowners or the new landowning class. Under these conditions, the struggle of sowing, planting, irrigating, harvesting, and marketing becomes all the more difficult for the small farmers.

Winter's Night ('Poos ki Raat') Is Severe

'Hori aur *1984*' opens up to a play of ironic and parodic discourse summoning in laconic idiom the times of harsh winters. The poor not only need the feed of toddy[10]—as in the 1930s but also—propaganda, in the December of 1984. The Hori of our times is squatting upon the cemented veranda of Pandit Matadin in the early hours of a winter's night. Winter nights are perennially cruel to the poor, reminding Hori of the harsh cold of 1930 in Premchand's 'Poos ki Raat' (Winter's Night). Hori is watching TV and eating prolefeed.[11] Prolefeed encroaches upon Hori's world in a gamut of discourses: advertisements, news programs, and spiritual Gurus that channel and shape a proletarian's response to his circumstances:

> Were these the days of 1934–35, Hori of *Godan* would be sitting under the cracked roof, in his village, Semri, warming himself by the fireside made from sticks and dry cane leaves. But in the year 1984, especially George Orwell's year 1984, Hori has changed. He is no longer sucking hookah, but bidi[12] after guzzling toddy (country liquor in the form of palm wine) pilfered from the river bank.[13] (Shukla, 55)

The writer's occasional remarks intruding into the narrative, serve the function of an ironic mediator, drawing a parodic analogy between Orwell's *1984* and the peasantry of Hori under containment, with the television serving as one of the more sophisticated and dispersed techniques of power permeating a common man's world. In Orwell's *1984*, the telescreen bruises Winston Smith's ears with 'statistics, proving that people today had more food, more clothes, better housing, better recreations—that they lived longer, worked shorter hours, were bigger, healthier, happier, more intelligent, better educated than the people fifty years ago' (p. 68). Correspondingly, in 'Hori aur *1984*', prolefeed announces the initial statistics of increasingly higher rates of growth that 'flow like autumnal leaves in Hori's thought-stream' (Shukla, 55). Hori listens: 'The average development rate of India had been 4.7%, while of America 2%, and England only 0.3%' (p. 55). Prolefeed goes on, 'The produce of grain increased to 15 crores' (55), to which Hori muses, 'must be rotting in the yards feasting rats' (55). That the state's claims are far from true is very well-known to Hori's community. Criticizing the state's proclaimed record surplus in 2001–03, P. Sainath, a specialist in agricultural and rural development, reveals, 'the state exported millions of tons of grain at prices lower than those offered to its own deprived. That grain fed the European cattle, the most food-secure creatures on earth, while hundreds of millions went hungry at home' (1996, 8). For the deprived, however, hunger and malnutrition are the normal contingencies to be endured. In the rural regions, customarily it is by toiling hard that the poor peasant earns food for himself and his family. The quantity of grain given to the labourer by his employer would be in proportion to the hours worked. 'In case of absence from work due to illness, no food would be cooked in his hovel' (Shukla, 55–56). The convention of the poor exchanging manual labour for edibles survives in all rural regions of India.

Usury Renders Them Refugees in Their Own Land

The state of indebted peasants was like that of refugees in their own land.[14] Harassment and mounting pressure forced them into compromising circumstances; their dwelling place, land, oxen, calves—all would be on auction, rendering them destitute in their own village. Hori reminiscences the days of *Godan*, in the 1930s, when he could not understand the tricks of usury; all he knew was the formidable fear:

> The fear of the loan from a Brahmin, fear of rushing back and forth to the police stations and the courts, fear of the shock of watching one's ready standing crop set on auction, fear of the other methods of extortion: the 'mother-sister' abuses and brutal thrashing; and the biggest thing: 'trapped in a vicious net; the more you wriggle yourself free, the more trapped you are'. (Shukla, 58)

Godan's Hori's debtors were Pandit Datadin, Dulari Sahuian, Jhinguri Singh, and Pateshwari. For a loan of Rs. 50, Mangru Sah extorted Rs. 300 and got his cane crop auctioned off. In spite of Dulari Sahuain's sweet tongue, it was Hori's repeated nose-rubbing alone that could fetch Rs. 200 from her. As a matter of policy, Pandit Datadin would extort interest on every paisa, demanded Rs. 200 for Rs. 30, in nine years. The exorbitant rates of interest forever dispossessed Hori from his land. He could no longer plant the cane and was downgraded from farmer to labourer: 'Memories of the tribulations of the past even today make his heart shudder' (56).

Tortuous Snare of Moneylending: Private Loaners and State Assistance Programs

In rural India, parents arrange the marriage of their daughters, and fathers of unmarried daughters are answerable to the community. Arranging a marriage involves settling the amount of cash and gifts demanded by the groom's family. Sometimes marriages fail to occur because parents cannot meet the dowry demands of grooms and their families. In the worst cases, if a marriage takes place and a material demand that was promised to a husband goes unfulfilled, the wife is put to death via burning or other methods. Hori's mind is gripped by concerns about how to settle the marriage of his daughter Sona and what would happen if he would be unable to pay back the debt.

In rural and semi-rural or urban North India, Hindu household perform varied ceremonies[15] (*'gouna', 'mundan', 'chhedan',* the *'tenth day',* the *'thirteenth day'*) that involve feasting and gifting. Loan from the local usurer remains the only option in this crisis, 'whose terms of agreement could be even more frightening than those of Mangru Sahu in the times of *Godan*' (57). Sainath's investigation into the business of lending finds that 'a peasant seeking Rs. 3000 does not have to run around for weeks; he will get precisely that sum (sometimes minus the first instalment of interest) from the local moneylenders. No one asks him to explain why he is borrowing the money—the interest will eventually kill him' (1996, 199). Sainath's itinerancy into the heart of Indian rural scene made it very clear to him that the professional ethics of usury never change. Amiable to their customer at the outset, the usurer could be extremely relentless in extorting interest. Coveting hefty interest has to be the dharma (religion-sanctioned law) of a usurer that disallows any sentiment towards the borrower other than the matter of profit. One who is involved in a deal with him has to accept this.

Panchayats to Rural Banks: Agencies of Rural Welfare

Hori's narrative tells us how the exploitation of generations of peasantry in the times of colonial India and even thereafter, since the abolition of zamindari never stopped. High hopes were posited in the role of Panchayat (Village Council) to ensure equality of all human beings. It was expected of Panchayat to guard the villagers against any kind of exploitation. It was however generally found to be languishing under the subservience to the wealthy landowners who possessed a specific triad: political clout, musclemen employed to physically or materially harm or intimidate the justice-seekers. In the world of 1984, to Hori, nothing could be scarier than the 'Assistance Programmes of the Nationalized Bank'. The prolefeed announcement delivers accounts of their proud achievements that 'pour upon Hori's consciousness like burning coal' (Shukla, 58). Dedicated to profit-making, the agents of micro-financing programmes inveigle the gullible, uneducated villagers by means of deploying touts and fixers who also happen to be the functionaries of the village governance/Panchayat in exchange for some commission paid by the banks. Hori is no longer the naïve and trusting peasant of the time of *Godan*. He knows that the assistance (loan), once sanctioned, will pass through quite a few mediating agencies and representatives assigned the delegation of the loan. His apprehensions are proven correct, but the gross facts he discovers reveal the true intent of the assistance program:

> The assistance never directly reached the deserving. Of the amount, two third reach the Gram Sevaks (the village servants), the development officials, branch managers, with which they would purchase trucks, build bungalows in the cities; the rest was used to make many luckless like Hori indebted. The Prolefeed announcement that on behalf of 24,000 branches of the Nationalized Banks, Rs. 45 crores as loan was distributed in the rural region during 1983 and 1984, reminds Hori of the damage he suffered on account of this. It was far more devastating than the despair suffered by Hori (of *Godan*) by Pandit Datadin. While pleading for mercy could make Dulari Sahuain of the time of *Godan* melt for some moment; the law-bound, faceless new clan of moneylender of 1984 is never visible. One could say nothing to him. His existence, however, is struck home in the notices to defaulting householders for recovery and through the summons of confiscation in the Newspaper. In 1935, the crocodiles on one side of the river bank would pounce upon him, but now—on both sides—crocodiles of different faces, but of one race are on the prowl. (57–58)

It was realized rather too late that the micro-finance scheme of the Gramin Bank was solely dedicated to profit-making. The bank's profit piled up through exorbitant rates of interest imposed upon destitute borrowers. There has been severe criticism of such programmes, for their style has shown the hiatus between rhetoric and responsibility. It is a known fact that the poor have often taken the tragic route to suicide to escape the humiliation caused by the coercive recovery of outstanding loans.

Doublethink in the Welfare State: Experts and Intermediaries

In *1984*, Orwell reveals that in a society, those who have the best knowledge of what is happening are those who are farthest from seeing the world as it is: It need hardly be said that the subtle practitioners of doublethink are those who invented doublethink and know that it is a vast system of mental cheating.[16] In general, the greater the understanding, the greater the delusion; the more intelligent, the less sane (Orwell, 1999, 195). Indeed, in the fictional society of Winston Smith's Oceania, the English Socialist Party, or 'Engsoc', claimed that the revolution happened to liberate the Proles. In reality, however, it worked under the surveillance of the privileged inner party elite and punished all individualism and independent thinking. The proletarian is made to believe that 'at all times the Party is in possession of absolute truth' (194) while it indulged in lies: 'To tell deliberate lies while genuinely believing in them, to forget any fact that has become inconvenient, and then when it becomes necessary, again, to draw back from oblivion for just so long it is needed' (Orwell, 195). The doublethink of Orwellian state characterizes the world of political class around Hori as well. The sarkar (state) in Hori's world in 'Hori aur *1984*' is a vast network whose centre is difficult to locate. It is assumed as sovereign, possessed with a distinct aura, and attributed with wisdom and superior purpose. It clearly works far more to the advantage of some individuals than it does to others. The state's doublethink to improve the lot of peasantry is brought to the surface by a group of appointed representatives. Awed by their presence, Hori calls them '*Divya Jana*'.[17] Shukla's contemporary, Kamleshwar,[18] sees this class of state functionaries as 'the logical heir to the elite nationalism, the progeny of messy policies, muddled governance and bad practices of implementation'. Their intent to exploit the gullible masses is concealed beneath a genial condescending exterior and benevolent sloganeering. 'They arrive in Hori's world armed with papers and files, to grant "divine loan"' (Shukla, 58).

Hori is apprehensive about the *Divya Jana*'s design, for it is known that their men might arrive at any time to confiscate his belongings for auction (59). Most vexing to Hori, therefore, is the rural development loan, called the 'divine loan' (58), imposed upon the peasant community by 'overenthusiastic urban experts: the makers of India's destiny, born with the genes of gods: the big officials of the Ministry of Finance, big, big bankers, well known economists, presiding white-clad multifaceted leaders, and the officers' (57). Hori sees the gregarious arrival of urban exploiters in Premchand's *Premashram*[19] replayed in the year 1984 when the entire retinue of the state Development Department descends upon the village. Near Semri, in Belari, a camp for the loan distribution is convened to distribute the loan of 20 lakhs to the farmers. It was the same place where the landlord Rai Sahab used to organize *Ramlila*[20] annually in the 1930s. Now in 1984, in the supervision of his MLA (Member of Legislative Assembly) son, who aspires to become a minister, it has turned into a camp for the loan distribution where vociferous campaigning is pursued as if it is not the loan but the charity sponsored by the benevolent *sarkar* (the state):

> The Bank employees were 'flitting here and there like frogs in the rain ... A khadi[21]-clad youth, serving as a volunteer for the noble cause of granting loan to as many people as possible displayed cheerful countenance, making grand announcements on the loudspeaker applauding the unity and integrity of the country'. (58)

Shukla's reference is to the khadi-clad youth and the loud self-congratulatory idiom he uses to tempt the villagers via nationalistic and patriotic slogans is indeed reminiscent of Squealer in *Animal Farm*: 'of the best known among the pigs, was a small pig named Squealer ... a brilliant talker, and when he was arguing some difficult point, whisking his tail, which was somehow very persuasive' (Orwell, 1999, 9). Squealer handles the propaganda machinery of the new rule and is sent round the farm to explain the new arrangement to all others after Snowball's mysterious expulsion. He argues in support of Napoleon, 'No one believes more firmly than Comrade Napoleon that all animals are equal' (Orwell, 37). The young man in 'Hori aur *1984*' performs the role of a fixer or a facilitator, an Orwellian official agency deployed to lure the peasants to the investors, to ensure the full success of the loan scheme.

Deal Done! An Ailing Buffalo with Three Teats

A calculation sheet displayed to Hori made a strong case in favour of the loan, proving that besides paying his debt, with the milk yield of the buffalo, Hori would earn several hundred rupees per month. As if acting on Hori's behalf and in his interest, 'they [the officials of the Bank] were not ready to take his no' (Shukla, 59). Hori was left with the burden of the bank loan. As he anticipated, the scheme was not without the pests inside:

> The first pest was the *Gram Sevak* (the village servant), whose commission of one percent in the deal was set. The second was the veterinary doctor, deployed to represent the interest of a poor peasant, at whose initiative in a big cattle fare, a group of buffaloes was bought—a buffalo with three teats was one of them and Hori was handed over its tether. At his dwelling since then is tethered the ailing buffalo that never yielded milk. (57–58)

Hori's experience of being persuaded into a deal and deceived by the whole network of people shows how, for an impoverished peasant, it is difficult to resist the influence of the one who speaks in the vocabulary of the knowledgeable and the educated. Sainath's findings tell us that the Panchayats acting in a farcical manner contributed to the failure in the operation of Gramin banks. 'Many of the Gram Sabhas involved in identifying the beneficiaries did much damage. In parts of Bihar, families of Sarpanch often became multiple beneficiaries' (197). The banks began with some promise but soon ran into the reality of village power structure; while some did benefit, the poorest got the least. 'In many cases petty government officials and local bank officer slice off their cut.

The beneficiary thumbprints a document saying, he received Rs. 8000 and pays interest on that amount though he got only Rs. 5000. In effect he is paying an interest of 20 percent' (Shukla, 197). In this Brechtian, drama is reflected what constitutes, according to Barbara Harriss-White, a 'shadow state':

> This vast assemblage of brokers, advisers, political workers, crooks and contractors surrounds the 'official state', deprives it of funds, and helps to ensure that it is run in part for the private benefit of some of its employees. The official part of the Indian state, hollowed out over the course of the last twenty or thirty years. (77)

Conditioned and disciplined in an unequal relationship, the poor are not supposed to actively claim their right to question, or right to justice or right to be heard. Policies and programs meant for them do not involve their participation. For Hori, the event makes even more poignant the memory of the days of *Godan* when he had lost the most cherished possession of a farmer—a cow. The loan from the village lender had enabled Hori to own a cow. 'Driven by jealousy, his brother poisons the cow; Hori could never dream of owning a buffalo in the world of 1984' (Shukla, 58).

Poor Peasants, Targets of Indignity of Vasectomy

During the period of 'Emergency which spanned from June 26th, 1975 to March 21st, 1977',[22] vasectomy became a stringent population-control measure. Large camps were set up for facilitating this mission. Officials of the Indian bureaucracy were assigned targets to get the largest possible numbers of vasectomies performed. Poor, deprived rustics proved the easiest targets and were often coerced into undergoing the procedure. To the villagers who faced the stunning impact of 'Bio Power, the experience was unforgettable'.[23] Hori remembers the popular sloganeering that made vasectomy sound like an ardently desired goal of the politics of Emergency claiming to structure a war on poverty. The memories of the period flash back to Hori in 'Hori aur *1984*':

Hori was forced into a vasectomy camp and it was like four strong men applying force to slit the gullet of a pig. In that operation, one of Hori's veins was cut off, but he was not much aggrieved. The torture though made him sterile was to be borne for the good of the nation. (58)

The poor were the easy targets of subjugation during Emergency. What was good for the country was decided by a group of politically powerful elite and interpreted as beneficial for the common masses. The political arrangement of the period was strongly reminiscent of Orwellian welfare state in which the inner party circle, official deception, secret surveillance, and manipulation were the modus operandi of a totalitarian regime.

Indirect Violence: Land Ceiling Act

One of the unforgettable violence against the farming villagers was perpetrated through the Land Ceiling Act[24] during the 1970s. Intruding into the rural life in the garb of a rural welfare program, it became a subterranean source of turning their lives upside down. Several fictional narratives of Markandeya and Damodar Datta Dikshit have provided moving accounts of the way in which the act fuelled various kinds of caste and class politics. The upper castes, through ingratiating relationships with the officials in charge, usurped the fertile portions of lands of small landowners by means of clever paperwork, smartly made claims, and bribes. For the victims, it was difficult to pin down the blame on any one individual; the Act turned into a source of indirect violence, pre-empting the aggrieved into taking legal routes to defend their lands. Hori grieves for his brethren who suffered betrayal and deprivation; several of them abandoned farming and left for the cities.

Rural Population, Streaming to Distant Lands

Rural Indians have been migrating to cities in small and large numbers since the late nineteenth century. Premchand's works reveal the causes for this phenomenon and poignantly evoke the disarray and vacuity that the displacement stirs in the life of Hori's son Gobar in *Godan*. Shukla's *Raag Darbari* (1969) concludes by suggesting that migration is the only option left to the peasantry. Several rural narratives in Hindi have explored the psychological dislocation the state of migration brought about. Hori's story in 'Hori aur *1984*' hints at the massive migration of the rural population to the cities in the last decades of the twentieth century. David Ludden (1990) ascribes mass migration to late nineteenth century transition to capitalism: Landless workers lived and died through the transitions from paternalistic to capitalistic labour control as bondedness remained. Landowners feeling the pinch of declining growth rates in agricultural surplus by the late nineteenth century, like their dependents, moved into the labour market, but sought jobs in professions, business, and government (171). Comparing 1984 to the times of *Godan* in the 1930s, Hori's narrative notes that:

> Dulari Sahuain, Mangru Sah—the privileged and resourceful of the village, during the times of *Godan* have now shifted to the towns. Their offspring have entered into the Indian Administrative Services or having obtained the degree of Management are reaching high places: the places that belong to the elite distributing the divine loan. (Shukla, 60)

Since the 1980s, villages have been fast undergoing transition. Both rich and poor are increasingly drawn to the city for different reasons.

Clearing of Forests Have Cleared Even Vultures and Bats, Neel Gai, or Even the Crowd of Deer

It is a sad fact that segments of woodlands that once thrived in the Indian rural landscape have vanished in a few recent decades. The thinning of forest areas in the villages due to the axing of trees, the girdling of barks, and the clearing of forests for purposes of agriculture and the creation of roads conspicuously impacted the congenial habitat of flora and fauna. The celebration of *Vana Mahotsava* (Forest Festival) in Hori's village takes place at the directive of the government. In the deforested surroundings, even vultures and bats do not stir. With the felling of trees and drying pastures, the crowd of deer and the forest cows are now no longer visible.

The Village, a Site of Crimes, No Police Patrolling

In Premchand's story, 'Poos ki Raat' (1–9), the peasant's misery in bitter cold finds resonance in Hori's braving the unsparing cold in Hori of 1984. Unlike the earlier times on winter evening, the village assembly does not take place by the side of fire. Sporadic bad blood or court cases as inevitable part and parcel of *pattidari* (co-sharing of farming lands) send many to jail. The cases remain untried for decades. The doors get locked in the evenings. Dogs' barking in the secluded nights makes one fear the terror, the darkness may enshroud. Gangs of bandits emanate from any village, with the intent to not just rob, but assault and plunder. The apprehension of menacing presence makes Hori anxious for the safety of his young daughters: 'villages unlike the earlier times of *Godan*, are no longer safe for women; Sona, Rupa and Silia used to live like unfettered birds' (59–60). Police cannot protect him, if he is threatened or hit by a bullet. 'For lodging a report, he is made to walk 14 kilometres to the police station; in the election times, to grab his vote however, the polling booth would be installed next to his dwelling' (61). It is commonly known, the police response to the complaints of the poor is dependent upon meeting their customary expectation regarding inducement—either First Information Report (FIR) is not lodged—or, if lodged, is of no consequence. Hori relates that the octogenarian Sanpatti failed to protect his daughters. Like him, Hori is incapable of protecting them. Matadin tells him, 'Let your daughters be in Gobar's care in the city; after settling their marriage, call them back to the village' (60). Now Hori is not only worried about the unpaid loans, but about the thought of his daughters being home alone. No longer does immoral conduct or the tomfoolery of village youth prompt the summoning of Panchayat. The offender can now escape to the city after hurling abuses at the Panchayat. 'After all, drawing rickshaws in the city yields more income than does labouring in the fields' (60). In the rural world, the poor are hardly listened to. Panchayat as a law-regulating authority generally proves ineffective in granting unequivocal justice in the cases against the perpetrators.

The Caste of Power Matters

In Hori's memory, the stringent and punitive caste equations of the 1930s keep flashing back. The moneylending caste determined how menacing the punishment for not paying the debt could be. Of all the usurers, the Brahman caste was the most formidable. Customarily, in the course of time, recipients of expensive gifts and fertile lands from wealthy landowners, the Brahman priest class, accumulated wealth and power. Superstition dictated that offending a Brahman was a sin:

> If a single paisa remains unpaid to a Brahman lender, it would break out from my bones. When Gobar dared to challenge Pandit Datadeen for the usurious interests of Rs. 200 for borrowing only Rs. 30, and decided to pay Rs. 66 calculating all interest, Hori of Premchand held the feet of Panditji, 'Maharaj, do not take the boy's words seriously. As long as I am alive, I'll return each and every paisa owed to you'. (56)

The most gossiped news in the society of *Godan* in the memory of Hori of 1984 was Pandit Datadin's son Matadin's notorious love story and seduction of Selia, a *chamain*.[25] Matadin's exclusion from the Brahman community as punishment and subsequently his father Pandit Datadin's invitation to the priests from Varanasi to perform the purifying rituals of his defiled son generated a lot of debate among people of Semri. Matadin however later publicly made a dramatic declaration of accepting Selia: 'I don't want to be a Brahman but rather remain a chamar' (57). The Hori of 1984 cannot figure out how 'Matadin has become a Brahman again' (57). The son Ramu, born of Matadin and Selia's union, turned out to be adept at studies. Adopting his mother's caste as his own, he sought employment as an Excise Inspector in the Reserved Category.[26] The son's elevation to inspector raised Matadin's status. It was agreed upon by all that 'Matadin can no longer be called a chamar; he was since then addressed "Panditji." Not only was the tuft on his back head was raised, his torso was also showing the *"three threads"*[27] with pride' (59–60). The cross-caste credentials of Matadin prompted him to be nominated as the suitable local president of the ruling party, for he can influence the votes of the lower as well as the upper caste: 'Now at his house, the matters pertaining to the village governance: incoming and outgoing bogus income are settled in larger number' (p. 61).

In the present era, though caste remains unthreatened as a value system, it survives more as an issue of political expediency. In contemporary India, caste is of no significant value to the poor. Whether upper-caste, middle-caste, or lower-caste, small peasants are in the same underclass as small landholders, tenants, or labourers striving hard for survival.

Toddy Sinks Hori into Unthinking Stupor, Prolefeed Lends Illusion

Villagers caught in the appalling worry of getting unmarried daughters married, paying back debts, or coping with problems such as disease and unemployment find arrack easily available. Leisure hours are no longer consumed by pleasant socializing, but stolen for television or the drinking of country liquor: 'Hori and ten more Horis (peasants) in the company of Matadin—all drunk with the pilfered arrack are listening to the sermons of a religious leader on television' (55). Most reverentially, Matadin interprets the sacred knowledge to the peasants; 'when the channel switches the program and begins airing an amorous song, redolent with the lover's desire, he turns off the TV' (55). In Orwellian terms, this could be seen as a moment connecting class, privilege, and control. Symbolically, Matadin has the choice to remain impervious to the TV (prolefeed control) that the peasants do not have. In Orwell's *1984*, it is Obrien's privilege to turn off the TV: 'Yes ... we [Inner Party members] have that privilege' (153). This is symbolic of the fact that the privileged class, a part of which is the mass media, determines what the proletariat see, hear, and, to some extent, do. The hope that more leisure time will compensate the worker for his estrangement has proved to be misleading. Indeed, the consumption of prolefeed and liquor allows hard labourers to become immersed in a haze of comfortable illusion. Liquor sinks Hori into an unthinking stupor. Observation of the lives of labourers and peasants make Sainath infer that 'for the liquor wholesaler and the client, there is hardly any concern for the societal values that prohibit man from drinking, rather it is taken for granted that for those engaged in tough labour, drinking offers solace' (287). It is common knowledge among Indian citizens that across India during the general elections and local Gram Panchayat (Village Council) elections, chicken and liquor are generously served to the poor as a way to court their votes. During this time, a huge stock of country liquor intended for wooing the village voters is often confiscated and deaths from alcohol poisoning increase considerably.

Dreary, Drudging Village, but There Is Surfeit of Bright Images to Keep the Blues Away

Hori's narrative is not unmindful of the spectacular achievements of the Indian state, substantially attributable to state initiative: 'Not everything is wrong with the prolefeed; of course, film actors, musicians, management experts, astronauts, industrialists, philosopher, specialists of law are contributing to the betterment of our lives' ('Shukla, 61). Sham Lal (2001) points out succinctly, that the increased presence of multinationals in many poor societies has jacked up the salaries of executives in the business houses, entertainment industry, 'provided access to TV networks as in the West. The political or economic situation may be pretty grim but there is a surfeit of bright images to keep the blues away' (232). And Hori's narrative wistfully submits: 'but call this the misfortune of Hori that upon his life reigns the regime of criminals, brokers, interest-profiteers, impotent intellectual experts, dacoits, insensitive policemen and political opportunists' (61). Seeking comfort in arrack and television, the poor peasant may be in possession of a mobile phone, but no security of subsistence. Even the middle poor need to rush to the cities for medical care, which costs a large chunk of their income. Oftentimes, the poor are forced to sell off their small farm holdings and possessions to meet healthcare expenses. Subsistence grows increasingly difficult with unaffordable healthcare, hygiene, and sanitation. Illness of a family member, the death of a dairy cow, or financial ruin of the sole breadwinner of a household can suddenly turn a rural family's livelihood upside down. Seeking comfort in arrack and television, the poor peasant may be in possession of a mobile phone, but no security of subsistence.

Despite the regimes of power producing the forms of subjectivity on which they can most efficiently go to work, 'the emergent'[28] or 'the left-over' remains subliminal in Hori, episodically spurring anger, bafflement, and derision. He feels wronged:

> People in authority have however three worries regarding his community: How can they [the villagers] be stopped from producing children; how can they be thrust with one bigha [five-eighths of an acre] of barren land in a state sponsored program; and how can they be made to owe the development debt for the land acquired? (61)

Through Hori's bewailing, 'the several lakhs of farming laborers and crores of tribal are living in the nightmare of 1984' (61), the narrator draws attention to fact that the exploitation of labour and the poor enforcement of law have been the norm in the unorganized sector which employs a much larger segment of the working population. In the interest of the unorganized sector, the mechanism of surplus appropriation in each epoch of history is reinvented.

As the story moves on towards the end, the diet of prolefeed is already standardizing Hori's consciousness. His thoughts edge closer and closer to dystopia: 'Struggling with insecurity, illness, debt and penury, Hori has as relief—only the TV set of Pandit Matadin, and the pilfered country liquor—brain resonating with arrack' (61). So is the plight of Orwell's Winston Smith, 'sitting in The Chestnut Tree Café, delivered liquor by the name of "Victory," the TV for his consumption however is installed at his place' (61). The ensuing reference to Aldous Huxley's[29] message to Orwell in 'Hori aur *1984*' offers the clue to understanding the crux of Hori's situation: 'in order to rule over people, arousing their childishness and stupidity may be more effective than incarcerating them or exposing them to the pornographic shows' (Shukla, 61). Huxley invokes a nightmarish world that is not based on fear, but on conditioning induced by propaganda and brainwashing, very similar to Orwell's doublethink and thought control. Sham Lal, with his comprehensive understanding of the poverty-growing endemic in contemporary India, sees how the crisis of the subaltern shifts from economy to culture as 'socially integrative means like religion, family or local traditions are replaced by the steering media, which rely on bureaucratic and market mechanisms to supply meaning and to secure compliance and identity' (231–37). The personal autonomy of the subaltern remains restricted by the essential structures of economic and cultural arrangements. The situation pre-empts the necessary space for the struggle to bring about reformation. Hori's life compels a realization that a small peasant's efforts to survive in extremely difficult circumstances is generally seen as natural, and the starvation and near-subsistence existence of poor farming, labouring community is seldom seen as worthy of respect, while it is in fact heroic, though conventionally we assign heroic virtues only to adventurers and military personnel.

In the death of *Godan*'s Hori, Premchand symbolically perceives the death of the old society—'the collapse of peasant utopia that could not be reformed from within'.[30] Shukla's Hori remains alive yet vegetating, alienated, and contained by the system. His plight suggests that the rural world's struggle with the native colonizers has been difficult, but more bewildering has been (and may continue to be) its struggle with the 'closure of the alternative', the imposed perception of the impossibility of ways of life that do not promise 'convergence' with global norms.[31] Shukla's transposing Orwell's *1984* in the lives of lacs of Indian peasants is a cautionary tale addressed to the injured and slighted humanity about the dangers of submission to one's plight. Hori's 'having won victory over himself' (Shukla, 61) may appear ironically a benign solution to his crisis, but it has grim implications for India's small peasant.

Notes

1. Maithili Sharan Gupta was a celebrated Hindi poet known for gentle description of the natural environment and innocence of village life.
2. Phaniswar Nath Renu, a recipient of *Padma Shri* award, portrayed the rural life of Bihar. He radically shifted the stereotypically prevalent narrative of the Indian villages as rigid and unchanging to a more gentle, sensitive, and detailed representation with rapid changes towards a modern era.
3. Shrilal Shukla (1925–2011), recipient of the 2011 *Jnanpith* Award, one of the two most prestigious literary honours in India, is known for his earliest masterpiece, *Raag Darbari*. First published in 1968, this novel has been translated into several Indian and foreign languages and is considered a modern example of fiction as an ethnography of India in the decades of the 1960s and 1970s. A series of intersecting anecdotes describe the events of insidious manipulation, corruption, and desperation in the agrarian rural township of Shivpalganj of the North

Indian countryside. His 'Hori aur *1984*' (55–62), 'Gram Varsha' (5–8) 'Pahali Chook' (123–25), and Umraonagar me Kuchch Din in the collection *Jahalat Ke Pachas Saal* illustrate the network of forces in newer permutations reigning in the rural world that preclude the possibility of genuine welfare of peasantry.
4. 'Hori aur Unnis Sau Chourasi' is translated into English as 'Hori aur *1984*' (268–73).
5. The views attributed to Shukla draw on Rajiv Ranjan Giri's interview with him in 'Vidambanaon Se Sakshatkar' ('Confronting Ironies') in *Samkalin Bharatiya Sahitya* (242–44).
6. This excerpt is from 'Swarna Versha'. Subsequent reference is from the same narrative.
7. This excerpt and the following are from 'Pahali Chook'.
8. The small- and middle-level farmers have meagre assets. In modern times, they find it increasingly difficult to earn money through agricultural means. While the income from agriculture is shrinking, the pressures of a consumerist society are bearing on the small and middle-level farmers and their families.
9. A *zamindar* is a landholder or landlord who has free hold of land and who is exempt from the payment of tax. He collects taxes from citizens of the British rule and is doubly empowered to unleash atrocities on peasants. One new law spurred by India's independence was the abolition of *zamindari* (landlordism).
10. Toddy and arrack both are distilled alcoholic beverages made variously from fermented rice, fruit, sugar, and palm. The craving for country liquor in the peasantry is a matter dealt in detail by Sainath in 'Despot distillers Poets and Artists' (271–314). The trade of hooch, toddy, and arrack in the rural India is widespread. Those who get hooked, consume at the cost of three quarters of a day's earning and daily in some seasons.
11. In Winston Smith's Oceania in *Nineteen Eighty-Four*, 'Prolefeed', the discourse of power, includes telescreen and propaganda and is considered the 'food' of the proletariat.
12. A 'bidi' is a thin Indian cigarette smoked mainly by the rural poor. It is cheaper and smaller than a regular cigarette and contains unprocessed tobacco.
13. The excerpts from are from Vanashree's translation of 'Hori aur *1984*' (55–62).
14. Shambhunath in 'Hindi Navjagaran ka Kisan Prashna' ('The Peasant Question in the Reawakening of Hindi') says that peasant society was driven to extremities of crisis due to indebtedness. In the journalistic writing of 1920s and 1930s saw their condition as almost akin to the state of refugees.
15. Until the child bride attains puberty, she is withheld at her parents' home after marriage; *Gauna* is the ceremony of the 'send-off' of a bride to the groom's house. The custom is still followed in the rural and semi-rural regions of north India and Bihar. 'Sixth day', 'twelfth day', *Chhedan* (ear piercing), and *Mundan* (head trouncing) are the earliest initiation ceremonies performed from infancy to early adolescence, meant to mark purification of the child and his/her entrance into the sacred order of the Hindu faith. 'Tenth day' and 'thirteenth day' are post-death

ceremonies that pay tribute to the spirit of the dead via feasting and donations to Brahmans. All of these ceremonies involve expenditure.
16. Orwell coined the term 'doublethink' in his novel *Nineteen Eighty-Four*. The term denotes accepting two contradictory ideas or point of views simultaneously (yet in different contexts), leading inevitably to the practice of double standards and hypocrisy. In Oceania, the Ministry of Truth is concerned with lies while the Ministry of Plenty is concerned with starvation; knowing means not knowing, and to be conscious of complete truthfulness means telling carefully constructed lies.
17. '*Divya Jana*' refers to the upper crust, the cream of Indian society: English-speaking, educated, wealthy individuals. These are the people who exude the confidence of elite power marked in material difference not only in ownership of capital, but in dress, housing, and transportation.
18. I have translated a quote from Rajiv Ranjan Giri's interview with Kamaleshwar, the noted novelist, critic and a film script writer of Hindi in 'Vidambanaon Se Sakshatkar' ('Confronting Ironies', 248–49).
19. Premchand dramatizes Gandhi's view of the exploitive role of Indian city-dwellers. In invoking the issue of the conflict between urban exploiters and rural producers, he reveals the ways in which the affluence of urban upper classes is drawn from rural sources: trade, usury, and absentee landlordism. See *Premashram* (54–55). Several fictional or non-fictional narratives in Hindi and regional languages reveal the way in which the urban dwellers in all epochs of Indian history have exploited the rural landscape and the rural poor. Kuruvilla Pandikattu, in rendering the biographical details of Gandhi in 'Global Village versus Gandhian Village' in *The Meaning of Mahatma for the Millennium* (180–89), notes that Gandhi thought that the cities had drained villages of wealth and talent.
20. *Ramlila* is a religious drama that performs the grand spectacle of the Hindu epic *Ramayana* organized on a large scale across India during the festivities of *Puja* or *Dussehra*. For ten days, Lord Rama's feats are graphically represented via histrionics, songs, and dances.
21. *Khadi*, homespun cotton, was promoted by Gandhi during India's struggle for independence as a form of resistance to foreign production and a symbol of simple life. In the free India, cotton is the preferred clothing fabric of the political class.
22. The controversial time of 'Emergency' (26 June 1975 to 21 March 1977) was declared by President Fakhruddin Ali Ahmed at the advice of Prime Minister Indira Gandhi. Invoking Article 352 of the constitution, with effect from Emergency, Indira Gandhi granted herself extraordinary power and launched a massive crackdown on civil liberties and political opposition. Parliamentary and state governmental elections were postponed. During this time, an inner caucus of the political class surrounding Indira Gandhi was empowered to manipulate the ordinary masses via totalitarian ideology. Tharoor's accounts relate that most of the real victims of Emergency were among the poorest in India. Several people who

most needed the protections of democracy were seized by the state in bazaars or in the fields and carted off into sterilization camps (37).
23. Michel Foucault reads 'bio-power' in the state's management of disciplinary power, deaths, population control, and expansion. In her interpretation of biopower, Sara Mills in *Michel Foucault* says that it is at the level of the body that much regulation by the authorities from the nineteenth century onwards is enacted: knowledge is accumulated, populations are surveyed and observed, and procedures for investigation and research about populations as a whole and of the body in particular are developed and made sophisticated. These activities combined the objective of the government to control population with the investigation of social sciences in population growth (82–95). Paul Rabinow in *The Foucault Reader* (257–89) historicizes biopower wielded by the state, arguing that it is without question an indispensable element in the development of capitalism. Capitalism would not have been possible without the controlled exploitation of bodies into production in terms of labour and the adjustment of the phenomena of population to economic processes (263). See Michel-Foucault.com.
24. The Land Ceiling Act, or 'Chakbandi', was a core part of land reformation in India intended to meet the land needs of the landless in rural areas. It was also intended to reduce the glaring inequalities in land ownership, with the goal of developing a cooperative rural economy and expanding self-employment in owned land as distinguished from subletting and tenant cultivations. Numerous debates have found the Act a failure.
25. In the Hindu caste hierarchy (one of the scheduled castes), female of the Chamar caste.
26. Reserved Category is set by constitutional laws and statutory laws wherein a certain percentage of total available vacancies in educational institutions and jobs are set aside for people from backward communalities. Scheduled Caste (SC), Scheduled Tribe (ST), and Other Backward Class (OBC) are the prime beneficiaries of the state reservation policy.
27. The '*Three Threads*' ceremony is an initiation rite into the *Brahmanic* code of conduct. The ceremony involves the pledging of sacrifices and a male adolescent Brahman wearing three threads across his chest as a reminder of that pledge. It is one of sixteen holy rituals of the *Vedic* Hindu tradition. The three threads, made of hand-spun cotton, are actually only one threads folded three times, braided together into a fine rope, and sanctified by *Vedic* chanting. It can rightly be regarded a holy covenant that binds the adolescent to the pledge of purity of thoughts, words, and deeds. The threads also represent the debt that a *Brahman* owes to the spiritual master, parents, and society.
28. See Terry Eagleton's 'Ideological Strategies' in *Ideology* for a discussion of contradictoriness of all social experiences, social formation, subjectivity, and the resistance to power (33–61).
29. *Nineteen Eighty-Four* (1949) is often clubbed with Aldous Huxley's *Brave New World* (1932). See Sham Lal's article on Huxley, 'A Bad Dream' (263–67), for an

interesting commentary on Huxley's relevance to understanding contemporary Indian society.
30. See P. C. Joshi, 'The Subaltern in Indian Literature: Some Reflections on Premchand and *Godan*' (111).
31. David Punter's phrase in *Postcolonial Imaginings: Fiction of a New World Order* (182) is modified to express the predicament of Indian peasantry.

2
Land Grab: The Dispossessed in the Spectacles of Jugaad

> For any peasant, ownership is the basic need, priced above tenancy and tenancy above casual labour.
> —James C. Scott

Folk narratives of land at stake, land disputes—issuing from contentions about land grab exploding in violent confrontations, murders, lawsuits pursued for life—resonate with fierce emotions in the memory of village folks. Losing land to money lenders has been the oldest story known to most battered households. Numerous stories however in telling details address the damage state-sponsored development schemes have wrought upon the middle-level farmers, small farmers, and that populace at large whose living depended on indigenously practiced vocations aligned with agriculture. The development programmes not only triggered environmental degradation but also their methods of execution messed with the very means of subsistence of those for whom dependence on the indigenous means was the substantive means of survival. It has not been easy to stop business houses from appropriating villages into their corporate image. The legally sanctioned acquisition of lands for 'public purposes'[1] promoted growth of hotels, public transport, industries, golf courses by covering areas which were principally forests or fields meant for farming. Land mafia thrived in the emerging conditions. Dalits, small farmers, and indigenous people being more vulnerable groups suffered displacement, landlessness, unemployment, and homelessness. P. Sainath[2] illustrates how the people chased by development received eviction notices, lived in threat of displacement, lack of food security, and increased levels of illness and disease. Loss of land, as we know, is not the only resource lost, when people are forcibly shifted, grazing grounds, fodder, herbs, forest produce, and community labour are also lost. The schemes of reimbursement are announced, but the loss of such assets is generally undercalculated or misjudged. However petty might be the area, a peasant's land is a symbolic mother, a source of self-esteem, traditionally giving him a sense of belonging for which he could even lay his life.

The two stories of Markandeya[3]: 'Bhudan'[4] (Land Gift) and 'Daune ki Pattiyan' (The Leaf Plate) as elegiac tales, take us to varied periods and decades of history. In both the stories, Markandeya captures the animated ambience of the time, 1950s, when a number of highly promising programmes and schemes raised hopes in the village folks who had faced turbulent times for centuries. The first story 'Bhudan' is a telling evocation of the time when the rhetoric running high in praise of Sant Vinoba's movement raised the hope of every downtrodden rural population in the magic that the spirit of freedom of India could bring about. *Bhudan* was launched as a movement meant to liberate the small farmers from age-old exploitation by ensuring that the big farmers—landowners of many acres of land—would donate some small plots to the landless farmers to help them become self-reliant. Infused with the images of traditional pantheon of folk culture, local deities, strange gods and goddesses—the hut, the rain, spirits, the hum, and buzz—gossips and intrigues, the peculiar histories of conflict with the oppressive usurping powers, resonate the consciousness of the communal past into the present, constructing a symbolic universe of peasantry. The legend of Chelik, a peasant, enclosed within Ramjatan's story, urges us to visit the distant period of 1860s in Indian history. Chelik's daring protest against the coercion of a colonial Sahib in those times still lingers in the folk memory. The following story 'Doune ki Pattiyan' shows how a peasant's small strip of land, a lone source of security and survival, is made a site to dig a canal under the State Development[5] Programme. The shock drives the peasant Bhola to a state of insane frenzy and he is jailed on the charge of an attempt to murder. Damodar Datta Dikshit's[6] 'Darvaje wala Khet' (Farm at the Door) coveys to his readers the anguish of small peasants at the arrival of *Chakbandi*[7] (Land Ceiling Act). For the land profiteers, it proved an opportune time to target small peasants to acquire the most fertile pieces of land. Despite making all efforts to save the field, which they cherished and nurtured most ardently since their childhood, in the end, they could not help losing it.

Faustian Bargain: 'Bhudan'

The initial principle of *Bhudan* movement was to secure voluntary donations of land to the landless. The revised norms proposed by the educated and influential people of the village stipulated that every owner however small landholding, he might be having, will have to surrender one-sixth share of the land, in return for which he would be awarded the land from the surplus land of the owners. Ramjatan is exultant at the thought of an extended land in the wake of Bhudan. He is unaware of the hidden intent of the revised norms of the *Bhudan* scheme which gave those in charge of implementation, larger power to dictate terms and to act as decision-making authority regarding the meagre possession of small farmers. This ironically turned out a nightmarish Faustian bargain[8] for Ramjatan. The Thakur heading the *Bhudan* committee had called in Ramjatan to assure him that by giving up sikmi[9] land to the Bhudan, he would be awarded five bigha land from the surplus land of a landowner. In fact, for ages, the custom of giving surplus land to the landless for tilling in the agrarian society had been considered a sort of 'moral economy'[10] of peasantry. Since the tiller pays the irrigation and revenue charges, called *sikmi*, he becomes a deemed owner of the land. As per the law of *sikmi*, Ramjatan is one such owner of one bigha of the land given to him by Thakur from his surplus land. He has been since then nurturing this land diligently which yielded adequately to his hard labour.

The narrative moves forward to illustrate how the campaign for distributing lands in the *Bhudan* to the landless becomes fraught with calculations and hidden agenda. On his way back to his hovel, the gathering in the *mohalla* (locality) of chamars[11] makes him stop by. The conversation of the elders here finds Thakur's loudly announced faith in social equality untrustworthy. The oppressed groups make sense of the 'hidden transcript',[12] as James C. Scott perceives in the peasants, 'the capacity to test and exploit all of the loopholes, ambiguities, silences, and lapses available' (1990, 138). What someone in the locality observes, obliquely hints at the crooked designs of the dominant:

Sant Vinoba is coming. The Deputy DM of the district is also going to be on tour. Deputy Sahib had a grand feast at Thakur's house; it is being heard that Thakur has given up his ten Bigha. His generosity was applauded by the Sahib who garlanded him. His photo and name will appear in the newspaper.[13]

The conversations of the village populace suggest more than what apparently seems. Thakur's caste stature and influence have already got him nominated as the President of the Bhudan committee.

They 'Hold Your Nose from Behind'

The past experiences had taught the people in *chamaroti*[14] (the locality of Harijans) that a committee headed by the biggies of the village could seldom be unbiased—besides, the Bhudan functionaries feasting at Thakur's house was a message that all was not quite right. When elderly Ghurhu probed Ramjatan further, Ramjatan admitted:

> when I approached the President of the committee seeking specific details, he sternly rebuffed me, warning: 'Don't you try argue with me. I'll drive you to desperation in the court of law. Better give up your one bigha, Bhudan Committee will ensure, in return, you receive five bigha'. 'I felt good about it. Besides, I don't have the guts to withstand a litigation. I have given my piece to the Bhudan Committee'. Elderly Douna Mahato said,
>
> 'All this is the play in bungling' or why should Deputy Sahib visit Thakur. You don't know, 'it is like holding your nose from behind'. As members of the village society, they are privileged to elect themselves the members of *Bhudan* committee and reallot the assembled land to who so ever they want. First, they'll give you a little land and then assemble all the donated land in order to extend it into a huge property. Ask me? No temptation even of two bighas can force me to move my limbs away from my home turf? (276)

The conversation however confused Ramjatan, since at the behest of Thakur he had given his one bigha land; little did he realize that Thakur was fervently eyeing its much-improved soil quality and tempting harvest and wanted to repossess it. To Ramjatan, however, the prospect of extended land was indeed tempting, he could not help visualizing: 'the fields of lush paddy! Hefty pair of oxen, around their neck—big resounding bells; "what would it be like to be a big farmer, owning a cow!"' (271). With rapid steps he walked home in the silence of the noontide heat through the flourishing meadows and ocean-like rising crops of April, reciprocating the strange happiness enveloping him. The feel of a long bottle gourd dangling by his shoulder, the small bag of lentils, and a pouch of mango sour powder made him feel good thinking of the hearth and home (271).

Resistance to Indigo Planting: 'Chest Stained with Blood'

On the way, Ramjatan spots the consecrated platform, painted in red known as 'Choura of Bansatti Mai'[15] (271) constructed in the memory of the martyr mother of a peasant named Chelik in the distant times of British rule. Deep devotional fervour stirs him as he pauses and bows his head. He vows to offer a Chunari (a colourful scarf to Mai after the grant of the land promised in the Bhudan scheme). The legend of Chelik flashes back in his consciousness. In vivid kaleidoscope, the image of the land warrior—thick moustachioed Chelik—appears, who despite merciless flogging adamantly refused to yield his land to the Angrej Sahib for the farming of indigo.[16] His tortured, bleeding chest made an appalling sight to the onlookers, who while performing the ritual of obedience[17] privately nursed strong resentments against the atrocious ways of Sahib. At his command, when his retinue begins to plough Chelik's field for planting indigo, Chelik rushes right into the middle of his field, holding his ailing mother in his lap and chokes her to death. Chelik's bizarre act of resistance stunned everyone watching—a crowd of villagers—along with the retinue of Sahib. It was as if the long meandering unleashing of Chelik's private woes tore through the landscape like wildfire, making him eerily a character in a supernatural lore.

The baffled village community as witness declared Angrej Sahib guilty of killing the mother of Chelik and a trial court's verdict forced the expulsion of Sahib from India. What is worth noticing here is the way oppressed peasantry resorts to dramatic measures in support of Chelik. Scott's (42) observations are as follows: 'when the disguised resistance fails, subsistence is threatened or perceptions of danger lessen'; thus, the public conformity of subordinates in such a scenario induces inner distance and swallowed bile explains the intriguing conduct of the peasants. Chelik's defiance shows the imponderable extremes to which a peasant could go to save his land from being snatched. One may assume that the peasants' support to Chelik was an explosive articulation of resistance that enacted an endorsement of ethical system or moral economy, specific to the oppressed or the subordinated and that could very potently impede the effectiveness of the easy course of power. Arguably, as Scott puts it, much resistance is absent from historical and official records unless carefully uncovered. The queer twist in the tale of a peasant's resistance still haunts the collective memory of peasantry. Reliving Cheliks' story, ' "a mother sacrificing her life for the mother earth"; "by dying she made the field survive" ' (273), stirs deep emotions in Ramjatan; he tells himself: 'Bhuyan (the land) is indeed our mother!' (273).

On reaching his mud hut, holding his breath in anticipation, Ramjatan awaits the paper signed by Bhudan committee. He steps in to find Jasvanti, his wife, in the noisy company of other women congratulating her. Handing over an almond colour paper in the hand of Ramjatan, she says happily, 'Good, that you gave up the small piece of our land, after all being "Sikmi" it was off and on called into question. Instead in return we are gifted with a fertile farming field of five bigha' (277) Ramjatan's exuberance dies down when the tragic irony descends a little later as he gets to know plainly that 'whatever land was declared to have been donated by Thakur to Ramjatan was only on the papers of the village accountant, in reality it was in the river bed of Gomti' (278). The collusion between the President of Bhudan committee and the village accountant succeeded in depriving Ramjatan of whatever belonged to him; left with no option to survive, he was reduced to becoming a labourer.

Nearly a year after, in the winter's chill, violent asthmatic coughing rakes his ailing, frail body. When moving the shovel into the earth, he feels drained. In the darkness of night, upon the broken cot by his side, he beholds the face of Jasvanti, pale and deathly. He has fevered visions.

Sant Vinoba of *Bhudan* ... 'Long, thin, sinewy old limbs, wrapped in wrinkles', 'shrivelled figure of Bansatti Mai', 'Angrej Sahib saddled on a horse, riding fast, raising dust as if conversing with the wind'. From the mass of miasma appears the 'visage' of Chelik's audacious, bleeding, bold chest holding his moaning, ailing mother in one arm. In the din of cries, he feels as if he is held in someone's arms and is being rushed towards the fields. (279)

This is how the life of Ramjatan is snuffed. Markandeya's ability to distil an emotional and psychological state into images poignantly renders to the readers the delirium of a lonely dying destitute. The enemy with which Chelik of the legend fought was at least not faceless, but the one who controlled and destroyed Ramjatan's life appeared in the form of a benevolent welfare programme lending power to the dominant mediators to grab surreptitiously whatever little land Ramjatan had. It is in the cleverly crafted papers that illiterate Ramjatan's ordeal is scripted and legitimized. Markandeya shows the subtle ways through which the poor and illiterate are made to enter a kind of Faustian bargain, taken off guard, cheated relentlessly. Even those who were educated and believed in the possibility of amelioration were in for deep disappointment.

The Grim Outcome of Development

Markandeya's 'Doune ki Pattiyan' (The Leaf plate) narrates the grim outcome of the Five-Year Plan of the Government of India. The narrative invokes a familiar sphere in village life when the development programmes were in full swing, tall claims were being made about improving the irrigation facilities by building canals but in the process, a number of small farmers suffered unexpected loss. Several years of labour, thrift, and self-denial could afford Bhola a small piece of narrow land of one bigha, which he cultivates with tender feelings. Its yield of plenty of vegetables and the hedges splashed with marigold and chrysanthemum, flowers of many varieties are everyone's envy: '"a golden piece of land!" The place so neat, artistically constructed is described as the "bride of the village"'[18] (199).

The background at the opening of the story makes us understand that the Five-Year Plan was about to end and it is of concern to the government that the accruing funds must not remain unutilized. It was the opportune time to start raising the soft soil since the peasants have sufficiently irrigated the fields. For over several months, the project of canal building was continuing but it got stalled since mapping for the sixty-feet-wide dam was taking place at the boundary of the village and the measuring ribbon fell upon the twelfth bigha of Tewariji's vast land. Tewariji's rushing to Lucknow and using his contacts and resources rescued his land. The engineer in charge receiving special orders from Lucknow in the interest of Tewariji now measured the site for the dam through an alternate direction and this time it was routed through Bhola's small strip of land. Bhola's appeal to the village Panchayat, proved of no consequence. During the early hours of the morning, rising commotion at her door startled Bhola's wife, Gulabi. Crowds of people made her curious with anxiety, for Bhola had not returned that night. What she saw appalled her. Their farm was razed clean. The dam appeared—into half of the field—into the middle of the thin strip of field.

> About twenty-five shovels at work, digging into the soft soil. She was spurred to rush to stop them. But who is to be stopped! There were so many.... Like someone deranged she ran into the field. At an adjoining area, some people were holding fast someone. It was Bhola in hysterics. The policemen looked vigilant, moving back and forth in stern posture. (203)

Taken off guard, bewildered, outraged, Bhola did not know who was to be held responsible for his doom. The knowledge of being forever dispossessed leads him to frenzy. In mad rage, he wants to strangulate Tewariji, but changes his mind and then rushes to the site where the engineer was camping, finds his wife sleeping blissfully. Undoubtedly, the chart of happenings is too baffling for the gullible Bhola and that defied the habitual way of holding any one individual or a group culpable for his ruin. He realizes soon that 'neither Tewariji nor the engineer can be held blameworthy for his ruin. "Or is it the state!" "But did it know that it was the lone space I owned? By starving myself for five years, I managed to buy it!"' (204). Ironically, at this moment, 'he is taken to be a thief and arrested. In the custody of police, he is to be tried on the charge of attempt to murder or theft' (204).

Whatever happens to his wife Gulabi and son Bhuller is nobody's concern. Bhola's desperate reaction gives away the idiosyncratic reasoning of an innocent man stripped for good of his basic means of subsistence, wronged, rendered in the world Foucault conceives of, where there are no determinate agents—the conspiring power remains dispersed, indifferent, 'heteromorphous subjectless'[19] and that controls. Power/knowledge is constituted through accepted forms of discourse through which power is legitimized and conducted. Even while in the state of despairing suffering, Bhola could sense this convoluted truth that the power to destroy him or likes of him is not invested in a lone authority nor it is wielded by people or groups but in the accepted, unquestioned norms and practices which do not see any anomaly if a poor man's small piece of land is sacrificed either to grant favour to someone influential or to facilitate a state sponsored project.

Chakbandi (Land Ceiling): Benami Holdings and Profiteering in Dikshit's 'Darwaje vala Khet' (Farm at the Door)

It may not be an exaggeration to claim that with the launch of measures of land reforms, various troubled facets of post-independence rural existence emerged in unforeseen permutations. Dikshit illustrates how in the name of land reforms, rampant cheating, corruption, and litigations were concomitantly coming into existence in the contemporary India. In the First Five-Year Plan, the constitution of the Land Ceiling/Consolidating Act was hailed as espousing a radical reform movement, meant to reduce the huge disparity between the income of large landowners and that of the small or landless peasants or rural poor. Its implementation in the 1960s however became the covert cause of displacement of small landowners. It let down the very purpose for which it was enacted. K. Venkatasubramanian's report issued by the Planning Commission (2012) finds multiple fault lines disabling this programme. Several of its crucial goals to help the tenants and landless cultivators own even a meagre piece of land failed. Ironically various provisions of the law helped the landowners to manipulate their sustained hold over considerable land areas under the various provisions of the laws. *Benami*[20] holdings (i.e. holdings without the legal papers of ownership) became the order of the day in many states. The officials supposed to facilitate these programmes mostly responded ingratiatingly to the influential landowners and to the bribe givers, solely concerned with saving the lands of big landowners from ceiling. Acting as fixers, the officials would facilitate the drafting of documents of dubious ownership that would make counter-claims on the lands of small landholders. The latter's life is thus mediated by the representatives of the state and is made to suffer huge losses. *Chakbandi* hurt the small peasants most. It was found that a lone individual was implicated in five court cases, where goons and *dabangs* (lathi wielding, gun trotting musclemen in the service of wealthy landowners) flourished. In the game of competing clout and money power, the small peasants were inexorably the losers, for it would take years and years of fighting messy legal battles.

In the village, Bhagupur of Uttar Pradesh, Ramesh and Deena Nath, the brothers, own a small farm. Ramesh is educated and works at an office in the town close to his village. When Deena Nath breaks out the news of the arrival of land ceiling, it was like a lull before the storm in the lives of two brothers. For the villagers, it was no less than a pandemic, no less than a huge threatening war. Deena Nath goes deep into the shell of silence, but his eyes were saying that this formidable threat had to be resisted. Ramesh knew the grief the land ceiling could bring about; they had experienced it a few years ago. He exploded, ' "Is it that once when implemented, it brought irreparable loss to many. Wasn't it enough to satisfy the belly of the government?" Deena Nath's eyes were not seeing either Ramesh or the veranda, but the blind past and the crumbling future (21).[21] He remembered the times when it arrived previously. In every alley *Chakbandi* was a cause of mourning. In the redistribution, in exchange for their long-serving fertile lands, several villagers were given barren gravel lands. The lands formerly close to the well or the sources of water were now the ones where there were no facilities for irrigation. Some were given the portion of a pond instead of the land. The norms of this programme distanced long-term neighbours, those farmers whose fields were adjacent to each other now found farming plots far distant from the other, at different corners of the village.

Spectacles of Jugaad: Surplus Lands in the Phony Names, Divorced, but Not Divorced Wives, Temple, Cats and Dogs

It was principally the upper caste, hefty landowners in possession of resources who could save their lands and annex more lands to their own by dubious means. The two upper castes saw to it that even before the ceiling arrived their landed property be registered on the name of their various family members, broken temples and platforms, phony names, even cats and dogs. Thus, dispersed among so many phony claimants their lands were now protected against any interference. Proud of their cleverness they consummately botched the project of *Chakbandi* and turned it in their own favour. Dikshit draws upon some real episodes to which he was exposed and Panditji's story was one of them.

In the hierarchized village society, two families of the village were however prospering with the onset of *Chakbandi* against which they never had any grudge. One was the family of Thakur Ganga Baksh Singh's and the other Pandit Ram Avtar Mishra's. Thakur Sahib and Panditji get the farming done by labourers. 'Thakur's land grew from 80 acres to 100 acres in the wake of *Chakbandi*. *Chakbandi* made him complete the century. Panditji was four times ahead of Thakur Sahib in completing double century' (22). The most fertile land, equipped with the best irrigation sources, went into the piggy bank of these two landowners. They were synonymous with clever plotting and insidious nexus and as a result, they benefitted from *Chakbandi* just as the traders gain during floods or famine: 'They are experts in milking with thousand mouths' (22). A curious blend of satire, irony, and hilarity ingrained in the narrative lets us see the absurd extremity to which the *Chakbandi* profiteers indulge in jugaad.

Manipulating Provisions of Law

Panditji broke all records in checkmating the Ceiling Law and gaining from it. In spite of that, some land was to be sacrificed.

As a tactic of countering this, he made his wife lay allegations of spousal cruelty and sought for her the decree of divorce from the court. As maintenance, Panditji was obliged to give a large portion of his land to his divorced wife. Though Pandit and Panditani live under the same roof, Panditani wears a *bindi* of the size of ten paisa, wears cartful of vermillion, twenty bangles, every morning after waking up touches her husband's feet, has the same privilege of wifely bantering and jesting with him, but on paper they are no longer husband and wife. Even after this clever move, some land was to be forfeited in the Ceiling. He got his elder daughter-in-law divorced from his elder son on the basis of harassment and torture. Son and the daughter-in-law were two units and the land could be saved from ceiling. Panditji was lucky in having obedient son and daughter-in-law. (22–23)

Class and caste equations also seemingly played some role in allotting and re-allotting the lands. While Panditji prospered:

The programme stalled the fate of Pawarun Pasi, Kunvare Kurmi and Chaturi Chamar. Chaturi suffered most. The shock killed him. Ceiling lost him the land dearest to him. The rest was now divided in his six sons. Whatever little piece of land came in their claim was not even worth 'wearing or spreading'. As a result, all brothers sold off their lands—ran to the city to seek their means of survival—selling ice-cream or gate keeping or riding rickshaw. Bechan Koeri's house collapsed but the assistance went to the second floor *kothi* (a spacious house) of Pradhanji (village head). A buffalo was bought in the name of Basheer Behna but was tethered at the door of the grocer, Tularam. Manure Gas Plant was set at the door of Shakoor but all he could have: some incense of the rotting manure and nothing. (23)

Thus, the laws which are made to facilitate and benefit the weaker and the neglected segments of the rural world turned hostile against them.

How can Ramesh forget that in the previously held *Chakbandi*, his land close to the dam got registered in the name of Panditji and as a replacement he was given a land which was full of alkaline soil. For years he devotedly applied treatment to that land and made it worthy of farming. The Land Ceiling committee chose to write his sloping field for the village society. Even after lakhs of appeals and applications, the officials of *Chakbandi* did not listen to him. The committee's decision to register Ramesh's piece of land for the village society was a cunning strategy. The fact was that the influential people in the process of *Chakbandi* would get the best pieces of land in the name of the village society and later on take possession of the same. The sloping land was lost in the process. Fighting a case in the court for seven to eight years, rubbing their ankles by taking rounds of the courts did result in favour of Ramesh and Deena Nath and yet in spite of the court's decision, the *Lekhpal* (Village Registrar) was most reluctant to register the declaration of judgement. 'He was arguing, "Where is the verdict in my court?"' (24). Only after taking a note of Rs. 100, the *Lekhpal* did the needful and the land was restored to the two brothers.

The Aggrieved and the Sahib; Sahib Has No Patience for Nonsense

Dikshit's narrative reveals how the local village officials from the Panchayat or even the civil servants at the higher level pressurize the vulnerable petitioner. When Deena Nath asks why the peasant's collective appeal to SDM (Senior District Magistrate) to revoke *Chakbandi* was not made, Ramesh tells him that it was made.

> 'What did he say?' He said, 'this is for your welfare'. We said 'our welfare is in not having *Chakbandi*'. Like a wounded camel he unleashed his annoyance: 'Schemes for welfare cannot be stalled due to your liking, you uneducated, stupid rustics!' We said, 'Sarkar, we are being looted'. He sounded stern: 'whether you're plundered or thrashed, land ceiling would take place. You—coarse people—challenging the planning commission!' Excessive rage brought thick spit over the corners of his lip. (26–27)

In the last *Chakbandi*, the farm at the door was saved. But seems in this one it might not. Its fertile soil always yielded vegetables in plenty. Both the brothers share tender feelings for this land. As children, they were involved in weeding, hoeing, and watering of this plot. The pampered farm generously produced for the family and the neighbours varieties of vegetables: okra, bitter gourd, cucumber, beans, spinach, brinjals, and fenugreek. By the side of this farm was a tree under which was planted a machine to grind sugarcane. During harsh winters they would stay close to the machine and savour the cane juice with lemon, its pieces rinsed in milk or in concoction of cream and jaggery. Mostly thereafter for the evening meal, his belly was seldom ready. The thought of losing this farm would not let him have a single moment of ease.

The Destiny of Marked Letter: They Reach Nowhere

While the brothers do not leave any stone unturned to stop *Chakbandi*, Ramesh is helpless because he knows that 'the appeal of a wasp like me at the collectorate will be thrown in the disposal bin and then a canker will perform the function of disposal' (26). Deena Nath however taking pride in his brother's capability of speaking English, posits hope that the formers' talks with the Sahib would perhaps give some solution. 'Sometimes some of the Sahibs are really kind and perhaps they might grow interested in the paper and make it move' (24). Desperate Ramesh meets with the most important individual of the village Panditji to seek his mercy, but nothing comes off to raise their hope. Meeting with the collector for his brother's satisfaction was necessary. With folded hands, he addressed the collector.

> '*Hujoor*', 'Sarkar'. He began his appeal. The collector snatched the application from his hand, raised his hands like traffic police in the pose of stop signal that stopped him from speaking any further. Ramesh kept standing intimidated, with folded hands. The collector read the application cursorily marked for someone else and put his signature and then putting the appeal in a tray he barked 'Go! That will be seen'. Whatever courage Ramesh had mustered now vanished; he knew the destiny of such marked letters. (Dikshit, 'Darwaje vala Khet', 22–30)

Ramesh informed his brother that the appeal was submitted but there was no hope. Deena Nath did not lose hope. He believed that sooner or later the letter would reach the officials responsible for *Chakbandi* and that some order would be issued in their favour and when the village folks would ask the whereabouts of his sources, he would keep smiling. Dogged by this hope, whenever any employee of *Chakbandi* visited, he would follow him as if spellbound and repeat his appeal even while snubbed rudely: 'Whatever is the rule of law will be done. Your repeated chanting of "the farm at the door" won't help' (27). They know how the memory of losing their lands still tortures the small peasants of Devraha village, when many villagers were deprived of their land or were allotted useless lands, gave up farming. In some cases, those who could afford the recourse to the court, many rounds of the courts for seven to eight years, sought verdict in their favour. The execution of Land Ceiling suffered the same consequences as the schemes for flood relief, house collapse assistance, and other assistance programmes. Barbara Harris White's (2003, 100–101) study of the so-called state in India as having 'already been privatized and turned into a vehicle, the shadow state for the accumulative projects of local capitalist classes', amply applies to the ways the wealthy benefitted from and monopolized the schemes of welfare in Dikshit's story of Bhagupur.

Numerous stories, a few mentioned here, representing the countryside of Bihar and Uttar Pradesh articulate the extremities of suffering the development programmes generated. They became the apparatus of flouting moral economy existing in peasantry. The big landowners in mutual solidarity with the state bureaucracy generally acted as office bearers and coercive authority, empowered by their retinue and the police who were happy to earn their shortcut profit. Ganesh Pandey[22] (1999, 75–82) discusses the stories of Viveki Rai, Surendra Sukumar and Vijaykant in the book, *Aathven Dashak ki Gramin Kahaniyan* (Rural Stories of the 1980s). In Viveki Rai's 'Tarikhen', (Dates), Bodhan says, 'The arrival of *Chakbandi* Courts in the villages has opened the portals of hell' (Pandey, 75). The story reveals the plight of losing his battle for his land at the local level. Bodhan approaches the district court and ends up losing whatever was left to sustain his family. First his field, then his fruit garden, everything was mortgaged, then the jewellery of his wife and lastly even the utensils. The prolonged pending court hearings transformed him; his sunken eyes and sickly appearance tellingly showed that the court system in our country only gives dates—dates after dates (*tarikh par tarikh*). Pandey's analysis lets us see how the rural elite in Surendra Sukumar's 'Hanka' collude with the officials of *Chakbandi* and manage to arrange the matters of land allotment in their interest. Chchanga's father, Babu, finds his fertile land snatched; he is ordered to receive a piece of barren land at one end of the village. In the meanwhile, Chchanga is charged with indulging in some rowdy activity and that leads to his father's imprisonment where the latter dies. Vijaykant's 'Beech ka Samar' (War in the Middle), another much-discussed story registers how the poor and landless felt cheated by the implementation of *Bhudan*. Beni Babu, a peasant does not endorse the leftist armed struggle against the rich landowners, for it would inevitably mean bloodshed. His dedication to the belief in the possibility of spiritual transformation of elite farmers however receives a severe jolt when on the land donated by Shivji Babu he wholeheartedly toils, irrigating, airing, and investing in fertilizers. When the crop is readied for a rich harvest, Shivji's musclemen armed with guns arrive on the scene and collect the harvest. The narrative ending on a note of peasants recruiting in the armed struggle hints at the onset and spread of Naxal revolution in India. The repercussions unsettle lives and create precarious situation for the small peasants.

Sainath writes that the loss of land 'over the decades has removed the one cushion of many people—their land' (369). James C. Scott's fieldwork enabled him to listen very closely to the peasants dislodged from their land. Scott argues that to survive solely on agriculture, a peasant needs to be able to rely on access to land, customary usages of life resources, and, subsequently, entitlements to produce, rather than transporting it to the marketplace. For any peasant, ownership is the basic need, priced above tenancy and tenancy above casual labour, because even though they may overlap in terms of income, each represents a quantum leap in the reliability of subsistence (1976, 10). The storytellers depicting the plight of the Indian peasantry are conversant with the terrain of lived experiences. Their writings testify how the impact of various agricultural transformations in post-colonial India led to disruption of self-contained rural resources, escalation of monetary pressure on the small peasants, large seasonal migration of agricultural labourers, bolstering of the hold of moneylenders, and litigations, prompting many to quit farming. Getting dislodged from their land was not just an economic crisis for the peasants; it was, moreover, an existential crisis, uprooting them from the terrain which had lent them an assured sense of identity.

Notes

1. Kalpana Sharma in *The Hindu* (3) discusses the onslaught of more virulent policies that would exacerbate poverty of the rural populace all over the country. That is the policy to forcibly seize thousands and thousands of acres of land from farmers and communities of special economic zones (SEZ). The provisions for compensation however are known to be vague or inadequate. One gets to know that even golf courses are forcibly acquired from the lands meant for farming. This was done under the archaic Land Acquisition Act, 1894, a British law meant to further colonial interests. The main complaint against the 1894 legislation is that it allowed acquisition in the name of public purpose without clearly defining what it was. The golf courses and commercial complexes have been termed as public purposes. A new bill has been introduced having provisions for better compensation and rehabilitation measures, preceding this the land was also acquired for non-state bodies.
2. In the three consecutive studies, 'and the meek shall inherit the earth', 'the problem of forced displacement', and 'survival strategies of the poor', P. Sainath (69–133) describes the disorientation suffered by the indigenous communities due to being rendered landless and displaced.
3. Markandeya (1930–2010) is described as one of the most prominent representative writers of Hindi, who after Premchand re-established rural life in Indian literature. Raised in a peasant household of Jaunpur, Uttar Pradesh, is also known for his missionary activism committed to the betterment of peasantry. See http://lekhakmanch.com/. His several collections of stories probe the varied kinds of struggles with which the farming community is endemically made to struggle. The two stories 'Bhudan' (Land Gift) (268–70), and 'Doune ki Pattiyan' (The Leaf Plate) relate the complex plight of small peasants who fail to deal with the problems brought about by the welfare programmes of the state: *Bhudan* and the building of dam for irrigation.
4. The idea of *Bhudan* was a noble experiment of Sant Vinoba, Mahatma Gandhi's contemporary. For more, see Chapter 1.
5. In 1950, the newly formed Government of India set up the Planning Commission to create, develop, and execute development plans, each for a span of five years.
6. Damodar Datta Dikshit (1949–), novelist and short-story writer in Hindi, hails from the village Atarauli in Uttar Pradesh. His much-acclaimed book, *Agriculture, Irrigation & Horticulture in Ancient Sri Lanka* was globally acknowledged as an authentic document of research. His knowledge of the miscellaneous issues of farm life and the village society is reflected in several of his stories.

7. Ledejinsky's report in Charan Singh's India's Economic Policy (23-24) finds that rampant corruption prevented the Land Ceiling Act from succeeding as a reform movement.
8. Doctor Faustus, a character in German folklore and literature, surrenders his soul to a representative of Satan. Faustian bargains are by their nature tragic or self-defeating for the person who submits to them.
9. 'Sikmi', is an aspect of 'moral economy', a term given by E. P. Thompson (see Introduction) to a custom practiced in south Asian peasantry. Accordingly, a small portion of farming land would be given to the landless from the surplus lands of those possessed with vast lands of several acres. It could also be regarded a gesture of subsistence ethics. The transformation of millions of peasants into indigo and poppy cultivators cannot be sufficiently explained without a closer description of the coercive power relations at play.
10. Moral economy is concerned with subsistence agriculture and the need for subsistence insurance in hard times. A moral economy is an economy that is based on goodness, fairness, and justice, as opposed to one where the market is assumed to be independent of such concerns. In the endnotes of chapter 1, it is mentioned with reference to E. P. Thompson, James C. Scott and Premchand. For more see Götz (2015, 147-62).
11. Chamars are the lowest among the scheduled caste in India.
12. It is from the examples in literature, history, and politics and culture around the world that Scott (1-204) observes the nuanced confrontations laden with deception between the powerless and powerful. Peasants, serfs, untouchables, slaves, labourers, and prisoners are not free to speak their minds in the presence of power. These subordinate groups instead create a secret discourse that represents a critique of power spoken behind the backs of the dominant—the mocking, vengeful tone they display off stage. This is what he terms as their public and hidden transcripts. Scott examines the many guises this interaction has taken throughout history and the tensions and contradictions it reflects. The oppressed deal with public transcripts in three ways: they use public hegemonic claims to extract concession, they create a 'folk culture' of ambiguous forms which would be on both sides of the hidden and public transcripts, and they explosively express hidden-transcript ideas in revolts (19-20).
13. The excerpt is from 'Bhudan'. All excerpts are translated by me. Subsequent references to the text are from this story.
14. The term refers to caste-based arrangement of localities in Indian villages. The upper-caste localities are generally at a distance from the lower castes.
15. 'Bansatti', a village goddess, in the rustic dialect refers to Sati Mother of the forests—who sacrificed her life as a mother—protector of the fields and lives of the inhabitants, supposed to fulfil the wish of her worshippers. Edible food is offered to the deity and then distributed to the worshippers as rituals of worship.
16. British East India Company (BEIC) started its production of indigo in Bengal and part of the current Bihar states of India and continued it until the second

decade of twentieth century. Bhattacharya (13–23) finds that in 1860, EWL Tower testified before the 1860 indigo commission, that 'not a chest of indigo reached England without being stained with human blood'. The greedy managers of BEIC forced the farmers to grow indigo in place of food crops by attracting them with loans on virtually non-repayable conditions. This caused considerable tyranny and torture of farmers and finally led to the Nīl Vidroha (Nīl Revolt) of 1857 and forced the British Government to appoint a Commission of Enquiry, which confirmed the atrocities caused by the British East India Company. The British Government closed the East India Company and took command of the country's rule in 1858. There was a second Nīl Revolt (Satyāgraha) the name given to this non-violent revolt) in Champaran, Bihar launched by Gandhi in 1917. The records document how north Indian peasants were forced to plant indigo and were not permitted to plant anything else. See Rajendra Prasad, 'Indigo—The Crop that Created History', 296–301.

17. James C. Scott observes that public deference or obedience of the subjugated groups towards the dominant is usually motivated by fear of retaliation rather than internalized compliance. The powerless feign deference because of fear of being punished, and the powerful subtly assert their mastery. See *Weapons of the Weak*, 26–27.
18. The quote is from 'Doune ki Pattiyan'. Subsequent quotes are drawn from the same text.
19. Best and Kellner (48–49) succinctly explain Foucault's perceptions which can be understood in the context of my discussion.
20. *Benami* plainly explained, means any transaction made by a person without using his name or by using the name of another person. As an example, a benami property is a property purchased by a person in the name of another person.
21. The excerpts are drawn from 'Darwaje vala Khet' (20–30). Subsequent references are to this edition.

3
Small Farmers of Cane and Paddy: Post-Harvest Delays and Non-Payment

Journey where the straightway was lost.

The consciousness narrative in the two stories, Damodar Datta Dikshit's[1] (2014 [1980]) 'Under weighment' and Suresh Kantak's[2] 'Kisan Kya Kare' (2018), lets us see the insecurities threatening the farmers who have to take several steps for the cultivation of cane and paddy. Their problems do not come to end with sowing, fertilizing, planting, and harvesting—braving drought or inundation—but the ordeal grows multiple in dealing with marketing the produce and receiving the due payment. The world of actual transaction with the local arrangers and the state-appointed agencies can bring about extreme hardship and sometimes death. The plight of cane farmers in an agrarian set up where local and state-appointed agencies and bureaucracy settle the transaction of cane produce from the fields to be transported to sugar mills remained perennially troubled. The paddy farmers too have related experiences of being harassed and roughed up very often when they visit the government paddy centre, where the rule of crooks and pilferers is rampant, and they successfully operate in the business of chicanery. Suman Sahai[3] (2011) identifies the plight of the aggrieved peasants in 'Good Harvest Do Not Always Translate into Money in the Bank'. Her astute analysis covers a range of issues integral to the harvesting of produce and then selling, to receive the payment holds true of not only the way paddy and wheat farmers undergo the tough trial but also the cane farmers. UP is blessed as a Gangetic belt where farmers have done great job in producing a rich harvest. There are important centres where rice and wheat are procured for the central pool. She reveals how the procurement has become an exercise to torment farmers rather than support them. Both procurement agencies and the market are aware of this and turn the screw on price as they know the farmer is left with no choice but to sell. Other strategies that are used to pull prices down is to tell the farmer that his grain has not been dried sufficiently and cannot be bought. 'But as soon as the palms get greased, the grain gets sold miraculously'. Other tricks are to declare the grain as being 'light' in weight, not fulfilling the standards set by the Food Corporation of India (FCI). 'The FCI's exacting standards are equally miraculously met once the farmers' pockets have become correspondingly lighter.'[4] One gets to know how delays and non-payment at several levels have caused the suicide or the cardiac arrest of the farmers.

Both paddy and sugarcane have been very dear to the farmer; the attachment with the sugarcane persists despite delayed returns, because one sowing gives two yields. The harsh and grinding experience of the two farmers—respectively, the sugarcane and paddy in the two narratives—reveal that those who work as the functionaries in the transaction of cane or paddy, with the covert approval of their bosses in hierarchy and in solidarity with them, dittoed the colonial system. Empowered by the system, they consider it their obligation to harass and discipline the poor peasants who catch up long distances for onward procedures for payment, are exhausted, starve, and wait for the deal done. These issues, intricately comprehended, find a moving rendering in the two stories.

Difficult Relationship with the State: The Bowl of Sugarcane Farming

Premchand's Hori was also a cane farmer; in the colonial times, the torture, they were made to bear with shattered their lives. In 'Under weighment', Maiku, a cane farmer's tale is based on Damodar Datta Dikshit's personal experience[5] as a Commissioner in the Sugar Cane Department of UP. UP is known as a major sugarcane-producing state in the sub-tropical zone. By mid-1970s, Dikshit's posting in Devaria, UP, a district adjacent to Bihar, made him gain more intimate understanding of the pains cane growers are subjected to. 'Under weighment' is the term, historically in use since the colonial time, as the weighing of harvested cane was always caught up in the system of underhand connections with some people from the bureaucracy at the higher level. Cane was customarily under weighed at the sugar cane purchase centre of the sugar mill. The harassment caused by the policies and practice of rate fixing and unfixing or the non-payment[6] from the mill owners keeps appearing in the news perennially. The payment for which would be delivered later.

Maiku's Travails of Wait: Such a Long Journey!

Carrying the bundles of cane from his village, Karmaha, to the cane purchase centre of the sugar mill in another village would indeed be tough in the harsh winter night. The nights most difficult to endure for those in farm labour remind us of Premchand's 'Poos ki Raat' (Winter's Night, 1936). Maiku's thoughts register the tough struggles of a small cane farmer. With great hesitation, his neighbour Shivcharan lent him the bullock cart, on the condition, it would be returned the same evening. Miscellaneous unfinished tasks of farming exasperate his mind:

> He had received the slip for supplying sugar cane from the mill four days back. The purchase center was far from Karmaha. But for not having a pair of bullocks, or a bullock cart with rubber tires, he could not make it on time. With some distress, he recalls, he had let a neighbour to plough his bullock last year, one of his oxen died. But when his time to plough came, none helped him. He could not plough when the field was moist; now that time was over. 'What would I do with the plough? Even manure was not accessible. Better pulling rikshaw in the city that would enable the children to stay alive'.[7] (9)

The entire night was spent in journeying by the bullock cart; when he reached the cane purchase centre, it was early morning, and the employees of the centre were sleeping. He laid down with both hands folded, trying to take some sleep, but cannot; he tried to lit up some fire, collecting dry leaves to seek relief from cold. The sound of rustling leaves awakened Kanta Babu (the weighment clerk of the sugar mill—Cane Committee clerk) sleeping inside. Maiku heard someone growling:

'Who *harami*[8] is making noises?' 'I'm from Karmaha'. Says Maiku. 'Trying to raise some fire, it's cold'. 'Why are you disturbing my sleep? At the twilight you're out to devour my head? Keep silence'. (Dikshit, 10)

When the purchase centre opened, a crowd of cane growers assembled at the entrance of the centre. Already strained from long journeys, and the delay in weighing, they watched helplessly as Kanta Babu left on a cycle for somewhere. After several hours, he was seen coming back, though the rules pasted on the wall said that by a certain time the cane must be weighed. Kanta Babu laid himself upon a cot, placed for his rest. The further delay made the villagers carrying bundles of cane restless. While waiting, growing desperate, famished, braving cold, those who were not having anything to eat or offer to their bullocks were miserable. The mismanagement at the centre worsened the problem of indefinite waiting. Those in charge had not even bothered to repair the damaged trough for feeding of bullocks. The handle of the hand pump was also broken. It was also a provision that the cane farmers and their bullocks are provided the facility of rest and a trough for storage of water for bullocks. The provisions as per the contract between the sugar mill and the government dictated that the purchase centre must open on time, and that the procedure of weighing the cane must follow the right standards. To guarantee the correct conduct of weighing, so that the cane farmer is not made to suffer injustice, the cane inspector's visit and monitoring were essential prerequisites of continuing with the license from the state to run a centre for further transaction of cane produce.

The Set-up Is Staged: Heckling and Manhandling

When the waiting farmers exhorted Kanta Babu insistently, describing their plight, the tremendous pressure, they were faced with, the latter said:

'Don't you guys lick my head; the truck is yet to arrive'. Maiku dares to approach Kanta Babu and complain. During the long wait, for having complained about the inordinate delay, Maiku was manhandled, heckled and abused by the employees of the cane purchase center, withholding sobs, bundled in one corner of extremely cold floor. (12)

The following day, the truck came, the clerk of the Cane Cooperative Committee sat next to Kanta Babu to monitor the proceedings and made entries on the register. Maiku noticed that they were doing all this without checking the weighbridge. Any query would meet with a snub: 'We know what's right'. One of them dared to ask for their turn in weighing, reminding the weighment clerk of what the rules dictate, 'Our Pradhan told us about the government rules, accordingly the weighing should be finished within ten hours. Here we are kept waiting for over 24 hours' (Dikshit, 12). This made Kanta Babu furious and he ordered the watchman: 'Push the cart of the farmer who recites the law, out of the queue' (Dikshit, 12). In the meanwhile, the Cane Manager also arrived and in a loud voice asked the farmers rudely to unblock his way, physically pushing them, hurling expletives, when a cart driver approached him with the desperate complaint, he utters: dismissively, 'nonsense' (Dikshit, 12). When the farmer insists on his appeal, the Cane Manager struck his back with a wooden cane hurling a barrage of expletives. Maiku witnessed the high drama of delaying tactics, insulting rebuffs, and ingenious manipulation of lies and cheating, enacted by the cane manager, the mill weighment clerk (Kanta Babu), the cane society clerk, and the watchman.

The names and village of the cane farmers were registered. The cane cart driver was giving his slip to the society clerk. The weighing was going on. Kanta Babu was taking note of the weight. When the cart driver asked:

> 'What is the weight?' '19.10' 'But Babu, the beam is showing 20 quintal and 30 kilograms?' 'Let the beam say anything.' 'It's a grave loss!' 'You want your cane weighed, or no?' barked Kanta Babu. (Dikshit, 14)

Threatened, the cart driver kept mum. His belly ached for not having eaten anything for the last two days. His bullocks were hungry, wife was alone at home, field was drying, needing water. The same practice of weighing continued when many carts were weighed after this. Suman Sahai finds that the farmers travel to different procurement centres with their goods, for it to be inspected, weighed, and lifted. If they do not own their own bullock carts, they hire or rent trucks or tractors to bring their grain to the centre. Everyday causes delay and bleeds the farmer. 'It is like the way ports charge demurrage if you do not lift your goods. Each day the port holds your goods, it charges you a fee.... Bullock cart, tractor-trolley and truck owners do the same. So, if they need to wait around till the farmer can negotiate the deal, the cost of hiring goes up every day. This eats into the farmer's profit', she adds.

Maiku is perturbed, since after a lot of pleading his neighbour had agreed to lend his bullock and cart on the condition that it would be returned the same evening; it does not seem a remote possibility. Soon after an officer-looking man addressed as 'Sahib' arrives on a jeep identified as cane inspector. His commanding presence made everyone alert. At the hut adjoining the weighbridge, he perused entries and other details. His reprimand to the cart drivers for creating a crowd showed he valued discipline and could enforce the right conduct. Everyone noticed how Kanta Babu was also admonished off and on. This made the cart drivers hopeful that after all Kanta Babu is getting what he deserves. Sahib once again weighed the cart full of cane and expressed his outrage at the cheating of Kanta Babu. 'Both of you and your mill owner will be put into jail and be punished for bungling. You will be made to grind grains in the jail' (17). Inspector Sahib appeared to be taking strict note of the grave defects in the management of the farmers' cane weighing purchase centre. To create a perfect semblance of 'all is well', on the scene were deployed two men wearing *gamchha* over their head. They came forward to give their testimony in defence of Kanta Babu and claimed loudly that there was no scope of any dishonesty in the business of weighing, as cane farmers they knew. Maiku could guess that they were disguised as cane farmers. The show of solidarity was stage managed to ensure that cheating could go on undisturbed and that rendered the complaints of other farmers and Maiku futile. Sahib's inspection declared that the purchase centre was violating the prescribed norms; the trough to get the tired and thirsty bullocks drink water was broken. Sahib's loud expression of displeasure and constant rebuke encouraged the cane farmers to believe for some moments that he intended to take the employees to task. After his inspection was over, while returning, Kanta Babu handed over an envelope to him. Sahib said in English, 'How Much'. Some exchange between them in whispers confused the cane farmers. Something was whispered; the cart drivers could not understand. The Sahib closed the inspection note but continued to upbraid Kanta Babu until he sat on his jeep to leave (16). What they could not understand that when the inspector was in collusion, why on earth was he continually scolding them?

The big difference was obvious between what the beam showed and what Kanta Babu announced. When Maiku's number came, he heard Kanta Babu saying, 'the weight is 18.80'. Daring to protest, Maiku whimpered:

> 'Hujoor', the right weight was 20.80 quintal. I'm a very poor man; from every one you have deducted one and a half quintal, why are you reducing two quintals from my cane. As if Maiku's objection was an offence, Kanta Babu roared: 'Are you willing accept what is declared or no?' 'Hujoor!' Maiku pleaded. 'Watchman! move his cart—move! Place it behind everyone. He won't be brought round without this. Let him rot for four days only then he 'll be set right'. (16)

Humiliated, Maiku kept crying, pleading, but Kanta Babu refused to relent. His cart was shoved aside as punishment. He was made to stay rolled up in the open, empty stomach. After much prostrating and begging, praying to be forgiven, his cane is weighed after two days. Totally numb with fatigue and feebleness, without questioning the obvious cheating in the scale and the beam, he put the receipt in his pocket.

Flouting of Moral Economy: Death by Starving or Cardiac Arrest

Cold wave was blowing. Spurring his cart, the thought of not being able to return the bullock on time scared him. The bullocks were visibly tottering, famished, and weak; he would be answerable to Shivcharan, who was for sure going to unleash his outrage on him. Maiku reflects on the ordeal of cane peasants like him:

> What kind of bargaining is this? When a shopkeeper sells a thing—he keeps the money first. Buy wheat—first pay the money. The sale of cane however is outrageous. Only a year ago, the factory paid the cost of cane after 8 months. There is no accountability for the wrong done to cane

farmers. Peasant will die of hunger or disease but will not be paid on time. (18)

He felt cold and sleepy. In the morning his cart reached home. The sound awakened Basantia, his wife. She opened the door, not finding him, she called out:

'Ramu ke Bappa!' The oxen were still not unyoked; when drawing them away from the yoke—she sees his shrunken body lying—eyes glazed. She sprinkles water, but there is no stir. Basantia's desperate wailing brings the neighbours rushing. People around gather, guessing 'but it wasn't so cold last night. One couldn't die of hunger; was it heart attack?' (18–19)

One can guess, it must have been a cardiac arrest. In the failed protest and tragic end of Maiku, we behold the protest of millions of peasant voices that are not heard. All across India, the cane growers have been historically in difficult relationship with the state. Dikshit's story is an authentic account of slighting and delaying tactics, the cane farmers are made to face at different stages of transaction: the weighing of the cane cart to the mill and thereafter the inordinate delay[9] in payment.

The Village Administration and the Profiteers: Hassles of Long Wait

In 'Kisan Kya Kare', Murari, a relatively educated farmer, is driven to frustration when even after waiting for twenty days, his paddy was not weighed at the government paddy sale centre of the village. The two markets function in the region, the private and the government owned. Desperately needing payment for the urgent treatment of his daughter in the city hospital, however, Murari was keener on receiving the due payment for his harvest from the government paddy centre. The private receives and weighs the goods at a lesser price than the government one. Suman Sahai (2011) finds that 'When the farmer's grain is held up, and he is desperate to sell, the private companies step in and buy the grain at low prices. In this way the backbreaking effort put in by the farmer and the little subsidy he gets on fertilizer and diesel to irrigate goes to the benefit the private companies'. Murari's desperation was growing since no amount of pleading worked. He was running short of time. The routine toil and matters requiring attention at the farming site and at home front do not allow the farmers to keep waiting for too long.

Middlemen, Grocers, and Dealers Slide Ahead of the Farmers

Besides, what is disgruntling is to watch that in the long queue intrude grocers and dealers who having given inducement to the handlers of the agency; they slide ahead of the small peasants and get the sale deed done before others:

> These men—basically the middle men—have already purchased the paddy at a lower cost, now que the government run agency to sell it at a higher price and make profits. The ruckus was gathering around Murari; amongst the people desperate for weighing their stuff were: 'Sarpanch, Mukhiya, BDC, some member of panchayat—none expressed solidarity with Murari, or—resentment against the arbitrary, unlawful ways in the paddy centre'.[10] (Kantak, 184)

Confident of being more informed about the transaction of his produce, Murari tried to deal with the inordinately long wait, by employing the conventional logic one applies in a democratic system. He tried to garner some support from the functionaries of the village administration who too were in the queue much ahead of Murari, but they sound indifferent, not concerned with the right or wrong. The misery of suffering unending waiting was too disheartening for the small peasant because they lack storage facilities and must sell their produce immediately after harvest. His plight was that of many such farmers. When their grain is held up, they are desperate to sell, the private companies step in and buy the grain at low prices:

> Murari was anxious because at the scheduled time, the center would close, instructing the paddy farmers to arrive the next day. But the

following day when the gullible peasant looks for his space in the que, he finds himself far behind everyone. In spite of having waited for 15 to 20 days, pleading daily—giving went to his frustration, Murari eventually draws the attention of the Manager, who agrees to weigh only one of the three trolleys of Murari—one third of his paddy. The weighing man announces: '32 quintals'. Rattled, Murari protests, 'When it was weighed at home, it was 41 quintals'. Some intruders join the weighing man, asserting loudly: 'the weight is less now because the paddy becomes dry'. (Kantak, 184–85)

Murari's voice got buried in the din, when he fervently insisted that his paddy was already dried up[11] when measured at home. It is an acknowledged fact that the farmers never get the payment for the genuine weight of their grain. But everyone around seemed annoyed with him. The manager ignored his plea and insisted on his paying the labour charge to the weighing man. When Murari refused to pay, arguing: 'You have already stolen my paddy and now ask me to pay? You're obliging those who are giving you inducement' (185). He was rudely asked to take back the already weighed paddy and told that the rest of his harvest too would not be bought; for the commotion he created, police action would be enforced against him.

Difficult to Seek Hearing: Sahib Speaks English

Murari decided to lodge a complaint with the MLA and the following early morning, reached the city. The MLA sounded concerned. Receiving a letter on MLA's official letter head, addressed to the RM (Regional Manager), raised Murari's spirits. He hoped, RM would surely act against the local manager and teach him the consequences of dishonesty. At RM's office however, in spite of begging for an urgent hearing, since his daughter was ailing and needed medical treatment, the security man did not let him meet the Sahib; he was shouted down rudely. He contacted Veerbhadra, a combative leader of the party due to whose campaigning, votes were given to a certain local candidate, and sought assurance that the meeting with the RM Sahib would be facilitated. The security man this time sounded humbled, told him, Sahib did not know Hindi; he would rather speak in English. Murari told him that he could converse in English being decently educated and added that he could have become an engineer had the financial crisis not prevented him from taking admission. This conversation with the security man warmed up the latter a little more in sympathy towards Murari:

> Murari's unkempt, sweaty attire, made the R M Sahib visibly upset. Murari explained: 'I'm a poor farmer and at the Paddy Sale Centre, the Regional Manager is refusing to buy my paddy since I'm not giving him bribe'. In somewhat broken Hindi, Sahib took his details. Murari's felt deep satisfaction hearing Sahib's solid reprimand and strict warning to the Manager on phone. He thought, there was delay in God's verdict but justice prevails. (187–88)

At the paddy sale centre, the following day, a scene stirred fright in everyone. A young peasant whose paddy was also shelved for a long time seemed to have lost his patience. Everybody was taken aback when he raised his shovel, threatening the Manager, 'I'll behead you' (189). People around tried to talk sense to him, but he rushed at the manager, the crowd also ran after him. The manager looked scared and meekly weighed the young farmer's paddy (191). When Murari approached him for weighing his paddy, the overbearing manager appeared so humbled and distressed. He told Murari sadly that the latter's complaint against him had been damaging and added that it was time to close. Murari should better come tomorrow. Murari perceived that the reprimand from the authority after all worked; he felt sympathy for the manager. But when he visited the paddy centre the following day, it was closed, locked up. Outside a notice was pasted: 'Paddy purchase closed, exceeding the storage capacity of 10000 quintal. No space to store.' 'Manager' (191). This showed the manager remained unrepentant, invincible. Murari had hoped that by taking the right approach to seek fair dealing, he had been successful in enforcing justice. He was however checkmated.

The officially announced minimum support price was never paid to the peasants in full, always less. Despite good harvest, a farmer does not make a profit. In Dikshit's 'Under weighment' the cane grower, Maiku harnessed to the life of hardship, nurtures the fear of losing his very small landholding for lack of resources, broods on abandoning farming, 'it would rather be better riding a rikshaw in the city than facing the life of rewardless hard labor' (18). The non-payment strengthens the stranglehold of the usurers. Maiku's narrative of immense frustration, humiliation, fatigue, and even death represents lives of many small sugarcane peasants. At the marketing arena, despite the prescribed laws of regulation, the tame submission of farmers is sought by threats of police or by harassment. Murari, the paddy farmer, in 'Kisan Kya Kare' being adequately educated is capable of taking his complaint to the higher office but at the end of the day, the villainy of the manager outsmarts him and he becomes just another aggrieved complainant with whom the veteran rogues know how to deal.

Notes

1. 'Under weighment' (9–19) is based on Damodar Dutta Dikshit's personal experience as a Commissioner in sugar. The story was first published in October 1980 in the magazine, *Aajkaal* edited by Dronveer Kohli. The norms of cane growing and processing, Dikshit finds, did no change since the colonial rule. The title of the story derives from a popular term for the customary practice of under-weighing of cane since the colonial times.
2. Suresh Kantak (1954–) known for his various stories and novels hails from the village, Kant, Bihar. His plays in Bhojpuri dealing with the peasantry in rural India are performed very often. He has won several awards for his writings.
3. Suman Sahai's blog post, dated 22 October 2011 (sumansahai-blog.blogspot.com) provides a detailed report about the subjection and the torture farmers face at the sale centres. Suman Sahai, a Convener, Gene Campaign, New Delhi puts it forthrightly in 'Good Harvest Do Not Always Translate into Money in the Bank'. (This also appears in *The Hindu*, 19 October 2011.)
4. I have paraphrased and drawn the matter from Sahai's blog.
5. Based on my conversation with Damodar Datta Dikshit.
6. Banjot Kour drawing on several field reports writes in *Down to Earth* (15 July 2018) that according to the Uttar Pradesh Cane Development and Sugar Industry Department, sugar mill owners owe more than Rs. 23,270 crore to farmers for 2012–13 to 2016. The farmers are put under tremendous pressure since despite the guarantee, the interest for the delayed payment was not paid. Roshan Lal, a farmer of Hardoi's Kunwarpur Basti village, mortgaged the last gold items in his house. He had given his sugarcane to Ajbapur mill that year; they owed him over Rs. 2 lakh. His payment is due to a bank from which he had taken loan to cultivate sugarcane. The labourers who helped him harvest are also to be paid. For more on

this, see 'Sugar farmer's crisis: Bumper harvest turns bane'. With the sudden fall of sugar prices, cane farmers have been incurring heavy losses.
7. The subsequent references are from 'Under weighment' by Damodar Datta Dikshit.
8. Refers to bastard, a usual rebuff used to insult poor and oppressed.
9. A report in www.aljazeera.com, 3 April 2017, 'Sugar Cane Farmers: cycle of debt and suicide', describes the grim situation in Vidarbha how all these sugar outlays ate into the cane farmer, Shivanna's profits, and he was forced to borrow money to cover the mounting expenses and eventually had to take out more loans to pay for his previous ones. In 2014, when his crops failed 10 due to insufficient rain, he suffered a loss of 1 lakh. The following year, the price paid by the factory dropped from Rs. 2000 ($30) a tonne of sugarcane to Rs. 1500, some of which was not even paid; factories can take months to make payments, and when he died in July 2015, Shivanna was still waiting to be paid for his January harvest.
10. Subsequent references are to the story, 'Kisan Kya Kare'.
11. Suman Sahai (2011) points out the well-played strategies of cheating. The foremost has been to declare the grain as light weight, not fulfilling the standards are equally miraculously met once the farmers' pockets have become correspondingly lighter. She observes a certain unholy nexus between the agents of FCI and private companies. The deal is that the procurement agency will reject much of the grain on one pretext or the other.

4
Women Peasants in Triple Jeopardy: Conmen as Philanthropists

> The Daroga said, 'Ask your husband why he produced a girl like the blossom of gular'. ('Kasaibada')

The notion, 'India is progressing', sounds like a truism, as much true as false, more conspicuously, with regard to the condition of rural women. Can the claims about progressing rural India, specifically in the regions of the Hindi belt, be considered accurate? While the urban women are ascertaining their rights in every sphere of existence, the same is not the case with rural women: it is not that they submit to wrongs, but the stakes against them are too convoluted and difficult to combat. Even though, women in peasantry comprise nearly 16 percent of India's female population and in the recent decades, seats have come to be reserved for elected women members of the Panchayat committee. The stories, Madan Mohan's[1] (2018, 55–78) 'Jahrili Roshnion ke Beech' (In the Midst of Poisonous Lights) and Shivmurti's[2] (1999) 'Kasaibada' (The Bucher House), unfold an inclusive spectrum of cultural and political information about the Panchayat[3] administration and the evolving rural scenario in the democratic India of our times that do explain the reasons of why while the measures to empower women show promises and yet in certain societal contexts their struggles are rendered helpless.

Saguna and Shanichari, respectively, the principal characters in the above-mentioned stories represent the struggle of village women under the circumstances where, due to an absent husband or being a widow or a with meagre means of subsistence or frail health, they are rendered

Rural India and Peasantry in Hindi Stories. Vanashree, Oxford University Press. © Vanashree 2023.
DOI: 10.1093/oso/9780192871572.003.0005

vulnerable to exploitation. Both face triple jeopardy, being *Dalit*, uneducated, and poor. It is a common knowledge that rapes and murders of Dalit women[4] in rural India had increased since the 1990s. Women from Dalit community, generally from the non-urban rural community, are made to suffer both physical assault and verbal abuse. The probes have shown how caste dominance can steer government machinery; how fraught with risk it is to challenge the guilty, despite the law being on the side of the victim. Several fictional works in Hindi and other Indian languages underscore that the women in the rural areas are worst casualty in matters of caste clashes, sexual assaults, human trafficking, land disputes, and land profiteering.

What is of conspicuous concern in the two stories is that in dominantly male-centric rural mores there is almost no space for women who do not have a male support system. Their oppression grows more complicated—due to poverty, illiteracy, and exploitation—both sexual and monetary. While in the context of the stories, female illiteracy in the sphere of rural India could be seen as the foremost cause of exacerbating their crisis, the tacit misogyny—directed at women, particularly belonging to the lower strata manifests in the attitude of the local functionaries of Panchayats—those responsible for maintaining law and order in the village society. Besides, anyone frequently visiting a village in the recent decades would confront the increasing presence of a fast-developing culture of parasitism and strong men. Not limited to the village administration but extending to several individuals and groups within a larger body politic: the police, big peasant/landowner, government officers, small engineers, overseers, excise inspectors, BDO (Block Development Officer), even school masters, headmasters, and lawyers. Their assets grow within a few years. The roots are deep set from village to the district of such people. Some of them, the traditional landholders who grow political clout act as the influencers, feared or respected and are described as *Bahubali*.[5]

Women and the Village Administration

The traumatic struggle and eventual death of Saguna and Shanichari unfold a vivid glimpse of a world where supposedly impartial judges at the

Panchayat (local assembly) secretly owe their allegiance to the power of the Pradhan, *Daroga* (Inspector of Police Station) or the MLA, where a cordial exchange of greetings at a formal occasion can in the blink of an eye turn into a nasty display of clout and deal-making, and where illiterate people are trained to parrot statements they do not fully comprehend. In such situations, the problems women in trouble face spiral out of control. In both the stories, the village administration, like predators, occupied in making most of the opportunity to earn money, targets those families which are headed by women.

The sharp innuendoes embedded in the narratives drive us to understand the mechanics of the Panchayat body's (village administration's) failure to perform its expected roles. We come to see how craftily the government aids or assistance schemes like MNREGA[6] (Mahatma Gandhi National Rural Employment Guarantee Act 2005) become the means of siphoning funds and how the village politics survives and absolves itself of all dubious activities. Studies have underlined most Panchayats as the hub of corruption and political hobnobbing. The massive investment in the election of the Panchayat, corruption and greed of the members, collusion between the workers of the Panchayat, the members of the ruling party, police administration, wealthy landowners, and the other mediators and handlers in the sphere of the village infrastructure build up a network that very often disrupts or distorts its essential goals. It is generally observed that Panchayat officials may come from humble origin or background but once they acquire a position, they become wealthy by misuse of funds, give advantage to their brethren and kith and kin. Once elected, their functionaries behave like rulers rather than public servants meant to serve the village society. Many of them thrive because of the blessings of a political party or a political heavy-weight.

Land Remains a Covert but Contentious Issue

We are familiar with the situations where the demise of a husband or his absence results in woman-headed households. In the absence of an adult male member in their family, or in the case of widowhood, whatever land they own is their main productive asset and a vital resource. It has also been found that in these situations, they are most likely to lose their land and other assets, which creates further difficulties in sustaining themselves and their children. Though women's land rights are legally endorsed, they own less than 1 percent of the land in rural India. While statutory law may be gender neutral, customary law prevails and is based on a patriarchal system. Customary law assigns property rights to men or kinship groups, dominated by men, and thus the ability of women to claim or inherit land is extremely limited. Securing land rights therefore can have a profound impact on the economic development of a family, as a source of identity and cultural heritage. It has been found that women who owned land had more domestic and economic power, for the land could be a means of investment and earning, in terms of leasing or producing, than those who did not own land. Accordingly, the resources[7] put in the hands of women, rather than men, are more likely to be used to the benefit of children and others. However, their lives as mothers and as lone earning members in their families, as owners of small lands, the drudgery at the fields and at home, render them defenceless in the situation of not being literate. Not being adequately trained to decide and act on their own, they are made the target of exploitation. Subsuming these critical issues, the larger matrices of the two narratives weave a dense but sinister political narrative. We are nudged into the labyrinthine networks of village politics, and confront how the reign of rogues and dissemblers like predators victimize the illiterate and the weaker segments of the village.

'Jahrili Roshnion ke Beech' foregrounds the subterfuge planned by the MLA of the region, Head of Gram Panchayat, and Lekhpal (the village accountant) in solidarity to dispossess Saguna of her two bighas of land. In 'Kasaibada', distraught with grief, Shanichari discovers that her daughter was trafficked into prostitution in the façade of the Gram Pradhan's welfare-scheme of mass wedding of the daughters from the deprived sections. Shanichari's complaint is not registered at the police station. In the meanwhile, a self-proclaimed leader of the village, who is a school master, in the pretext of garnering support for her case, manoeuvres to obtain her thumb print on her land papers. The bizarre end of Saguna and Shanichari in their respective narratives could be seen as predictable, being the politically strategic means of absolving the perpetrators of the most heinous crimes.

Saguna's Derangement and Death

Several sequences in the story, 'Jahrili Bijliyon ke Beech' construct the topography of a village in UP at some point of time during the recent decade. The disquieting news of the death of Saguna coincides with the grand celebration of the growth story of the village Ghamolia and the neighbouring villages.

> Around the dead body of Saguna at the field, a crowd of villagers stands in silence, a silence that is only interrupted by occasional whispers. Saguna was seen roaming into the alleys of the village, appearing distraught, in a rumpled saree, sometimes wailing, or holding strangers, imploring them to help her get her land back. Several villagers guessed that the cause of her derangement was the loss of land, treacherously usurped, but there was some confusion about it. The crowd watches Saguna's children, exhausted, silent, sitting around the body—the youngest, Chhutka, oblivious of the mishap, was fast asleep—beside the body of his mother.[8] (58)

Saguna was the wife of a small farmer, Kisanprasad Muravon with a family of four children. They owned a plot of two 50 bighas. Pleased with the laborious services of Saguna's landless father-in-law, a big landowner had donated a piece from his surplus to him. The two bighas since then has been the source of subsistence to the family of Kisanprasad and Saguna. In spite of the reluctance of his family, Kisanprasad decides to leave for Punjab in search of greener pasture to fulfil his dream of having a pucca house and a decent life for his children. Despite her frail physique, Saguna labours in her two bigha field in the scorching month of *vaishakh*, (mid-summer) when it is raining fire. All by herself, she struggles to deal with the rising cost of fertilizers, irrigation, and seeds. Besides, the precarious weather, either the floods or the parched earth aborted all efforts for the expected yield. She tried to grapple with the sowing of paddy by hard labour, but the investment made in seeds, manure, irrigation, and the labour broke her courage. All efforts did not help much; the yield was not enough to feed the family of five beyond three months. Working at MNREGA would cause her fatigue and she could not continue regularly.

During the initial five months since Kisanprasad's departure, she received a few thousands from him. She could get to know his whereabouts through the cell phone of the elderly, Manesar Mahato, the *lekhpal*,[9] also called *Munshi* (the village accountant). Manesar belonged to Saguna's caste. Soon, Kisanprasad stopped sending any message. The money from Punjab stopped coming in. With no resources at hand, Saguna's worry grew intense since the date of her daughter's *gauna*[10] was approaching and the roof of her hovel was in ruins due to heavy downpour. The greater worry was how to feed her family.

Treacherous Plan to Usurp the Land

The milieu of the village is teeming with the clamour of long-winded rhetoric of the politics of development, MNREGA, the construction of mobile towers, of roads, etc. The story nudges us to the background and in a kaleidoscope emerge the secret meetings, first between the MLA Lallu Tewari, called Baba and the Gram Pradhan, Sampat Yadav and thereafter, between the latter and the village accountant, Manesar. The MLA, Baba is conversant with the greedy money making of Pradhan in NREGA and summons him for a private chat. Obviously the three of them underhandedly serve each other's interest and Sampat's plundering of the government funds was no longer a secret. One day he was called up on phone, Baba speaking:

> 'Tell me about MNREGA? The CDO (Chief Development Officer) talks about social audit? Now be cautious'.
> 'When your blessings are with me how can it be possible?' Pradhan's voice trembled. 'Last time you had saved me from going behind the bars, snatching from the Collector the charge sheet against me. This time please save me from the audit. I hold your feet', groveled Sampat Pradhan. 'Don't you act smart. Meet me tomorrow at my residence'. (59)

The innuendoes let the reader understand what would be the end result of these meetings. The huge bribe is likely to satisfy the MLA.

Saguna's Plot of Two Bighas Is the Target

One gets to know that Pradhan would be granted impunity on the condition that he fulfils the MLA's desire for a plot in the name of his wife to build a petrol pump which could avail him a regular source of income. To ensure that their business of extorting money through fraudulent means continue with impunity, Pradhan and the village accountant move ahead with the assigned job. Saguna's land at the centre of the village, by the roadside is a coveted spot that the MLA wants for building a petrol pump. The trio use all the political manoeuvres and machinations to dispossess Saguna of this land. In the absence of a husband, whose whereabouts in the last few months were not known, she becomes their easy scapegoat. One day during her visit to her field, she finds Manesar standing close by. He speaks to her in a voice suffused with compassion:

> What is troubling you; you've become so sickly, like a dry stick? Your husband is having a merry time in Punjab and you're suffering an ordeal in your hovel. Manesar's sympathy being unusual, irritated her. She however replies, 'It is not the lone belly I feed, but five creatures. How can Rs 100 from NREGA be enough for all?' She was moved to tears. (67)

Manesar could sense that as the opportune moment to convince Saguna of the practical benefits of mortgaging her land and in a complicated vocabulary, he explains that mortgaging her two bighas could get Saguna Rs. 50,000. But for procuring that much, she would have to give the commission of Rs. 5000 in advance. He being an accountant of the village was supposed to be well versed in all the knowhow and sounded trustworthy. He added, 'I'll help you apply for the Kisan Credit Scheme. Regarding your ramshackle roof, I'll ensure that you seek benefit from Indira Gandhi Garib Makan Yojna'[11] (67). Desperate for funds, she readily agrees to it. As the story moves further, Saguna happily puts her thumbprint on the relevant papers as guided by Manesar *Chacha*[12] believing, him, someone elderly, who belonged to her own community, a senior village official, an educated person in the village. Who else could be trusted more? Her credulity however by no means lets her assume that her thumbprint acquired with a stamp upon her property papers (the document of ownership, *patta*) meant that the land no longer belonged to her legally.

With Rs. 50,000 as mortgage money, however, her most immediate household problems were seemingly resolving. Besides, there was the assurance: sooner or later, her land was to be freed from the mortgage. Within seven months of this deal, a flustered Manesar appears at her door feigning sympathy for Saguna, and informs her that it is being discussed that her land is to be prepared for the installation of a petrol pump. 'I'm worried about saving it' (72). He volunteers himself with alacrity to join her in defending her land and even writes an appeal to the Collectorate. Assuming him to be a reliable, elderly well-wisher, she obeys his instructions. The prospect of any deceit does not sweep over her.

The Stronghold of a Race of Parasites: The Handler-Manipulator

It can be inferred from the hush-hush instructions of Manesar that he does not want Saguna to seek advice from elsewhere. The village accountant's demeanour and his theatrics really represent how the con men manipulate and victimize the scapegoat. What is worth notice here is the perverse pleasure he derives in playing with her naivety. The drama of Saguna's lodging her complaint testifies to the magnitude of damage that could be caused by someone like Manesar who belongs to this clan of parasites. His acting as her well-wisher shows how adept he could be in the art of deceiving.

> The appeal was read, her name was called out. The District Collector asked Manesar standing beside her: 'Who are you?' 'I'm from the same *tola* (locality); her husband has gone to Panjab to earn Huzoor'. Munshi Manesar concealed his real identity.
>
> Sahib asked Saguna: 'Have you brought the papers of *Patta*? (The legal document endorsing the ownership of the land) Let me see', extending his hand towards her. Saguna looked behind at the Munshi. Sahib, growing impatient, raised his voice, 'I want from you the papers, why're you looking that side?' 'Sarkar my hovel caught fire and all the documents and papers got burnt up'. Mimicking the demeanor of

Munshi, she also joined her hands. Writing some remark on Saguna's paper, he asked, 'When did it catch fire?' 'Ten years have passed'. Said Manesar. Moving the papers towards the steno, Sahib said, 'Your complaint will go to the *tahsil* (town area). They'll look into the case'. (73–74)

This scene at the collectorate in the company of Manesar is the example of how handlers could themselves be the offenders or who surreptitiously help the offenders, smoothly managing the complainants—the victims. Saguna's hearing is just a case in point in India where millions of such appeals from the rural/backward regions have been of no consequence because of the intrusion of the know-all, and the braggarts.

In the next visit to the town, they were told that her appeal was sent to Bahadurganj police station. Manesar maintained a façade of profound sympathy; even his bombastic speech grudging the misuse of power of the MLA (Member of Legislative Assembly), addressed as Vidhayakji displayed as if he was even prepared to go against the MLA. As another ruse to sound sincere, he insisted that she ought to ask Pradhanji to escort her. This was to confirm that she is pre-empted from harbouring any doubt in Manesar or Pradhan's main part in the most sinister conspiracy against her. She gratefully thought that after all Munshi's (Manesar, the accountant's) support gave her the courage to go against Vidhayakji. At the police station, she was asked to wait. The police jeep turned up in the compound after two hours, and everyone greeted Darogaji. She nervously wobbled forward. Daroga demanded her application:

Who wants to capture your land? Saguna stammered the same line she had learnt. 'It's the goons and loafers of the village. I'm told, that it'll be a petrol pump'. Daroga smiled, 'Now get lost. Don't waste our time. Come here, when someone you can name captures your land!' 'Your name is not on the land; don't you accuse anyone! Don't think of visiting us.' (75)

When she reported it to Manesar, he laughed, 'Daroga is right, when it happens, let them know'. (75) Manesar was now relieved that Saguna's case was dismissed. He treated her with kachori and chai. She was grateful, thinking that being the Munshi of Pradhan, Manesar had made the utmost effort to protect her land, taking her complaint from village to the district.

Land Declared Benami: No Scope for Damage Control

Then some more time passed. Within everyone' sight were the trucks arriving, laden with labourers and then cement, rods, and bricks being dumped into Saguna's land. She rushed to Manesar. 'Munshi Chacha, do something', she was sobbing. He said 'I'm not responsible for your land; it is used as without any name: Benama'[13] (76). Feigning complete distance from his participation in the plot, he advised her to meet the senior Daroga. 'I can't escort you against the MLA, our Netaji. You should candidly call the name. Don't be scared' (77). Her visit to the senior Daroga was the endgame.

> He said, 'See, the pump is being built up with the sanction of the government on the name of MLA's wife. You don't have the papers of the land. How can it be proved? Ask the entire village?' 'Everyone knows the history of our land' Saguna replied. 'You can go to the court, we can do nothing', said Darogaji. (77)

One assumes that Daroga could make sense of the game played with Saguna but the matter now involved the MLA (Vidhayakji) and hence did not leave any scope at the end of Daroga for damage control. These episodes also indicate that the mistrust of ordinary rural populace which had been a colonial style of governance remained perpetuated in democratic India. The reader of a story like this comes to understand that the police in ingratiating relation with the MLA and the likes of him had scant respect for the oppressed and the victimized. Evidently, most people from the backward and poor rural world have experienced the indifferent, bullying, or servile police tantra.

Bouncing between deep hurt and helplessness, her world disintegrating, Saguna's was in a state of breakdown. Desperate, she would hold the feet of every member of the Panchayat and Pradhanji, pleading with him to pity her, and save her land. People were noticing her standing quietly or sitting there daily, staring at her field without batting her eyes, watching the masons and labourers carrying building material for the petrol pump. The neighbours talked about her suffering; how her grief at the loss of her land deranged her. She would stop by any stranger, cry bitterly, or hysterically plead: '*Kaka, Chacha*! save my field' (78). Metaphorically, the alienation of Saguna from her land is the alienation from her life force. Her children in tears wanted her to get back home, follow her; she would throw away *rotis* and refuse to return. Her roaming into the alleys made some educated youth of the village curious. They could make a good guess and got at the root of the whole plot of cheating to which Saguna was subjected. When their interest in Saguna's abject misery made a story, her picture appeared in the city newspaper, under the heading, 'A woman is fasting to retrieve her land' (78). The Pradhan and the Munshi (accountant) threatened those youth. They were shown the fear of police and the MLA. Since then, for quite some time, the youth were not seen in the village. On the 27th day, the grief-stricken Saguna in whose belly no grain had gone for days was found dead. The police came but the real culprit in full control of the situation maintained that she died of sickness. At the procedure of panchnama (a record of witness testimony during police investigation of the cause of death), it was but imperative for the twosome, the Lekhpal and Pradhan, to indulge in more apparent show of histrionics, grieving for the death of poor Saguna, to save their skin. Though privately they were rejoicing.

The Development: Reality Check

The story of Saguna runs parallel with the story of development. Within a year as if some magic occurred, the pucca roads, bridge, television, installation of electricity, and mobile phones in the pocket of every village youth displayed development. Every house availed cemented walls and a mobile set. Even those who had small lands of no more than two bigha, possessed tractor or trolleys. One having a cycle was seen riding a motorcycle. Mobile companies were actively erecting mobile towers. The initial indifference of the peasants to mobile phones did not deter them. They smartly bargained and purchased the portions from the fields of farmers, to build towers just next to the main road. Whatever money was paid pleased the peasants for it fulfilled their craving to feel the cash in hand. At hindsight, however, one can reckon that getting land at such a cheap rate was a big business incentive to the multinational business houses, but it also resulted in the waste of fertile lands and gradual distancing of the youth from farming.

The narrative comes to an end when the police is winding up Saguna's *panchnama* (post-mortem) and at some distance, simultaneously, the loudspeaker is announcing invitation to the village folk to assemble and participate in large numbers in the celebration of the village success story. A huge gathering under a pandal greets the MLA, the head of the Panchayat, Pradhan, and other village functionaries. A series of speeches describe the achievements of the ruling political class. The MLA Lallu Tewari hogs the maximum limelight giving credit to himself, congratulating the villagers for all the developments. The gossip of the villagers showed that they were well aware of the motive of Pradhan, MLA, and Manesar but dared not raise their voice for until a person is proved guilty in the court of law, he cannot be persecuted, whatever be the public opinion.

Human Trafficking and Murders: Underbelly of Rural life in 'Kasaibada'

The story opens with 'The news spread across the village that Shanichari was on *Aamaran anshan*[14] (Fast unto Death)' (Shivmurti, 2020). Appearing as her mentor, the school master cum an aspiring leader, known as Leaderji, announces:

> 'Until her daughter is returned, she would not give up fasting'. For the last one week, he has been inveigling Shanichari to sit on fast unto death, and now he has blown into every ear that 'Shanichari's protest has nothing to do with Pradhan, but a non-violent Gandhian struggle for justice and against exploitation. It is every villagers' duty to support her wholeheartedly. (Shivmurti)

One can sense the politically correct tenor of his speech. Though the villagers put their thumbprint or signature on her appeal of three pages prepared by Leaderji, the complex caste equations or fear of the biggies do not allow them to actively associate themselves with her grievance. The villagers were appalled at the knowledge that the big show of mass wedding of girls from the poor families in which several young daughters were married, was actually a cover-up to facilitate trafficking of young brides. Shanichari, a *Dalit* widow peasant, was, in a state of shock and totally devastated. People were curious, seeing her seated on a tattered sack, at the gate of Pradhanji's double-storied house, holding a small picture of Gandhiji. One could however guess that the show was directed and staged at the behest of Leaderji to achieve his personal mission to shame and oust the village Pradhan from his position and replace him in the subsequent election. The narrative gradually exposes the underbelly of rural life: how village rogues in collusion with the criminal elements exploit vulnerable households.

Pradhan had fulfilled one of the generous promises before his election that he would organize the wedding of poor village girls without dowry. The reader is also informed that before his election, he was a moneylender known for his unrelenting usury. In this subtly drawn narrative, the cloak of humility the Pradhan wears is vividly portrayed. His care for the deprived is seen as worthy of applause and described as

> 'a new chapter, testifying to the progress villages are making'. The village was resounding with the announcement BDO sahib was making on the loudspeaker: 'Your Gram Pradhan KD Singh's untiring efforts made it possible to abolish the curse of dowry and caste system. In a backward region who could ever think of this radical reform'. (Shivmurti)

After the mass wedding was solemnized, in a big fanfare, SDO (Sub Divisional Officer), BDO (Block Development officer), the midwife from Aangawadi and officials participated in the event. The event was described as a new chapter in the village's history. Everyone was touched when BDO praising Pradhan's act of philanthropy declared in an emotional speech that it was an unprecedented move towards the upliftment of poor and Dalits which aimed to bring social equality through inter-caste marriages without dowry. The village women saw Pradhan as their saviour for hosting dowry-free ideal marriage (Shivmurti). Collective wedding was indeed a huge assault against orthodox dowry system and casteism. For Shanichari, an illiterate, poor woman, her young, tender daughter, Roopmati, married to a handsome groom was the ultimate fulfilment. It was a fascinating scene to watch—ten young and handsome grooms, ten brides, decked up in colourful bright sarees—from the deprived sections of the village. Parting of her daughter gave heart-rending pain to Shanichari. Since it was to be a marriage without dowry, no gift was allowed but so emotionally moved was that she stealthily stuffed three kilos of silver, the only precious possession she had, into her departing daughter's small box.

In less than a fortnight however, a furtive visit at her door, around midnight, of a girl, Suguni, who too was wedded in the same programme stunned Shanichari. Suguni's story was scary. She disclosed that the grand show of mass wedding was fraud; in the name of social service, the bargaining of innocent rural girls had taken place; they were then thrown into the sinister world of prostitution. Suguni wanted to file FIR, but she went missing since that night, her plight along with nine other girls remained unknown. It was suspected that she was probably murdered.

Women Complainant: No FIR at the Police Station, but Sexual Expletives

When Shanichari approaches the police station to lodge a complaint about the missing Suguni and her daughter, Rupa's whereabouts were not known, and also that they were the made the victim of trafficking, the Daroga (the police inspector) refuses to take her complaint. Treating her flippantly, his speech is redolent with offensive slighting. In the rural world, most expletives uttered at women have abundant sexual connotations. That gives away the subconscious sexual perversions and depravity of a character holding a position in the police service.

> 'Sarkar! Ai Pradhanji has sold off all the poor daughters of the village. Do hang him or better shoot me and kill me. My daughter is like the tender blossom of gular'. As if the matter for Darogaji was easy to understand. 'Hunh, Saaali![15] Now, after selling your daughter, you're here to lay the blame on others!'
>
> After shutting up Shanichari, Darogaji gains confidence in his chosen line of rebuke. One infers the derotatory style of dealing with the women from the lower strata of the village society.
>
> 'Ask your husband why he produced a girl like the blossom of gular'.

'It was Pradhanji who fathered her. My late husband was out of the village in *Pardes* to earn'.

'O, so you want me to write a report for free. Likes of you—better get a loop tomorrow in the loop camp of the police station'.

'Pradhan is the one who needs a loop'. (Shivmurti)

The extremities of sexual crimes against women and more uninhibitedly against defenceless women remain contained in the parochial societies; it is however an obnoxious disclosure that Pradhanji indulged in selling off his own daughter.

Further complication begins when the school master whose political activism has given him the name Leaderji initiates her case, masterminds the staging of her fast unto death, fervently inciting her to sit on fast unto death to draw the attention of the media and the police until the police takes action against the criminal act of Pradhan and brings back her missing daughter. Shanichari, distracted with immense grief, was seen sitting at the gate of Pradhan's double-storied house with a picture of Gandhiji. On behalf of Shanichari, Leaderji's speech addressed to the villagers at the site is replete with politically correct sentences, 'Until Pradhanji returns her daughter, she would be on hunger strike until death. She has nothing personal against Pradhanji, her protest is for justice, a Gandhian nonviolent fight. It is the duty of the entire village to support the poor widow wholeheartedly' (Shivmurti). The news in the city newspaper summons the reporters on the scene. A letter to the DM (District Magistrate)—with the signature campaign or the thumb impression against the criminal act of Pradhan, burning of dummies of Pradhan and his son—all accelerate the protest of Shanichari. The influential villagers however are reluctant to give their overt support to Shanichari's cause; even among the poor, those families whose daughters were married in the fraudulent ceremony and were missing since then are scared of joining her. In some quarters women in her own community were critical of her protest. She was described as brazen and, who was unnecessarily raising a storm.

Leaderji's empathy for Shanichari stems from a motive; he has his own axe to grind. He aspires to appear as a prospective *Neta* of the wronged and he is not leaving any stone unturned in drawing attention of the state authorities to destroy Pradhan's vote bank, hoping that within twenty-four hours, Pradhan would be in handcuffs, so that he himself would become Pradhan in the near future. Being unscrupulous he harbours and executes a more sinister scheme: In the pretext of forwarding Shanichari's appeal, he takes her signature (thumb print) on a stamp paper—to facilitate usurpation of her land—her only means of survival.

Special Connect with the Police: Villages, the Site of Roguery, Addiction, Arrack

It has been a known practice in the rural societies that to reinforce one's power and authority, it is essential to develop a close relationship with the police. Flaunting a special connect with the police allows the local functionaries the license to indulge in lawlessness arbitrarily with impunity. Lest the scale further tilt in favour of the complainant, when summoned to the police station, Pradhanji, desperate for the dismissal of the case against him, elaborately plans to please the Daroga (the police inspector) who happens to be easy going, given to petty avarice. A visit to Darogaji's residence has to accompany goodies. His wife is made a cohort in his plan: 'Listen, some rustic goods like blackberry vinegar, mango barfi, badi (spicy balls of black lentils) are liked by Darogain (the wife of the Inspector). This not being enough, solid wads of notes must be added.' (Shivmurti) Darogaji was sitting at Puja and after some time appears twisting his moustaches.

> 'Yes Pradhanji, what a terrible unrest have you spread in the village! A criminal village like yours which sells its daughters for money! I haven't seen in the last twenty-three years of my service', 'Pradhanji kept standing with folded hands'. 'Hujoor first listen to what I'm saying'.
>
> 'Who cares for what you say! Who so ever comes here, appears empty hand[16]. If the old woman dies, you will be in jail at least for ten years. And it'll be the government's liability to pay for your coffin and last rites'. (Shivmurti)

Pradhanji spins a tale, laying the blame of his disrepute upon Leaderji, who determinedly conspired to oust Pradhan from his post. The narrator lets us know that the offerings of money, some most coveted rustic edible stuffs, and the promise of building a temple in the vicinity of the police station pacify the Daroga. Darogain (the wife of Daroga) appears holding the curtain, looks approvingly, and gives Pradhanji the *prasad* of Lord Satyanarayana.

The scene of confrontation between Leaderji and Daroga is a familiar one. Pradhanji now absolved, Darogaji threatens Leaderji with dire consequences, if the latter does not give up his pursuit of Pradhan, his personal file would be readied, charging him of indulging in anarchist or Naxal activities. He would be sent to CRED headquarters where he might be declared dangerous for the country on the charges: "guilty of spreading rumours, against inter-caste weddings, promoting violence in public against the policies of the government, keeping opium, weed, and arrack. 'It would lick your leadership and your mastery. Destroy your future Shivmurti'). That very afternoon, Leaderji too hosts for Darogaji a lavish chicken party and serves a fat bottle of whisky at his house in the presence of his beautiful wife. Instead of visiting the victim, Shanichari, to act on her grievance, Darogaji chooses to take a trip, strolling into the adjacent forest, hunting for woodhens. In the thick of night, Pradhan's wife cajoles Shanichari with her insistent appeals, 'O, my sister, forgive us, tomorrow he'll bring back your Roopmati, and forces a glass of milk into Shanichari's gullet' (Shivmurti). Shanichari was found dead in the morning.

The narrative unfolds the dynamics involved in cheating, cloaked in the rhetoric of philanthropy. The idiot of the village, Adhrangi, however, can see through the façade and yells: 'both Pradhan and Leader ji are venomous snake and coloured hyena' (Shivmurti). The series of events justify the title of the story. 'Kasaibada' is synonym of the village. Pradhan, Leaderji—the would-be Pradhan, and the police inspector—the trio are the true parasites of the system—in their pull and push, the low caste, Dalit Shanichari loses not only her daughter but also her small piece of land and life. None in this hubbub is concerned with the mysteriously missing Suguni and Rupa and many other girls. The reader suspects that Suguni must have been the victim of gruesome killing for raising alarm. What is lamentable is that the villagers at large are not willing[17] to be an active party in Shanichari's protest, for fear of their dishonour; the scandal would affect the prospects of the younger siblings of the girls, trapped and victimized in the façade of mass wedding.

Illiteracy of Womenfolk: The Literate Offenders Defend Their Crime

It is the literate offenders who explain matters, defend their crimes in convincing rhetoric, and remain unpunished. The community of Saguna and Shanichari is a prism that shows the perverse reality of rural existence. Of these, the foremost is female illiteracy which is cojoined with caste. Both Saguna and Shanichari belong to the lowest caste (schedule caste) in terms of the system of caste hierarchy. Education for them therefore has never been regarded as a priority. None questioned the Sarkar (the State) as to why women folk of the village were not trained in the intricate nitty gritty of what is the legal meaning of *patta* (lawfully valid papers that declare ownership of a land), although the crude facts remain that in every farming family, women are the principal care takers of children and older relatives. We need to ponder over not only their drudgery in the household chores but also their diligent cattle care which is legendary. They work in the fields sharing their menfolk's all labour from sowing to harvesting, through thick and thin. The principal reason of their adversity is their ignorance, illiteracy. The traditional belief in the supreme wisdom and authority of men ruins them. Though one is aware of the scores of events of exploitation of village women, nothing much has been done to protect them from predators.

New Class of Rich: 'Progenies of Parasitism'

The narratives of Madan Mohan and Shivmurty dealing with different social contexts however collectively hold those culpable who blindly obey the men in power despite knowing the truth. The subtle detailing of the relationship between the triumphant persecutors and their victims in the narratives seems familiar even to those who never visited the village. The malaise of parasitism is not limited to the village administration but has seeped into the policing system: from the lower constable to the middle level or even higher police people have not escaped the temptation of cashing in on the crisis that vulnerable face in the village, displaying bias. The stories reveal close correspondence with the studies that illumine how a new class of rich and influential people is rising in the villages, labelled as 'progenies of parasitism',[18] having an evil nexus with the men of power who destroy the innocent and vulnerable. The most sinister crimes flourish with impunity. Ganesh Pandey's (1999, 70–71) study of post-colonial rural India identifies them:

> When peasants labour in farms, they pretend to put on the responsibility of the village, are in contact with the higher ups in matters of recommendation, appeals, religious work dharna, strikes, protest, lockout, matters of excise, addiction, arrack, addictive edibles, tari, employment of unemployed. As the representative of the village, they claim to have access to bureaucrats, Collectorate, even ministers under whose mentorship they flaunt power. (70–71)

Pandey's telling portrayal of the contemporary village society also draws from the astute fact findings of Kumar and Shrivastava (1980).

> The new culture of parasitism flourishing in the rural societies is even more heinous, menacing, more secretive than the earlier times of Sahukar, Zamindar or Purohits. The new exploiters are varied. They are representatives of the state government but in close contact with the police. Some of them are local coordinators and the panchayat officials from humble origin or background but once they acquire a position, they become wealthy by misuse of funds and giving advantage to their kith and kin. The list of such parasites thriving on their exploitation of others includes: Sarpanch (Pradhan), *lekhpal* (accountant) Big peasant/landowner, government officers, small engineers, overseers, police inspectors, Excise Inspectors, BDO, even school masters and headmasters. They grow their assets within a few years. The list could also include some one knowing law, or an advocate, who earns a lot of money by applying his knowledge of criminal cases, involving land disputes or the broker flaunting his familiarity with the nearest SHO (Sub Inspector of Police station) or someone, who moves in between the lawyers and their clients, a commission agent, an elected leader or even in the office of Sarpanch, Pradhan, Head of District Committee. Their race prospering today, can be identified as wearing white Khadi, a *gamchha* (a towel made of coarse fabric) as head gear, no longer riding cycle but a motor cycle. With years, they grow their assets, become the owners of

lands, collect expensive jewels, build good houses, a jeep or a noisy bike, called bullet. (70-73)

The above finding is first-hand—unequivocally empirical, and it aptly supplements Shambhunath's (2005, 123-40) and Shrilal Shukla's (2005, 117-18) comprehensive experience of the village, 'the notions conjuring villages as romantic or revolutionary—both are redundant today. Villages in independent India are not a romantic dream but a harsh nightmare. The village, I know of in the contemporary India is a dissolute arena of roguery, violence, selfishness, sloth, cunning, affectations, superstition, and cowardice. *Raag Darbari* is the icon of this village'. Shukla's shrewd seeing is amply illustrated in the woman centred narratives of Madan Mohan and Shivmurti. Undoubtedly, hundreds of conmen or dissemblers prosper in the rural society in varied guises. The lives of both Shanichari and Saguna are destroyed by the perverse greed of those who were the custodian of righteousness and justice. The analysis of John Rawls[19] cannot be contested by any stretch of logic, What move the evil man is the love of injustice. He delights in impotence and humiliation of those subject to him and relishes being recognized by them as the source of their degradation' (qtd. Eagleton, *On Evil*, 94). Eagleton's reflection adds another dimension to it: 'Evil is pure perversity. It is a kind of cosmic-grainedness. It may claim to invert conventional moral values; injustice becomes an accomplishment to be admired' (Eagleton, 2010, 94). Saguna, Shanichari, Suguni, Rupa, and many like them have struggled and were terminated not fully comprehending the ingrained evil of those who were supposed to be their well-wishers.

What is remarkable about the stories is that they portray the incredible violence perpetrated upon the souls of the women which goes unpunished and unchecked, as if it were absolutely ordinary and 'normal'. The effect turns out to be all the more powerful. We feel the tension behind all that is not said and fill in the gaps. At times the narrative voice is disengaged, the tone uninflected, the style economical, understated—the writers nonetheless understand not only evil but the extravagance of tricks with which evil presents itself as good. One feels that they cut right to the heart of the matter, to the essential rottenness of the world.

Notes

1. Madan Mohan (1947–) hails from Banbasia village of Uttar Pradesh. The story 'Jahrili Roshnion ke Beech' (58–78) is an in-depth study of the rural existence during post-liberalization, when a lot of clamour was created to display the achievements in rural development. There is no exaggeration in the portrayal of the lies and frauds in which the village officials, accountant, and headman indulge. The village Panchayat officials serve the interest of the legislature not only when he sought their vote, but after his victory as well. The nexus grows stronger when they have the same goal of making money by hook or by crook.
2. Shivmurti's (1950–) belonged to Sultanpur Uttar Pradesh His novels and short stories dealing with village life created a great deal of interest in *dalit* and gender studies. A realistic portrayal of village life is the special merit of his stories. 'Kasaibara' has been enacted on the stage for more than 500 times since its first publication in 1999.
3. In the Indian democracy, Panchayati Raj (the local self-governing bodies) was established to ensure the full participation of people in all activities which could produce development and equal opportunity. The brass tacks however expose us to a very different story. Within five years, since its inception, its institutions began to stagnate. Pinto's study (pp. 179–94) finds that Panchayat 's objectives were rendered in disarray. It turned out, 'new grafting, on the traditional system', The administration remained colonial in spirit. Given the pervasive presence of political factionalism, corruption, inefficiency, casteism and parochialism, Panchayati Raj is more of a caricature of the local government. See *Indian Political Science Association* (Stable URL: http://www.jstor.com/stable/41.)
4. The fallout of the rape and murder of a woman in a village in Hathras, Uttar Pradesh (14 September 2020), allegedly by the upper caste men showed how a ghastly event was diluted the way it usually does when a Dalit woman is assaulted and murdered. Initially it was described as a fake news and that the event was twisted to stir caste-tension. The Police showed reluctance to register a complaint; investigations were tardy; officials raised doubts there was a rape; there were insinuations it had nothing to do with caste; and authorities seemed complicit with the upper caste. The family alleged that they faced threats from the upper caste goons. Only when the state government and Supreme court stepped in, the investigation was steered.
5. Bahubali in our Dharmic tradition was the son of Jain Tirthankar. The name means a strong man. In the contemporary context it refers to a people like Vikas Dubey or Mukhtar Ansari who were feared in the eastern UP.
6. NREGA, also called Mahatma Gandhi National Rural Employment Act turned out to be an opportunity not only for the village bureaucracy but also the postal services to siphon funds meant for the poor and landless labours who sought employment under this scheme.
7. It has been observed that women smallholders are more effective and entrepreneurial than men and that they more often use their earnings to improve their

enterprises, provide health care for their families, improve their families' nutrition, and ensure their children's education. The prevailing practices in India however reveal that most women remain dependent on the existence and good will of male relatives for access to the land.

8. The excerpt is from Madan Mohan's 'Jahrili Roshnion ke Beech'. Subsequent references are from the same narrative.
9. The newspapers and youtube abound in the reports of Lekhpal (the village accountant forcing the people to pay bribe. In recent months of 2021, in several different parts of Uttar Pradesh, bribe taking Lekhpal were nabbed by anticorruption team. For more see: www.amarujala.com, www.reportwire.in, timesofindia. indiatimes.com.
10. In UP, and Bihar, customarily, girls, who were married at a relatively young age stay with their parents and after a few months or some years, they are sent to their husbands' home accompanying several gifts and cash for the husband's family.
11. Allotment of houses to live and the funds for the repair of the house are the schemes, guaranteed for the poor. It is however reported that the head of Panchayat, the Pradhan, has in most rural regions allotted houses to his relatives and not to the really deserving.
12. *Chacha* and *Kaka* mean uncle, father's brother. In the Indian society, in the course of social interaction, elderly males and females are addressed in kinship terms as a custom of curtsy.
13. That land which does not have a legally endorsed owner is prohibited according to law (benami Transaction/Prohibition Amendment Act). In other words, property purchased by an individual not under his or her name but under another person's name is benami asset.
14. The excerpts are from Shivmurti's 'Kasaibara'. *GadyaKosh*. https://www.Sahity ashilpi. 5 April 2020. First published in 1999.
15. It has been customary to hurl expletives upon women from the *dalit* community; it has not been uncommon to refer to their genitals in terms of expletives.
16. It has been the experience of many aggrieved people that police acts fast if paid bribe. In several cases one hears that even for lodging FIR some bribe is to be paid.
17. The recent events which occurred in Hathras and Unnao demonstrate the reluctance of the general public to side with the victims. Thousands of such events remain unreported, when women were subject to exploitation, sexual abuse, deceit, and destruction.
18. Pandey cites Harishchandra Shrivastava and Manjit Kumar's comprehensive survey of rural existence in UP and Bihar in the article, 'Gramin Samaj me Parajeevita' (Parasitism in Rural Society), published in a Hindi magazine, *Samajika* (Khand-1, 45). The excerpt is translated by me.
19. John Rawls' (1921–2002) *A Theory of Justice* (1971) is a serious reflection in the area of political philosophy and ethics. He rejects utilitarianism in advocating the imperatives of distributive justice. Here he is quoted in Peter Dews, *The idea of Evil* (2007, 4).

5
Why Do Rural Poor Continue to Remain Poor and Uneducated?

> Guruji declared: 'Can Studies make a crow sprout the peacock's wings?' ('Shadayantra')

Illiteracy is the foremost among the multidimensional causes of perpetuation of backwardness and poverty in rural India. The Census Commission in India (1991) defined a literate person as the one who is able to read and write with understanding in any Indian language and not merely read and write. India aspires to be a hub of global education. While the urban English educated privileged in India having imbibed global culture gained legitimacy in the society, even the current generation of our middle-level poor, like the very poor, remains grossly uneducated. Deprived of a decent level of education, the poor will continue to be poor and more so in the new forms of knowledge. Indeed, unequal education is one very major means of maintaining profound undemocratic streak running through and smudging India's development process. P. Sainath's[1] (1996, 21) perception that India's elite saw the education of the rural poor with contempt, is an astute judgement based on his extensive exposure to a spectrum of social milieu and mores across various rural regions. This sounds compatible with the assumption so pronounced in George Orwell's (1999) world of *1984*, 'Proles are natural inferiors, who must be kept in subjection' (1–7). This ethos, generally speaking, applies to any political dispensation or class/caste-elite's relationship to the poor, subjugated, or relatively low in assets. We cannot argue with the blatant truth that unequal education and unequal opportunities produce and reproduce poverty.

Rural India and Peasantry in Hindi Stories. Vanashree, Oxford University Press. © Vanashree 2023.
DOI: 10.1093/oso/9780192871572.003.0006

It has been perceived that our brain develops the most in the first eight years of life. Our experience endorses what several studies maintain that children gain most from early education of quality as they grasp a range of growth-related appropriate abilities and are therefore more likely to finish school successfully. With refence to this aspect, when the state of children's education in rural India is considered, one finds rural India with 65 percent of the population is dependent on the *anganwadi*[2] network for its pre-primary education needs. The government's investment is manifest in the opening of many schemes to ensure early childhood education, but it needs a lot more. Regrettably, the very purpose for which *anganwadi* was launched has been defeated, for its overburdened system has to invest itself in activities such as vaccination, maternal health, and malnutrition. Instruction time takes a backseat. As regards, the primary schools and above, only lately, the matters pertaining to the apathy[3] of the school system to the poor is being talked about.

The irretrievable damage that unequal education has wrought is inexorably facing us now with the onset of COVID-19. Girija Gaurav Shukla (2020, 9–10) in close working association with rural education relates the facts that school dropouts in the rural areas are already high, and post-lockdown they might go up further. It is not just because the closure of schools has confined children to their houses, but because unlike the urban school children, the digital classroom measures are unavailable to them. They suffer from severe deficit of guidance; since their teachers are neither adept, nor equipped with the digital methods of teaching.

The four chapters of Sainath's *Everybody Loves a Good Drought* deal with the nitty gritty of the regrettable state of literacy in the rural India. He mentions his meeting with a doctor serving the village populace, who submitted that illiteracy[4] was the biggest killer disease. 'Even if medicines do reach these villagers, the dosages are a mystery to them. The village health workers can barely read or write. Sometimes people have swallowed chlorine given for their *matkas* (pitcher to store water). Several times they do not take vital life-saving tablets due to ignorance' (362–63). The failure of education in rural India is aligned with the failure of the state to monitor the processes of implementation of the basic infrastructure for schooling to ensure that the schools could function and achieve their goals.

In spite of an aspirational law, the Right to Education Act (2009), the state of education in UP and Bihar remained pretty grim. Generally, the prevailing opinion in the urban world holds the rustic temperament and sloth responsible for the backwardness and illiteracy. One gets to know however the indifference of rural primary schools in enrolling and then ensuring the presence of the rural students. It is found that the financial crunch forces the low-class people to use the services of young children either for earning money or looking after household chores or infants in the family, instead of admitting them to the schools.

Balani's survey[5] (4 January 2017), drawing on several reliable sources of information finds the siphoning of millions of pounds of aid for education under *Sarva Shiksha Abhiyan*[6] (SSA). She finds that the literacy rates and learning outcomes are some of the lowest in the ailing states, that is, Bihar, MP, Rajasthan, and UP. Bihar is India's third most populous state. In the countryside, the ratio remains invariably even much lower. It could be attributed to the lack of adequate number of classrooms—primary, upper primary, secondary—all coexisting in the same space in the vicinity. The teachers' being on temporary contract make it impossible to achieve the objectives of schooling. The tendency has been to overlook the depressing, uninspiring condition of the primary educational institutions in the countryside.

Wrongs, since the Foundation of New India after Independence

What is significant is to reckon that historically things went wrong. Wrong at the very beginning when the foundation of modern India after independence was being laid. Prabhas Kumar Choudhary's[7] (1991) 'Pita' (Father), and Vipin Bihari's[8] (2000) 'Shadayantra' (Conspiracy) unfold the processes of rural development, specifically in the field of promoting education, amply pointing at several convoluted motivations and reasons of the failing education mission in rural India. Both the narratives spring from the first-hand experience.

The sombre narrative of 'Pita' (Father) is a muffled up elegiac obituary of a father, a son writes. The news of his father's death awakens his memories and the rendering of which in undertones suggest the deep disappointment of a generation of all those who posited hopes in the promises of free India. A son relates how his father, a school headmaster, reposed absolute faith in the promise of Swaraj for the betterment and progress of the rural populace. For him the freedom movement was aligned with the idea of emancipation from colonial rule, clubbed with the idea of education and upliftment of all. In every cultural activity and program, he would take initiative, ensuring the participation of the entire village community. His persona exuding enthusiasm for building up a new nation touched everyone. For the village youth with his initiative, labour and skill, a store to house books was built up which he hoped would one day develop into a decent library. The village populace of the time responded exuberantly to the climate of change. The narrator's reminiscences invoke the moments when the villagers gave a ceremonial welcome to the union finance minister who arrived to address his constituency; it was however noticed how watchful he was, 'about maintaining distance from the sites of dust and dirt' (Choudhury, 'Pita', 56)[9]:

> It was in the fitness of the occasion that an emotional appeal for a much-desired improvement of the school was made by the Pita (father). He emphasized that the objective to build an organizational groundwork for the school needed the financial incentive from the government. This hope was not without a basis. Independent India raised hopes of the oppressed and the downtrodden for a better life. It meant for them: better schooling, installation of electricity, paved roads. The exultation over the prospects of great India and equal India reached momentum in the electioneering season. The atmosphere was charged with the excited conversations of the artisans, the small shop owners over the prospects of a better life; loud sloganeering was on full swing, as the elections were approaching.... ('Pita', 57)

Subsequent events in the reminiscence convey that 'Pita's hopes like that of many villagers died down and turned into silence and despondency' ('Pita', 58–59). The city dwelling writer in his following visits notices the sickly, frail figure of his father, heartbroken and lost. Soon after, he hears of his demise. The summary span of the story conveys a lot more than what appears on the surface. The reader gets an inkling of the scenario.

The subtly portrayed conditions of a village society enable us to discern how the rural India was let down by the newly independent democratic state.

Gyan Prakash's discerning study is informed with how the process of going wrong was further catalysed since the 1970s. As the state-sponsored appeal of populist slogans and programs were making noisy proposition for its authority, its institutions were gradually decaying and their legitimacy was made to appear dubious. In the milieu, the political parties, the electoral process, parliamentary bodies, the bureaucracy flourished but their role as representatives and functionaries of the ordinary or deprived population received severe jolt and that allowed the groups possessed with agency and political clout to usurp opportunities (1994, 1475–90). Education for the poor in these circumstances suffered most. In spite of the right to education, no visible headway in the reform process could come into being specifically in the eastern UP, Bihar, and the adjacent regions. Probing the multiple visible and invisible obstacles to the goals to educate the rural poor can make us confront foremost a determined drive of the authoritarian caste clique who callously disregard the human rights of the underprivileged and marginalized that concomitantly furthered the conscious bid to maintain caste and class dominance. In the circumstances, the state of deprivation continued unrelentingly messing up the most elaborately structured programs. This is a common knowledge that in UP the funds allocated for the schools were spent on projects that had nothing to do with SSA (Sarva Shiksha Abhiyan) which means the project for education of all. There is no dearth of stories as well that let us know how the village Panchayat and Pradhan[10] or the local bodies in charge endowed with ample funds misused the money, blatantly indulging in granting favours to their kith and kin or in the weddings instead of those for whom the money was allotted.

Interestingly, the stories not only precede most of the academic surveys in understanding the mess we find in rural education system, but also serve as the most immediate idiom informed with the complexities and the solution to this problem. The incidents illustrated here invoke images of even more oppressive spectacles than the ones we find in Charles Dickens' repressive school scenario. The situation has not been very different in most such government or low-level private schools. They may not be indulging in physical violence but are capable of granting the child a subhuman status, crippling his ability and urge to learn. Even the teachers coming from the background where they suffered discrimination, but who hail from towns and cities, internalize the conventions of treating children from the subaltern group superciliously and as unwanted. 'Shadayantra' not only ferrets out the dynamics of failure of education in rural India, but also offers a discourse on the caste-based bigotry that prevailed in the historic times of 1980s and 1990s, when Mandal Commission[11] report was constitutionally endorsed and the reservation for SC, ST, and finally OBC was creating uproar and immense discontent in the upper caste of the society. Bihari's story illumines those grey areas of our political and cultural and psychosocial configurations[12] which were generally side-lined in the academic surveys until the recent times.

Dearth of Adequate Number of Schools: Village School in Debris

Sainath's findings in 'Here we go to the school' (47–58) is literally dramatized in Vipin Bihari's story, 'Shadayantra', that vibrantly brings to the fore the deficient infrastructural facilities and resources for teaching the primary and middle-level government schools in the villages of Bihar. The Brechtian episodic structure of the story enables us to make sense a lot more than is apparent. A series of spectacles akin to a burlesque reveal the varied ways the school is managed. The opening of the narrative lets us have a feel of the caste configuration in the villages.

> The Primary cum Middle school is the only school located within the vicinity of five villages. Satbarva, Mangi, Simra, Pulandar, and Saidabad. All at the banks of Vahrahi river; it flowed at slow steady pace like a raindrain, but during rainy season, it's overflow would be a menace to the populace. These villages have been mainly the localities of the Schedule caste (Dalit), Schedule tribe and the Backward. None apparently exploited by the other. All shared the same economic status—struggling with their subsistence—except Baniyas since their business takes care 'of salt and oil'.[13] (Bihari, 2000, 64)

One notices however that the settlement of the upper caste—Brahmans, Bhumihars, and Rajputs—was at considerable distance from those belonging to the lower strata. The number of pupils is fifteen or sixteen. Going to the school means catching up long distances; during heavy rains or the season of extreme heat, many would be absent.[14] All masters are from the forward community. Since the inception of the school periodically, the number of masters increased. In spite of four of them, Ramji Mishra, the headmaster and the rest, Ramratan Pande, Chandesar Dubey, and Sarup Singh even basic learning could not be imparted to the children of these five settlements; majority from small peasantry—from diverse groups of scheduled class and tribe: Chamars, Dusadhs, Musahars, and Bhuiyan and Gond—who still remained illiterate and used thumb impression. The children of Kurmis, Yadavas, and the shopkeeper class could manage to train themselves to some extent. The pupils from the lowest castes and status were habitually described as undeserving. The narrative proceeds to guide us closer to this school at Satbarva, and one faces a familiar sight of a school with almost tumbled down building.

> But is it a school or debris! It could crumble any day. Here are three rooms with clay roof tiles. Only one room remained by and large intact; the second susceptible to heavy wind or rain, nevertheless was considered sufficient for housing children. The third one in complete ruin; the debris was tumbling down. A veranda with vanished roof faced the front; Funds for the repair were sanctioned by the block every year, but where did they go remains a mystery. None was concerned about the repair. There was no toilet. The teachers nonetheless did not mind using the thickly outspreading foliage of mahua tree facing the veranda as toilet. (64–65)

The narrator notes that the absence of toilet was of no concern to either the teachers or the people of Satbarva. 'Nobody knew, how the boys managed. There were no girls. After all, how many boys were there?' Besides, who wants to learn or to teach … !'[15] (64). Mishraji appeared disinclined to raise the number of pupils, complacent with the fact that 'the overall number did not exceed sixteen or seventeen. (65) Accepted as normal, it would not surprise nor outrage those used to the primary or middle school infrastructures in the rural UP and Bihar.

Caste Identity, Branding, and Expletives

A series of spectacles akin to an outrageous farce reveal the varied ways the school is managed. On a highly dramatic note, the routine sequences of the school begin at a little before 10 a.m. Being the headmaster, Mishraji had arrived and was standing under the foliage of mahua tree. He asked the two boys holding a slate and pencil at the door of the classroom to open the lock and bring the chair outside under the shade of the tree. Both of them took their turn in trying to open the door. It could not open. Mishraji's anger now mounting unleashed on one of the boys. He gave him a hard slap and began hurling choicest mother–sister abuses: 'Ssala[16] does not know how to open the lock. He'll rather open his mother's skirt!'[17] (2000, 65). Desperate Mishraji applied himself in unlocking the door but it could not open. Kerosene oil was brought to open it. Time and energy spent in struggling with the lock made Mishraji boil with rage. He could not desist the urge to slap Phenkna facing right in front, charging him of changing the lock, uttering mother–sister expletives. Phenkna dared to argue: 'There is only one lock in the school; it hasn't even rained and so it cannot even be rusted' (65). The lock eventually opened.

The scene makes us conscious of the way the boys specifically from the lower-caste group were slighted or treated with casual cruelty. Even the dignity of a proper name would not be assigned to them. In the folk customs of rural India, the odd names—Booten, Phenkna, Muchiya, Nagesar, and Ajudhya—are either given to them by their masters or based on their castes or community. Names were often allotted to them on the basis of the day they were born, or their skin colour or the vocation of their father. Booten derives from boots or shoes meaning a cobbler's son. Phenkna, a name, means worthy of being cast off. Muchiya also means the son of a *chamar* (cobbler). Those among Dalits who have entered higher education and have acquired good positions as teachers and professors have vivid recollection of how they were off and on the targets of *castiest* jibes of the upper-caste headmasters or teachers. In UP and Bihar, even the last name could be an issue of acerbic remarks.

The narrator's mention of Mishraji's domestic life, 'congested with routine ruckus, 'a demanding, taunting wife, two brawling daughters-in-law and sparring sons,' make him flee to the school. Riding his bicycle through the bumps and turns of a zigzag gravel path makes his limbs ache' (66), debunks his overt show of dignity. His disdainful attitude to the children proceeds from an assumed superiority of his caste. As far as his duty as a teacher is concerned, he is worthless. 'Seated on his chair—his feet upon the table, he cannot help feeling drowsy. The boys waiting for some lesson to begin, grow unruly and exchange blows with each other. "Guruji, he's hitting me." "You too beat him." For a moment Mishraji's eyes opened and then closed in a state of stupor' (66). Then he remembered to order one of the boys to massage his feet: 'Ae Muchiya, press and massage my limbs' (66). The boy meekly obeys. Irritated, Mishraji rebukes him:

> Can't you learn anything! Not even the job of massaging! Press with some strength, or I'll give you a good thrashing, you'll remember for life. Hasn't your father taught you anything? Nagesar! 'you're the son of a cowherd; do press with the strength of your caste'. Stretching his arms and limbs, he continues yawning: 'No comparison between a Koeri and a Yadav!' (66)

Mishraji then conveys his wish for pure ghee from the Yadav boy: 'tell your father to deliver one-kilo good ghee. It is your obligation to serve a Brahman and a Guru' (66). Invariably, the caste equation lent the upper-caste teachers some authority that justified their slighting and bullying the pupils. Mishraji's character is in fact a prototype of hundreds and thousands of teachers in India in schools and colleges who get away with impunity in spite of shirking from their basic responsibility. Unfortunately, it is a known fact that in spite of spending several hundred corers on training teachers, the spectacle remains depressing. Many remain morally and cognitively untrained. Teachers, serious about their vocation, have expressed their exasperation over the poor quality and irrelevance of such training programmes.

Casual Cruelty to Inhuman Punishment: 'Can Studies Make a Crow Sprout the Peacock's Wings?'

The following episode resonates with grim implications in describing the way the lives of these adolescents is damaged by a crass group of so-called teachers. It occurs when those students who are generally in the class also arrive, extending the number to nearly fourteen and fifteen. Attendance here hardly mattered. Many students would arrive only after 12 noon, after tending cattle, goats, or pigs or doing other household chores. Guruji's sound of snoring confirmed that he was fast asleep, and that day no lesson would be taught. The boys stopped pressing and massaging him, and it was the opportunity to play. They started jumping and knocking each other, shoving, scuffling, and thrashing. Ajudhya and Nagesar were tossing each other and exchanging sister–mother abuses. Other boys were watching the scene as spectators. In the meanwhile, the new Guruji, Sarup Singh feared for his brutality barges in. His late coming is due to another business that holds him at his farm at the time of sowing and planting. It is worth noticing that most of the teachers have some side business. From some distance he had seen the wrangle between the two boys. The boys clashing and hurtling is a fitting scenario that demanded his disciplining. Those who ever became the target of his frenzied thrashing had left the school. He would make his victims bleed.

> 'Go and get the pain-remover (the cane to beat) If I don't make Ajudhya remember his mother's milk, you change my name; what will you gain from learning—become a Brahmin or Rajput?' Muchiya rushed to bring a sharp cane. Ajudhya was ordered to perform a *murga*.[18] With full strength Sarup Singh struck his back. He fell headlong. 'Rise up *Sale!*' A single cane cannot hurt a Dusadh. You've just fallen down. This is only a Sri Ganesh.[19] Stretch your palm. Ajudhya raised his hand the cane was struck harder. He cried, 'O Mai O Babu Re Babu!'[20] 'Don't remember your mother and father'. 'Not again Guruji', he cried miserably. Guruji rose up and insanely began hitting him harder and harder. Ajudhya whimpered. It appeared as if he would faint. The boys were dumbfounded with scare. Guruji announced: 'Learning is not for everyone. Can studies make a crow sprout the peacock's wings?' Ajudhya had stopped sobbing but gasping with wrenching pain; his back was badly bruised, bleeding in one or two places. 'Study is devotion and is beyond your capacity. Why Mishraji, am I not right?' Mishraji smiled; Sarup Singh laughed loudly. (68)

What is appallingly outrageous is the pleasure these teachers brazenly derive in torturing and demoralizing a human being. The friendly conversations of the twosome let the reader know that the other two teachers, Dubeji and Pandeji, were absent that day without any prior information. Teaching here is deemed as a leisurely vocation and teachers drop in and out of classrooms and school according to their convenience, what becomes more lamentable is that many times they do not teach if it does not suit their mood. In the subsequent days they are either late or absent or even if present, do not engage with teaching. The teacher's register happens to be a book of lies—the records they mark on paper have no correspondence with reality. Subramaniyan Giridhar cites a 'Probe Study' that also found out that in 48 percent of rural government schools no teaching activity takes place, even when the teachers were present. It proposes that the rules under Right to Education Act 2009 (RTE) can ensure a mechanism for effective monitoring of such parameters by the school monitoring committee.

Pairavi, Jugaad: The Crafty Deal to Manipulate School Inspection

Pairavi[21] and jugaad[22] in this environment is discussed with relish and self-congratulatory air—a potent means of seeking appointment in the government run school—in spite of the fact that the job seekers have no interest in teaching. Strong lobbying in the capital, Patna, made it possible for both Pandeji and Dubeyji to get appointed here. The closeness of the school to their farming lands helped them deal with both. Recently, the school was granted the level of middle school, though the teaching was only up to class seven. It was being heard that an inspector of schools intended to arrive on a surprise check to supervise the condition of the school building, the level of teaching, and the regular presence of the teachers. Though there was no formal information in advance, through his wily sources, the headmaster Mishraji had come to know, two days in advance, the arrival date of the inspector. For the existing staff of the four teachers, it was an unsettling news since the school in its present condition could not fulfil the basic requirements of being labelled a middle school. For Sarup Singh and Mishraji, it was imperative that the school in its present condition be not subjected to the negative reporting. They could easily escape from all accountability being in a backward region.

The absenting pupils or the teachers were never seen as answerable to the villagers. Besides, proximity with their site of farming and business is possible here without any hassles. Pandeji says:

> Nobody wants to study, and, brother! Who wants to teach! This region is of backward and Harijans and Adivasis, our presence has many advantages. 'Brother! They are forbidden from reading Vedas. If they study, they'll become Bhasmasur'.[23] (Bihari, 69)

Pandey's reasoning impressed everybody. The conversations here fully exemplify the in-built bias against the tribal and the *Dalits*. In Godda, Bihar, an officer in Tribal Welfare Department confided in Sainath:

> Many teachers here always keep a casual leave slip ready and updated. If an inspection takes place, they fill in that date to explain their absence! It (the school) is simply not meant to retain tribal children. They join the school but the system drives them away. The contempt for the tribal and schedule caste students is more explicit in the attitude of the teachers, but generally even when the overt decorum of conversation is maintained, it has been found that the students from the oppressed section are systematically demotivated to stay away from education. The greatest fear is that if *dalits* study, there would be no one to work in the fields. They would then demand better wages and rights. (Sainath, 63)

'Shadayantra' makes one infer that all the teachers get and save their positions by licking the boots of those above and kicking the backs of those below them. Notwithstanding their backwardness, the students recognize their hypocrisy.

Trying Times Force Us to Call 'a Donkey Our Father'

The schoolmasters now devise the ways of making the school presentable so that the negative report of the inspector would not damage their existence. They planned in advance a strategy to win the villagers.

Let us put on the veneer of the teachers with a mission—the worshipper of education—determined to serve the society selflessly and to contribute to the emancipation of rural children from ignorance. That would impress the gullible villagers and they will not be able to give any adverse report about our performance. In the tough times it is better to call a donkey our father. ('Shadayantra', 71)

As planned, they visit the villages in the vicinity and personally plead with the parents of the girls and boys of all castes and communities, convince them of their commitment to the mission of enabling everyone to read and write. Subsequently, the numbers of pupils begin increasing unexpectedly, especially of the girls. The wish to make her daughter learn prompted Sarna Godain[24] to send her daughter Nimia to the school. Sarvant Saab, Nandlal Jadav, and Hemant Mahato—all sent their daughters. For the time being, the four teachers too pretended to teach. Dubeyji's pattern of teaching inspired mimicry: '*Ka for kauwa, Kha for khajur, Ga for Gadha*[25] … He could not help obsessively ogling the girls in the first row; his constant focus would be on their bodies' (71).

The arrival of the inspector was indeed sudden and all these teachers had made a range of arrangements to cover up the deficiencies of the school. The inspector appeared a no-nonsense man and sounded concerned with the neglected infrastructure and tumbled down school building. The number of students was also not up to his satisfaction. Mishraji's explanation developed into a kind of discourse on why education in the rural regions for the backward and *Dalits* is waste of the government's money. 'These boys are truant; some will come after a gap of two days and some would run away in the middle hour' (72). The narrator, Bihari, enables us to draw inferences from Mishraji's innuendoes. It is imperative for the likes of Mishraji to clock their failure and entrenched bigotry by laying the blame on the innocent and oppressed, 'Other'. An apparently hilarious episode testifies to the downright failure of the rural education. When the inspector asks the boy, named Booten Ram to stand up, Mishraji's running commentary promptly lets the inspector know that the boy was a '*chamar*' (72–73).

'In which class do you study?' 'In 3rd'. 'Now tell us who had broken the bow of Raja Janak?'[26] Nervous Booten peered around, 'I have not broken it'. They all suppressed laughter. The inspector asked the other boy standing next to Booten, 'you tell us who broke the bow? Even I have not broken it'. When the inspector in a sharper voice asked the third one, he said, 'I have not broken it' and began crying. (72–73)

In a stern tone, the inspector tells Mishraji that the standard of teaching here is very bad. 'Pay attention; children are the pillars of the nation. One of these may turn out to be a Nehru or a Gandhi. A huge responsibility is bestowed upon the teachers' (73). One infers that the show of servile obedience of the teachers demonstrated here was hardly sincere. Neither the teachers nor the inspector was serious about their duty. Mahashweta Devi (1985) could recognize the covert intent of the privileged in preserving the rural poor's state of ignorance. In her *Imaginary Maps,* an itinerant journalist protagonist, Puran visits an obscure village in Chhattisgarh and finds that the rural and tribal people are ignorant about what is theirs by right. He realizes that a deliberate intent to maintain the status quo has been successful so far with the active collusion of all those who are resourceful. He puts it: 'What an immense deal of labour and money is spent to keep up this directive of non-information!' (Mahasweta Devi, 110). In the school milieu of 'Shadayantra', one confronts a tragic waste of human resources where corrupt mindset destroy and damage young lives which could otherwise be harnessed to a purpose.

What is required in such conditions is the review of the right to education. S. Giridhar's (2009, 11) view that that Right to Education Act will merely guarantee schooling, not education as long as the rules are not very explicit. It has to be fortified with clear guidelines about learning outcomes and learning standards of children. It is indeed worth great worry that a survey report 2018, called the Annual Status of Education Report (ASER),[27] submits that more than 50 percent of students in fifth standard attending rural school are not capable of reading a second standard textbook and nor solve basic mathematical questions. The stark fact is that very few government schools can show that their children's learning can commensurate with their age or grade.

Post-Mandal Storm: Forged Upper-Caste Solidarity

The ambience at these times was also charged with the aggressive rise of *Ranveer Sena* (1994–2000) in Bihar in the 1990s. Resultantly a paranoia was sweeping the psyche of the upper caste. Even the college students and the educated middle class harboured the visions of real or imagined threat from the *Dalits*. Naxal militia was also active in these times. The state's endorsement of Mandal recommendation amounted to turning upside down the age-old caste system. During those decades, most crowded places, trains, and public forums clamoured in heated, belligerent debates defending the status quo. In this climate, many upper-caste elites and men from the police force supported and funded the armed ventures of *Ranveer Sena*. One can discern how the operative energies of the time manifest in the self-aggrandizing speeches of the teachers spewing venom against the young students from the lowest strata.

The story moves on to unfold how craftily the four teachers played out their roles as manipulators and rescued the school from negative reporting. The foursome applied their cunning to find out the caste of the inspector that could give the masters the clues to his tastes, and accordingly, a special chicken party and, in addition, country liquor were arranged. The feasting and drinking in togetherness made them all shed inhibition. They gregariously exchanged views on national politics, and the post-Mandal regarding the forward and the backward. The inspector, who also belonged to forward *Kayastha* caste now more vocal, endorsed the casteist prejudices of Mishra, Pandey, Dubey, and Singh. He departed after having given his approval on the state of the school.

Male Teachers: Lower Female Attendance in Rural India

It has not just been the lack of toilet facilities or the menstrual problems that restrained rural girls from attending schools, it is the male masters' offensive body language and gestures towards the female students that remain traditional deterrent. The state of female literacy[28] in rural India in Bihar and UP is constantly lamentable. The reasons are varied. Acute poverty is one of them, but the outstanding reason is that even those who can afford, and would like to educate their daughters, are reluctant because of the concern for their safety. Dubeji's abortive attempt to sexually molest Nimia becomes the cause of gradual withdrawal of other girls. Dubeyji, finding an opportune moment when he presumed that his act would not be witnessed, since the boys were under the thick shrubs of mahua tree and Mishraji was in the office. He sent the boys to bring their slate and pencil and summoned Nimiya. 'With rapt attention he ogled at her breast, that her frock, loose at the neck was showing. In the pretext of explaining something, he persuaded her to come closer, then began tickling her breast and then pulled her into the debris ... Horrified Nimiya began screaming...' (74–75).

This episode compels many parents of girls to withdraw their daughters from the school. The apprehension that male teachers could inveigle their daughters or exploit them always worried the parents more specifically in the rural society though it was not forthrightly acknowledged earlier. What is condemnable here is the way the other colleagues of Dubeyji encourage his lurid, boastful accounts of earlier exploits and voyeuristic caprices. 'First case!' Whispered the headmaster, Mishraji. 'No, in the previous one, a case happened.' 'The girl was *jawan* (youthful)?' 'Of which caste? ...' (76). Mishraji protects Dubeyji when Nimiya's outraged community is out to kill him, seek dire punishment for him. Scared, Dubeyji goes into hiding and disappears for more than a month. His well-wishers advise him not to make appearance until the scandal dies down. Only after a month, he is seen stealthily visiting the school office to collect his salary, late in the shadow of darkness. The registers however corroborated the evidence of full presence of all the teachers.

Status Quo Challenged that Calls for some Shadayantra (Conspiracy)

In the midst of these events, the arrival of a Dalit master, Dhanesar Ram, takes the story to its end, as his idea of education is contrary to what had been going on until then. His caste/category becomes the senior teachers' principal topic of discussion. Dubeyji could not curb his curiosity: 'To which caste do you belong'? 'Amongst Harijans also there are many castes' 'Now that I am Dalit, what for is the caste?' replied Dhanesar Ram (78). But his way of conducting himself and his seriousness towards the vocation of educating the village children offended the group of the forward caste teachers. His punctuality, sincere efforts to encourage the school children, and willingness to involve their parents in the learning process of their children, even if they are not educated raised the spirit of the parents: 'The school is in your locality—yours and your children's. Whether they teach or no, keep a watch; they won't mind if your boys and girls remain illiterate' (81). As the *Probe* report[29] cites that 98 percent of the rural government schools, they surveyed, had school monitoring committees, the parents of the children are the members of the committee, but were unaware of the systems, roles, and responsibilities, unaware of the concept of measuring learning outcomes as a means of assessing whether schools are delivering on their commitment.

Dhanesar Ram's determined effort to arouse the oppressed and illiterate from their current state of stupor, to instil in them the urge for learning, was showing some positive results. When persuaded by the senior colleagues to take it easy, 'enjoy vacations, for the rural populace does not deserve learning' (80), Dhanesar Ram said:

> Master Saheb, the state has appointed me. Given me my means of subsistence. It is our moral responsibility as a teacher that we perform our duties with full accountability. If we don't do it, it amounts to cheating the state and the public. I will stay here and teach. I cannot accept a salary for free. This is my new job. I come from an economically weaker section and cannot risk losing whatever is the source of my survival. (Bihari, 78)

Dhanesar Ram's presence was now promising the possibility of a positive change, equity, and equality. But it posed a challenge to the existing practices of the veterans which served their vested interests. The situation demanded some strategies to drive Dhanesar out.

In relating the subsequent events, the narrative continues with the pattern of caustic humour. The older teachers are hardened in their practice of shirking from responsibilities; they are not open to any transformation or introspection. Their ingrained intransigence remains sustained. It is the times of 1990s, no matter how stringent were the laws against caste-bigotry, the caste and class system nonetheless sustained its stranglehold on people's thought, perpetuating prejudices. Ending on a Brechtian note, the narrative summons us to witness a scene, where the disgruntled teachers, Mishra, Pandey, Dubey, and Singh decide upon a conspiracy to drive Dhanesar out, and at the moment the best ploy sounding most effective was to label him a Naxal,[30] who is inciting the villagers and emboldening them against the state.

Fault Lines in the Rural System of Pedagogy

The story reveals a canny awareness of the fault lines in the education methods of those regions which have had a prolonged history of illiteracy. In an increasingly knowledge-based global economy, driving IT revolution, relevant for the dynamics of the market, inequitable access to quality education is the principal deprivation of the excluded in our country. Unequal education is a clear marker of rural–urban divide in India. How to change the current situation which has seemingly become 'given' deemed as normal in most educated circles? Our engagement with this sphere lets us understand that a majority of rural schools will change if they have a clear path and clear vision. The subject of grave concern to India is driven home in a series of spectacles in 'Shadayantra' which resonate with melodramatic tone and tenor, satire, double-entendres, bawdy humour, but do not fail to stimulate a rethinking of how to galvanize the languishing rural education. In ferreting out the underlined brass tacks, why rural schools in the Hindi belt largely failed in educating and imparting skills to children belonging to the poor and backward sections of the society, the narrative yields some fundamental information, unveils some unsavoury truths which were only lately acknowledged in several findings. One has to accept the fact that even in the current decades, though education is no longer confined to certain classes in our society, it still fails to genuinely station itself within the walls of rural schools.

Notes

1. The rural poor are doomed to remain trapped in an insufficiently funded and flawed educational arrangement in India. Sainath finds that the primary schools in the poorest districts of Bihar and Uttar Pradesh were schools without teachers or schools without teaching or schools without any students, or, to put it in a simpler way, *no schools* at all. Of every 100 children of school going age, about 70 enrol into Class I, half of these drop out even before they complete primary school in Uttar Pradesh. The situation failed to improve substantively.
2. I have drawn on Ashish Dhawan's article, dated 14 February 2020, the TOI, on the role assigned to *Anganwadi* which it failed to perform due to being under a lot of pressure. In the context, he underlines the responsibility of the state education department which must ensure that quality childhood education is provided to all children.
3. Ganesh Pandey's *Aathaven Dashakki Hindi Kayaniyan* (Village Life in Hindi Stories of the 8th Decade (1980s)) brings to the fore the heavy cost that illiterate people were made to pay. The moneylenders would take the thumb impression of the illiterate villagers and extort thousands instead of hundred. Or a roguish character or a self-appointed leader who boasts his connections and his ability to fix problems, pretending to be an educated advisor, implicates a simple illiterate villager in litigations and dispossesses him of his land. A Maulvi operated as the functionary of the state to befool the illiterate villagers.
4. In the chapter, 'There is no place like School' (54–59), in *Everybody Loves a Good Drought*, Sainath renders his experience of a visit to a middle school in Damruhat, Bihar, where he finds a school in total disarray, which drove home the collective tendency to betray the purpose of a school. Indeed, the attitude is 'who wants to teach', is amply exposed in the absurd arrangement: eight classes, the teacher student ratio—seven teachers, four students, two classrooms, and one broken chair—reserved for the headmaster, which remains vacant. Its occupant had been suspended on charges of embezzlement. The middle-school headmaster looked after the disbursal of teacher's salaries in a given area. The Deputy Commissioner, discovering that the salary was paid to non-existent teachers, tossed him out. The Unified District Information System for Education (UDISE), Flash Statistics: 2015-2016, reported the second highest teacher absenteeism (31 percent) in rural public school among 19 surveyed states in 2010.
5. A recent survey of Khushbu Balani's (7 January 2017) confirms the disappointing outcome of the Right to Education Act which was launched in 2009. Only 55 percent of students attended government school in 2014. Jaivir Singh also writes on 'Why rural India still has poor access to quality education?'
6. Sarva Shiksha Abhiyan (SSA) has been Operational since 2000-2001. It is Government of India's flagship programme for achievement of Universalization of Elementary Education for the children of the age group of 6–14 years, a fundamental right (www.aicte-india.org).

7. Prabhas Kumar Choudhary (1941–98) a recipient of Sahitya Akademi Award 1991, for Maithli literature, belongs to the village, Pindaruch in Darbhanga, in the Mithila region of Bihar. His novels and collection of short stories and the edited magazines, *Anam* and *Katha Disha*, relate to the sensibilities of rural India. Some of his works in Maithili are translated in Hindi. He is known more significantly for comprehending the middle-class restlessness and the psychology of the oppressed. The story, 'Pita', is in the collection, *Kosi ke Us Paar (Across and Beyond Kosi)*. The excerpts here are translated by me.
8. Vipin Bihari (1952–), based in Bihar, is acknowledged as a well-known writer of Dalit literature. He has published six novels and several plays. *Marod* (Wrenching) is his much-acclaimed novel. The story, 'Shadayantra', enacts P. Sainath's version of the plight of schools in the backward areas of Bihar and makes us recognize the immense damage the malfunctioning of the education system caused in the rural society.
9. The subsequent reference is to Prabhas Kumar Choudhary's 'Pita'.
10. Rakesh Bharatiya's (1954–) story, 'Itminan' (Assurance) (146–151), represents scores of such news reports about the members of village Panchayat or Pradhan or local bodies in charge of ample funds, misusing the money to favour their kith and kin instead of those for it was allotted. Bharatiya served in Indian Administrative Services. Most of the experiences of his native village near Azamgarh (UP) are rendered in his articles and short stories.
11. On 16 November 1992, the Supreme Court upheld the Mandal Commission's 27 percent quota for backward classes, as well as the principle that the combined scheduled-caste, scheduled-tribe, and backward-class beneficiaries should not exceed 50 percent of India's population. The Supreme Court also ruled that 'caste' could be used to identify 'backward classes' on condition the caste was socially backward as a whole, and that the 'creamy layer' of the backward classes could not receive backward-class benefits. In September 1993, it was constitutionally enacted.
12. Among the miscellaneous categories and sub-categories within Dalit are Dusadhs, also known as Paswans. They are primarily landless agricultural labourers and messengers who supposedly reared pigs to ward off the Muslim invaders. 'Chamars' (cobblers) deal with leather work and the task of disposing of dead cattle. Mushar are one of the lowest in SC, known to eat rats. Bhuyan and Gond are the forest people from the tribe, an indigenous farming community. Backward (OBC), a collective term, used by the Government of India, refers to Koeri: traditionally cultivators, also called Kurmis, and Yadavs, a pastoral Community of India, who are traditionally cattle keepers, but are also peasants and landowners. Baniya is a community with occupations usually of merchants, moneylenders, and dealers in spices and grains. Customarily in the Indian village demography, the locality of the upper caste would be at marked distance from those of the lower castes; it may not be so distant from the OBC class.
13. Refers to their being capable of affording meals for two times.

WHY DO RURAL POOR CONTINUE TO REMAIN POOR? 125

14. Sainath reports that quite a few rural children have tough time reaching their schools. Existing data hardly cover this fact. NCRT 1989 found that 94 percent of rural population was served by a primary school within one kilometre. Better still 85 percent have middle school within three kilometres. The terrain for walking distances however demands hardship, p. 47.
15. In the chapter, 'There is no place like School', pp. 54–59, in *Everybody Loves a Good Drought*, Sainath relates the experience of visit to a middle school in Damruhat, Bihar, where he finds the school in total disarray. He observes a general tendency of the people in charge to betray the very purpose of a school. The attitude, 'who wants to teach', is amply exposed in the absurd arrangement: eight classes, the teacher student ratio—seven teachers, four students, two class rooms, and one broken chair—reserved for the headmaster, which remains vacant. Its occupant had been suspended on charges of embezzlement. Middle school headmaster looks after the disbursal of teacher's salaries in a given area, is a travesty of the very objective of education. outraged Deputy Commissioner, finding them disbursing them to non-existent teachers tossed him out. Unified District Information System for Education (UDISE), Flash Statistics: 2015–2016, reported the 2nd highest teacher absenteeism (31%) in rural public school among 19 surveyed states in 2010.
16. 'Ssala' meaning brother-in-law, is generally used as a slang to curse.
17. This amounts to mother-sister expletive of sexual nature.
18. Murga '*Murga*' is a stress position used as a corporal punishment mainly in parts of South Asia (especially in Northern India, Pakistan and sometimes in Bangladesh). It is used primarily in educational institutions on students of both sexes, and occasionally by the police as an informal punishment for petty crimes committed by boys such as eve teasing. The punishment is usually ordered in public view, the purpose being to deter the offender by inflicting pain, deter recurrence of the offense by shaming the offender and providing a useful instance.
19. 'Sri Ganesh' is chanted in Hindu customs to invoke the elephant God's blessings for the success of any significant work.
20. Desperate cry of pain and humiliation invoking mother and father.
21. *Pairavi* means obtaining recommendation from an influential politician or people in power in order to get some benefits such as suitable posting in government jobs, promotion, or transfers to the place of one's choice.
22. 'Jugaad' here is employed to describe devious manipulation including bribing.
23. '*Bhasmasur*' is the name of a mythic demon who was blessed by Shiva with the power of destruction: his touch could reduce anyone to ashes.
24. *Godain*: female gender of *Gond*, a scheduled tribe, known as forest people.
25. This is the Hindi equivalent of teaching alphabets as in English: A for Apple, B for Ball, C for Cat.
26. In the epic, *Ramayana*, King Janaka of Mithila, the father of Sita hosts her Svayamvara (in which a bride would select the best and bravest husband from an

assembly of suitors). Fulfilling the condition of the Svayamvara, Rama broke the bow belonging to Lord Shiva and won Sita in marriage.
27. See 'Education Today' news, *India Today*, 5 August 2019. '50% Students cannot Read texts of class 2': 10 Highlights from the ASER. Amandeep Shukla also writes that 'One out of every four Class 8 students from rural India cannot read a simple text'. 16 January 2019.
28. It is surprising that the researches and surveys concerned with female literacy seldom refer to the voyeuristic interest of male teachers in the female students which has been a deterrent of female literacy.
29. Subramaniyan Giridhar's 'The Way Forward', in *The Hindu*, 22 November 2009, p. 11 refers to the Probe Report which emphasizes that the role of the community in contributing to an effective school will become more important in the post Right to Education Act scenario.
30. The tribal interior of Bihar (now Jharkhand) was notorious for fierce Naxal activism (a Maoist militant separatist group) since the mid-1960s. The security crackdown on Naxal violence led to an increased casualty figure in the tribal regions.

6
Rural Migration: Dismantling Rural Resources

The wreckage it leaves behind/the closest bonds break,/young people migrate, a way of life ebbs away

In many rural stories, Hindi[1] and Bhojpuri films, songs, and folk memories, migration of the rural gentry has been a moving theme. Ironically, for decades, the interest of the elite and intellectuals had generally been only in the job seeker Indians settling down in the western world for larger monetary gains. The studies in the Indian diaspora abroad figures in the disciplines of social sciences and literature, while the obvious exodus of millions[2] of rural population—the largest diaspora in the history of Asia remains a nondescript event, until the period of COVID-19, when thousands of migrant workers, were noticed walking on the roads towards their native places. P. Sainath (2020) rightly regarded their plight as 'one of the most telling human stories to have surfaced from the outbreak of the pandemic'. In the wake of the lockdown, fear of being impecunious or facing starvation gripped the migrant villagers. The resultant desperation made them leave for their villages and the subsequent scramble caused the death of many, if not by the pandemic, then by accidents.

Chinmay Tumbe's (2019) research tells us that in the hinterland India, the vast Bhojpuri-speaking belt of eastern UP and western Bihar form arguably the world's largest pool from where migrants arrive for employment in textile and industrial belts around Mumbai and in the fields of Punjab (much like the tributaries of the river Ganga) (205–6, 207). Rural people have been migrating to cities in small and large numbers since the nineteenth century.[3] Tumbe's research while probing the positive and the negative aspects of it provides us some perspectives on migrating rural populace. Not that those migrating have not been successful. Migration alleviates poverty, in the source region through financial remittances poverty is reduced. It has been a definite improvement in economic well-being and escaping from poverty. On most dimensions, the average slum dweller (rural migrant) in India is better off than his counterparts of the same social group in India. However, with reference to another survey,[4] he puts it that the migrants are prone to severe health risk due to the consumption of non-nutritious, less caloric food; children and mothers are also prone to health risk. 'These risks are compounded by the fact that "footloose labour" in informal jobs in the urban sectors faces a high degree of income volatility and a very real prospect of downward mobility' (207).

The Presence of Migrant Subculture in the Cities

Rural migration to the cities in the last quarter of the twentieth century therefore expedited at a faster pace. Fragmenting land ownership,[5] division of land among siblings and other kin, and indebtedness drive a massive supply of tribal and other migrants, who have no other recourse to employment and are forced to work in wretched conditions existing in the construction sector. One gets to know how seasonal migrants enter into the low-paying, hazardous and informal market jobs, in key sectors in urban destinations, such as construction, hotel, textile, manufacturing, transportation services, domestic work, etc. One could watch, in most big cities, a routine gathering of nearly fifty to seventy villagers in several groups at a spot in the city, to be hired by the contractors or builders. The middleman fixes their rates, mutually agreed upon, and they work according to the set rules. Either they go back to their village in the evening or stay at the site of the work for a few days or even months. They have poor access to healthcare services, which results in very poor occupational health. Since they cannot afford private hospitals, they often go back to their villages once they fall sick. This affects their employment opportunities, as well as the loss of wages. A large number of migrants find work as unskilled labourers since they enter the job market at a very early age, experience no upward mobility, and remain stuck in the most unskilled, poorly paid, and hazardous jobs for their whole work–life span. Most rickshaw drivers in cities are migrants from villages; auto drivers of Mumbai are from UP and Bihar. In the times of Premchand, the same people would rush to Calcutta for pulling hand rickshaw. This circular form of leaving the village for work is the circular[6] migration. It implies the experience of living perilously, near the margin of subsistence and being exposed to the threats of disease and death, or living away from their nearest family members, year in and year out.

Peasants, Non-cultivators Associated with Farming, Buckled under the Pressure

It is to be understood that the agrarian crisis is not only about farming. Farming, once an employment hub, an industrious society of peasantry that allowed countless peasants, and local artisans-non-cultivators provide for their families has been in the process of fast depletion. The crisis in the rural world has not only affected the agriculture but also significantly impacted that segment of the rural world which is associated with farming. The end decades of twentieth century could be conceived as the period since when the livelihood of a huge population of non-cultivators in allied vocations: weavers, carpenters, potters, braziers, blacksmiths, and many others linked with the farm economy also buckled under the pressure and they were in the process of being rendered redundant. The gradually crumbling old order generated desolation and confusion in all of the peasantry; even the age-old practice of cattle-keeping, a basic component of village life, is no longer considered affordable except for the better off. The methods of conventional agriculture are gradually vanishing, resulting in conspicuous decrease in the regular occupation of the villagers. Premchand's works sensitively illumine the disarray that the displacement stirs in the life of Hori's son Gobar, in *Godan*. Shukla's *Raag Darbari* (1969) within a few decades after India's independence concludes rather ironically that migration is the only option left to the peasantry. The three rural narratives here explore the varied contexts of agrarian crisis on the rural families, faced with the insecurities about *dal-roti*; for them migration is the only resort though it does not prove a viable solution.

Straddling Country and the City: Mansaram's Craft and Labour is Not Wanted

Punni Singh's[7] 'Mansa Badai' (Mansa Carpenter) is the story of one such circular migrant. Alluding to his earlier, childhood recollection of Mansa carpenter, the narrator Punit shares with the readers how the fast replacement of machines for manpower impacted the subsistence of a carpenter-blacksmith and stripped him of the dignity and pride that his physical prowess and craft gave him. Mansa Badai (Mansa Carpenter) exhibits the turmoil of that segment of peasantry which has been carving the tools meant for farming, for over thousand years. In the current age, anvil, hammer, shovel, sickle, spade, axe, rasp, hoof, knife, pincher, nipper—the conventional tools of use in the village culture and farming—are rendered irrelevant as the acceptance of modern machinery is gaining momentum. Since the incursion of globalization[8] has within decades contributed to the closure of village cottage industries, leading to fast decreasing opportunities for employment, and with less and less scope for work, the labourers are facing a time of terrible frustration, due to lesser scope for earning their livelihood. With the transformation in milieu, the lives of people are also changing.

Once a carpenter and a blacksmith in high demand, Mansaram's workmanship, with the changing times, remains no longer relevant. The image of Mansa *chacha*[9] at work, at his anvil, remains etched in the adolescent Punit's mind. Mansa exuded power and diligence when one watched him harnessed absorbedly to his smithy.

> Oblivious of the commotion around him, he was solely absorbed in carving, chiseling and sharpening scythe, spade, shovel and other farm instruments. The crowd around him bending at his fireside, waited for their tools to get ready—watched him captivated—deeply immersed in the tempo of his work. When the work was nearly over, the boy steadily pulling the wheel of the fan was exhausted, and the people dispersed, then sweating profusely, he would give a break to his work, pulling his body backward, lie flat on the floor, fold both his knees upon his chest and with both his hands gently press his tired muscles. He would then be seen shifting to his sleeping position, drifting off to deep slumber, begin snoring. At this time none could dare wake him. (Singh, 179–80)

The value of Mansa's skill dropped inevitably as the plough and oxen were now rendered useless in the village farming and the age of tractors began flourishing. Depleted of the source of earning, Mansaram's smithy was gradually running out of customers. Watching their ancestral work crumbling, the frustration goaded his son, Rajpal, to leave the village for the city to explore the prospects of livelihood. After a few months, the narrator visiting his village learns that, in the city, the police raided the workshop where Rajpal worked with his maternal uncle and discovered the equipment meant for building guns, *katta* (country pistol). It was known to everyone in the village that Mansaram was so hurt by Rajpal's engagement in the unlawful activity of making firearms that he did not even try to bail him out. When advised to bail out his son, taking a deep breath, he said:

> 'Bhaiya, I'll comply with whatever you say now, but don't say that same thing again! Punishment is a very small thing. I wouldn't even shed any tears if he is sentenced to death. My ancestors never committed a crime like this ... the penance of my several generations has been destroyed'. He cried bitterly. I wasn't able to meet my gaze with him. (Singh, 184)

The times were that of the emergence of technology of tube well and tractor, since then the value of Mansarams craft and art was undermined. As the time passed, the condition deteriorated further. His smithy previously visited by numerous customers now lies empty. Only rarely is his smithy's furrow singed. The workshop is seldom swept and very often the stray dogs of the village are found resting there. Now Mansa was in real crisis. For dearth of resources even to afford meals made him feel ashamed; the stability and peace of the older social order do not exist anymore. Now jobless, he too straddles between the city and the village to raise enough for his subsistence. Carrying his lightweight tool box, he is seen peddling in the alleys, and even then, he cannot manage two square meals; in this situation, his wife Gangapurvali suffers most. His son now after having spent his prison tenure had left for the city. One could see Mansa sometimes travelling to the cities and coming back in the late evening or taking round of the village carrying a bagful of instruments.

Times Have Changed the Village and the Values

The tone of the narrator Punit registers the shift of atmosphere which have come about in the village with the changing times. Unlike the earlier decades, now until late night, tales are not told around the fireside. Nor does one hear the remote sounds of *dhol-majira* or singing, none even gives to crying openly.

> Fear—so subtle, minute, that it could enter—through the hinges of the door, and terror so invincible that it can roar on the roof top. I'm into my quilt after evening meals. Bhaiya has gone to sleep in the closet of the farm tube well. The two children of my brother are sleeping inside the room next to the veranda. While leaving, he warned me not to open the door even if I hear knocking.

Lately, the villagers have ceased to feel secure and safe when the evenings descend. On one such winter night, Mansa knocked at his door. The visit of Mansa *chacha*, wrapped in a frayed blanket, was a surprise to Punit. The overall decay in Mansa's sinewy physical appearance disturbs him, as the image of his sprightly figure, his awe-inspiring energy was still in the narrator's memory. " 'Mansa steps in furtively, worn-out, fatigued, and suffering'. 'His eyesight had become weaker'. 'I remember his sparkling smile, now two of his upper teeth and one lower has disappeared' " (Singh, 178–79). The narrator felt a sense of unease when:

> Mansa removes his blanket from his shoulder and shows a double-barreled gun, one *pauna* (a multitool toy rifle) and a *katta*, lays them on the quilt and sitting at the footboard says: 'look at the fine craft of Rajpal! He is a specialist in firearms'. I insisted on his sitting on the chair, but as if he did not hear: 'There is a lot of demand for these in this region; life is no longer safe. The cost is not much; this double-barrel gun at 500, *pauna* at 300 and *katta*, Rs. 150 let us not talk about money with your brother, he has also given his approval'. (Singh, 179)

The instruments manually built for thousands of years have become obsolete and the hands that forged them are moulding weapons to kill or to defend oneself from goons and adversaries. Here, we come to see how a man proud of his honest work, earlier thronged by villagers, is forced to peddle his dubious goods in the town and village stealthily to earn some money.

> And yet the strange look in his eyes conveyed immense desolation; his visage still resembled Shri Ramakrishna Paramahansa. While leaving, closing the door, he said, 'This is what is written in our destiny and we've to depend on this for our subsistence'. (Singh, 184)

The episode also gives us the clue to understand that the composite cultural life which earlier supported varied vocations in the rural society has been dismantled. The clandestine manufacturing and sale of firearms indicate the growing approval of guns and goons in the village scenario where land disputes and caste rivalry very often culminate in violent bloody clashes.

For *Pardes* (Foreign Land): The Tough Toiling, Precarious World of Migrant Labourers

Shailendra Anand's[10] narrative, 'Uttha Puttar' (Wake Up Son), an elegiac story, opens in an idyllic, slow-moving, relaxed village environment of the 1970s, when people would gather at the choupal[11] under a huge banyan tree where Muktesar Kamat, a peasant, a known storyteller of the village would be surrounded by many listeners, both children and elderly, as the assembly of storytelling would begin in the evening. He had one son and two daughters. The daughters were married off. The continued drought conditions for three years had turned the life of Muktesar upside down. The earth was parched, for there was not a single drop of water. People were desperately pining for heavy showers. Clouds appeared, thundered, and left. But, it seemed, their prayers could not reach the rain gods. Even the auspicious planetary positions of '*punarvasu, Purva, hathiya*'[12] were not bringing rains. During the drought, a year before, his cow was sold off; in the following one, his buffalo. In the third year, the dilemma over the situation of unpaid debt mounted to such a crisis that he was made to sell off his ox. His worry was:

He does not own a piece of land, rather he survives on the leased land of 10 acres on the condition that if he fails to pay back the rental—the produce from the harvest—he would have to surrender his ox. Even the ox is not his, for it was bought after he sought a loan from the Grameen Bank. Besides, in spite of paying the share of the village head, the local official, the veterinary doctor, and the manager sahib, he had to borrow Rs. 200 from the money lender to buy the ox. How was he going to pay the money lender? (Anand, 42)

Muktesar's burden unfolds the warped circle of 'share' (secret commission) operating in the network of loan system.

In the customary folk saying, it was now the call for leaving for *pardes*. People were flocking towards Punjab. Most of the young population had fled the village. To give relief to his father, like many other young men of the village, Muktesar's son Ramsaran decided to leave for Punjab[13] to join the work as a labourer. It was heard that plenty of jobs were available there. After the son's departure, the neighbours found Muktesar's liveliness and verve missing. While telling stories he would be distracted very often. The story of a fairy would stray into that of a *panduki* (a variety of dove). The story ran like this:

> Once a woman was pounding rice in a palace for the king's kitchen. Slogging the entire day, she and her young son were tormented by hunger, the latter could not resist the temptation to eat a handful of rice. 'Lest the king's rice be reduced, she would be punished'; the fear made the woman desperate and she slapped the boy too hard. He fell down flat on the floor. Engrossed in the work, she muttered, 'take offence I don't care'. At last, when the rice was weighed and turned out the same weight, swaying with great happiness, the woman said to her son, 'wake up son, its done'. But how could he wake up! In one slap the boy's life had left him. The woman's heartrending cry was heard in every nook and corner of the palace. In the next life, she took birth as a dove who kept singing '*Uttha Puttar, pura hua Uttha Puttar, pura hua*' (Wake up son, it's done; wake up son, it's done). (Anand, 141)

Muktesar's repeating the same story of the rice-pounding woman and her child, or ending each with the song of *panduki*, '*Uttha Puttar*' or drifting, while telling the story of a fairy, into something else, now reduced the interest of the listeners. His *choupal* was no longer able to draw the same crowd. People could make out from his gloomy eyes and voice heavy with deep melancholy that his stories had also departed with the son Ramsaran.

He received money order from his son, two or three times in the last several months. Every time, Ramsaran would write that from the next month onwards, he would send more money to rid his father of the debt. Then suddenly the arrival of money order stopped. After sometime a letter was received from another labourer, Ram Charan, who too had left for Punjab. The letter carried information that Ramsaran was missing. His employer, Sardarji[14] said that he disappeared after stealing the jewellery and money of Sardarni. Muktesar became unconscious on hearing the news. When he gained consciousness, he found people around him discussing, 'Whatever happened, Ramsaran was not capable of stealing' (Anand, 143). People also talked about the reports that when the labourer in Punjab demanded payment after rigorous servitude of two to four months, the employer would accuse him of theft and the labourer would go missing.

> Coming back to his senses, Muktesar heard around him sympathetic voices. He looked at the sky, his gaze, unmoved, agonized, pleading in deep sorrow: 'come back Ram Saran, the loan of the money lender has been paid .... Now never go to Punjab'. Upon the banyan tree the dove was repeatedly singing, 'wake up son, it's over, wake up son'. (Anand, 143)

Muktesar's compulsive repetition of the tale of rice pounding, the grieving mother, and the pensive song of the dove symbolically resonates with a father's tragic pining for his lost son, and can be seen as symptomatic of a traumatized soul,[15] possessed with the past and threatened with a future of impasse. Even without indulging in graphic details, the narrative reveals the magnitude of grief, bringing to the fore, with visceral power, what migrating to the city means to the kith and kin and invokes the vulnerability of the rural labourers.

Harassment at the Hands of Employers or Police or Anti-social Elements

Muktesar's grief is the grief of many whose sons leave the village to raise funds to help their families seek relief from the burden of debt or the financial burden associated with their daughter's wedding but never come back. From Gurpreet Singh Nibber's (2018) findings, we come to know that 25 percent of migrants are found to have faced harassment at the hands of employers, police, or anti-social elements. Even during illness or injury, they approach the quacks or cheap private medical facilities because they cannot afford to spend time waiting at government hospitals. It is likely that Ramsaran's grinding labour could have caused illness, and hence, displeased with his absence from work, his employer punished him severely. One suspects that, behind a simple villager's disappearance, there must be something sinister but it was not a matter of any interest to the police, and none bothered to trace him.

Drift into Criminal Route: 'The Boats Capsize, Where? Nobody Knows!'

Salil Sudhakar's[16] 'Khari mein Gaon ki Kashtiyan' (Village Boats in the Gulf) maps the lives of two such peasant families from the Bhojpuri belt of Bihar. Chinmay Tumbe's (2018, 149) research informs that 'in the past decade the locus of emigration to the gulf shifted from South India to the North; Bihar once again dominates annual labourer flows outside India, much like it did a century and a half ago and of late, have overtaken Kerala in supplying migrants to the Persian Gulf'[17] (149). It is well known, how rich remittances from all these places flow all through the year to thousands of villages and small towns.

The foremost factor that spurs the urge to earn money and seek employment in distant pastures is the need to support the family struggling for subsistence. In all likelihood, weddings of daughters, debts, and lack of substantive scope for employment in rural regions create dire financial distress in peasant homes. The vast wage difference between India and the Gulf is tempting for those who have watched some other migrants in the village neighbourhood, growing overnight rich, building houses, and funding generously in the education of their dependents. Sudhakar story however relates that several of these migrant labourers are not so lucky.

Weavers Made to Abandon Their Work

Sudhakar's narrative subtly hints at the gradually decaying tradition of indigenous industries that divested a segment of rural India of the means of survival. The fast disappearance of workshops that ran indigenously after the advent of the computerized age has given rise to a feeling of worthlessness in the village youth.

> Several generations of Hanif's ancestors were in the profession of weaving bed sheets, famously known as 'Bhagalpur sheets'. The earning was enough to feed the family. The advent of high technology of textiles undermined the value of the locally woven sheets; the woven sheets were no longer in demand. The families of weavers were made to abandon their work and seek jobs elsewhere. Luckily the money Hanif's father had saved with his weaving business helped buy a few bighas of land for farming and that gave them some assurance of survival. (Sudhakar, 229)

Many small land-owning farmers and farming households and weavers were descending into poverty due to the shocks in the wake of globalization. The decaying tradition of weaving with the advent of technologically produced textiles had damaged the weaving industries as woven sheets were no longer in demand and the rural world found itself divested of a major source of economic support. The conditions exacerbated because they were not prepared or trained to perceive alternative income earning opportunities in comparatively better performing states in India. In the situation, where households were able to sell assets, borrow, or generate income from alternative employment opportunities, the impact of such shocks had been temporary. However, if the household had no assets to sell, no access to credit, or was able to borrow only at exploitative rates of interest, it got into a severe debt trap, and the jolts could have extended outcome, generally that of shoving the households from the level of being middle poor to below poverty line. The worst form of coping with this crisis culminates in suicides.

> Haroun and Hanif were childhood friends. Previously Haroun Mayan was seen dealing with a very small business of leather. With great difficulty, his six family members were making their ends meet. Haroun Miya's son, Iqbal had left for a gulf country. The money he was sending home helped Haroun build a house that was everyone's envy, though he confesses that the source of Iqbal's earning was suspicious and that it proceeded from some mysterious activity. However, 'with the remittance received from Iqbal, the family was now in possession of Aladdin's magic lamp. Now Haroun Miya is seen sitting in the AC cabin of a big shop of leather ware'. (Sudhakar, 228)

How could the neighbours contain their curiosity? They got to know that, fed up with the misery of poverty, Haroun forced Iqbal to leave for Dubai and since then the family fortune had transformed. The most talked about topic that interested everyone in the village was:

> How to leave for the Gulf country? 'Let us look for some jugaad to enable us to sail to Dubai, Muscat, Riyadh and Sharjah and get us some work ... everybody appeared in competition to garner the possibility of connection'. (Sudhakar, 229)

Hanif's farmland hardly provided any income since the consecutive years' drought had ruined all crops, and the selling of goats and eggs was the sole means of survival. The prospects of rain were bleak; hoping for a good sowing and harvesting was futile. The two weddings in the family further generated a lot of anxiety about the means of raising resources for survival. Junaid, Hanif's caring and concerned son, thinks of emulating Haroun's son Iqbal, giving up farming and leaving for the Gulf. He learns driving heavy vehicles to make himself worthy of employment in Dubai. Though Hanif is apprehensive about the future of Junaid in Dubai, the promise of big money makes him give in to Junaid's earnest wish. The cattle are sold to raise money to pay the broker and yet it is not enough. It was difficult for Hanif to muster the courage to mortgage the land to arrange money for Junaid's journey.

Restraining his inner turmoil, he faced his son with the property papers of lands: 'Listen son, I know it's time for departure to Mumbai. But the truth is I could not muster the courage to mortgage the lands bought by the sweat and toil of my ancestors! I hardened myself, but my conscience doesn't consent! Son, for us our farmlands are as dear as our parents! ... That's why my emotions prevent me, after all, many don't have the courage to mortgage their parents' legacy .... But I have learned, in the present times one can't live with such emotions; your desire to go and earn in the gulf country is also not wrong. And being your father it's my duty to help you in this mission!' (Sudhakar, 237-38)

Lives Hostage to Anonymity, Could Have Sinister Ends

For the following two and a half years, very rarely would the family receive a few thousands. The hope that the gulf money could get them back their mortgaged land turned into despair. Nonetheless, they hoped that possibly Junaid was saving money. The family however is in high spirits when Farzana Bi, Junaid's mother, receives a phone call that he was at Chhatrapati Shivaji Terminus, about to board a train for home. 'The dreadful sounds of continued gunshots petrify her whole being. The conversation with Junaid meanwhile comes to an abrupt halt; she realized that the contact with the latter was snapped. Thereafter Junaid's phone never responded' (239). A few minutes later a TV news channel conveys that a major terrorist attack occurred at the Terminus and numerous waiting passengers were killed. Since there was no information of Junaid, his whereabouts being uncertain, the family had no means of knowing what happened to him. It was however not difficult to guess that he was killed in that terror attack.

The story ends with the scene where Hanif and Haroun, after a long period of estrangement, come together and the stark truth of the latter's prosperity is disclosed:

Hanif could sense Haroun's voice steeped in deep anguish. For some moments he forgot his own pain. 'What happened to Iqbal .... He is doing good business in Dubai?' 'All that is a lie Hanif; Iqbal was brutally gunned down in Bangkok six years back by a hostile underworld gang. I've received the punishment for the money acquired through crime'. (Sudhakar, 243)

Both remain silent. The common loss brings back some empathy between Hanif and Haroun. The papers of his mortgaged farmland are with Haroun and he had no problem with Hanif tilling it. Hanif is still not at ease with the offer of Haroun in spite of being reminded of their old bonding. One infers that the reluctance of Hanif to seek any help from Haroun is because he cannot help feeling that it was the big show of Iqbal's newly acquired wealth from the Gulf, which aroused in Junaid the earnest resolve to leave his country for better prospects. 'Junaid could have been prevented from going to the Gulf, if he could have resisted the temptation for wealth that Iqbal acquired' (Sudhakar, 244). Temptations lure the youth into unknown but tantalizing trajectories without any destination: as one of the characters, Haroun says, 'We are all sailing in different boats, Hanif... which one would capsize, where! nobody knows' (Sudhakar, 243). The narratives of rural boys being led astray into unlawful activities, in exchange for good money, used for illegal activities by mafia kingpins and political musclemen, or, ideologically brainwashed and instrumentalized by certain terrorist groups are not unusual.

Notes

1. One of the oldest films, released in 1953, 'Do Bigha Jameen' (Two Bigha Land) was directed by Bimal Roy. Its story written by Salil Choudhury in 1940s and songs by Shailendra invoke the social context of a small peasant's life in Bihar and Uttar Pradesh who leaves for Kolkata to earn his livelihood. The opening lines of one of the songs translated here, 'Leave your stories here/leave, some of your sign/who knows you would ever return', resonate the pensive longing of those who missed the presence of their migrant kith and kin.
2. Sainath's lecture, 'Migrated Laborer in India', 10 June 2018, substantively backed by his empirical research and fieldwork indicts the bad economic policies since 1991-liberalization that accelerated the gradual process of the collapse of agriculture in India. His analysis invokes the scenario of 2011 and thereafter 2016 demonetization that inconsolably destroyed the agriculture and hastened the migration further.

3. David Ludden (1990, 171) ascribes the migration of rural populace to the late nineteenth-century transition to capitalism. Preceding the system of ownership, village lands were supposedly free for every individual's ploughing and planting; they belonged to every inhabitant of the village. With the capitalist system of ownership, the fragmentation, division of lands, and the multiple problems entailing the cultivation brought about a reckoning that farming could no longer promise a decent level of subsistence. Tumbe's graph of the migration of the Indian population traces the contexts of early nineteenth-century history and topography. His specific mention of the migrations of peasants from the Bhojpuri regions of Bihar (48–51, 61–63) is of significance to this chapter.
4. I have drawn on Tumbe's chapter 6, 'Migration and Development' (201–30). Tumbe draws on the research finding in David Atkin's 'The Caloric Cost of Cultures: Evidence from Indian Migrants'. Krishnavatar Sharma (2019) also finds that the migrant working life tends to have severe inter-generational implications, since their lifestyle in terms of vulnerability, poor health, and low level of skills is transferred from the parents to children.
5. The arable plot size is decreasing with each successive generation, mainly due to inheritance laws. The land owned by the parent is inherited by his/her wards and gets divided into fragments. These lands eventually become economically unviable in terms of agricultural produce. Since the first agriculture census 45 years ago, the number of farms has doubled from 70 million in 1970 to 145 million in 2015 and counting. This implies a greater number of people in an ever-shrinking land holding, leading to increased population pressure, and rampant underemployment. The issue of small landholdings is rampant in areas with dense populations, especially in states such as Uttar Pradesh, Bihar, and West Bengal where the average landholdings are abysmally low. See Urvi Shrivastav, *Business World*, 16 December 2020.
6. Drawing on the Economic Survey of India 2016–17, Tumbe submits that there are hundred million migrant workers in India, of which most are circular migrants. Such migration is highly circular, with migrants working in multiple destinations during their lifetimes, and retiring in their native places. The durations can be as short as a day or a week, in which case they are referred to as commuters, numbering in the tens of millions, who frequently board trains and buses bound towards a nearby town or city. A few more tens of millions migrate seasonally for work—for a few months of the year—drawn disproportionately from the scheduled castes and tribes and from particular clusters in central India. They work in precarious worksites in sectors ranging from construction and brick kilns to rural harvesting operations. Currently, Surat is a classic example of a smaller town turning into a migrant hub.
7. Punni Singh (1939–) belongs to the village, Milavali in Mainpuri (UP), and is a writer of Hindi fiction, mostly dealing with rural experiences of failing peasantry. 'Mansa Badai' (178–84) is in the collection, *Katha me Gaon*. The references are to this story.

8. The foreword (8) by Manager Pandey in *Katha me Gaon* conveys the disruption of rural life specifically in the Hindi belt in the wake of globalization (5–14).
9. *Chacha* and *Bhaiya*, respectively, mean uncle and brother. In the Indian semi-urban and rural ethos, they are polite addresses extended even to strangers.
10. Shailendra Anand (1952–) is a Maithili writer who hails from the village Lohana, Madhubani (Bihar). 'Uttha Puttar' is in the collection, *Kosi ke Us Paar* (*Across and Beyond Kosi*). Anand has published several collections of stories. He has also received awards for his plays. The excerpts are drawn from this story.
11. An open verandah under a huge tree where villagers have assembly.
12. They are *nakshatras* (stars) in Hindu astronomy, regarded auspicious for good rains.
13. The onset of Green Revolution in the fields of Punjab demanded farming labours in the 1970s. Gurpreet Singh Nibber reports in *Hindustan Times*, 15 October 2018, that majority of the influx of people to the cities of Punjab is from Bihar and UP. Thirty-five percent of migrants are illiterate, 36 percent have middle-level education and only 7 percent are graduates. Nearly 47 percent of the migrants come to the cities of Punjab due to poverty and 42 percent shift due to lack of remunerative employment opportunities in their respective villages. The reason behind large-scale migration is low remuneration in the unorganized sector. A recent report by Nibber on 11 June 2020 in *Hindustan Times* tells us that despite the COVID-19 threat, hundreds of migrant labourers are arriving in Punjab every day from Bihar and UP for paddy transplantation since Punjab has labour crunch.
14. One from the Sikh community and the female: Sardarni. Or any person in charge, a contractor for example.
15. I have drawn the concept from La Capra's studies on trauma, absence, and loss (712–13).
16. Salil Sudhakar (1968–) belongs to Aara, Bihar. He is a Hindi poet, an essayist, and a short-story writer. 'Gaon ki Kashtiyan Khari Me' (2008, 221–43) is in the collection, *Katha me Kisan* II. The excerpts are from this edition.
17. An extensive study of migrant workers in Gulf countries figures in Tumbe's 'Diasporas and Dreams' (113–62).

7
When Hunger Hits the Rural Poor, Aged, and Disabled: The Meal of Mice and Dead Cow

Work is seasonal, but our hunger is not.

Hunger is a harsh reality that the modern civilization has not been able to deal with until now. In spite of tremendous advancements in science and technology, mankind could not do away with the humiliation of hunger. Chris Arsenault (2015)[1] writes in 'Why are most of the world's hungry People, Farmers'? that the largest number of people, the small farmers—the people who grow much of the world's food—go hungry. The newest figures on international food insecurity, released by three UN agencies, show that 795 million people worldwide who don't get enough to eat are, in fact, farmers. Three-quarters of the world's hungry is living in rural areas; most of them depend on agriculture for their livelihood' In the Indian democracy even in the recent decades, the rural, landless[2] poor have to worry about the daily arrangement of *roti*; they cannot think of having the daily intake of *dal*. Previously, *dal-roti* was described as a moderately staple diet even for the poor, but now it is no longer affordable.

Premchand's 'Kafan': The Indignity of Hunger; the Joys of a Good Feast

The stories of hunger quintessentially relate to rural conditions when either drought or hostile weather generates great difficulty to deal with

Rural India and Peasantry in Hindi Stories. Vanashree, Oxford University Press. © Vanashree 2023.
DOI: 10.1093/oso/9780192871572.003.0008

hunger for the people who are poor, old, or disabled. Premchand's 'Kafan' (1932) translated as 'The Shroud'[3] is a moving example of the abject misery of hunger as a condition of the rural poor in India. The scene of the illiterate, abjectly poor, and indolent father and son to whom the terrible aches and wails of the wife in labour do not mean as much as the intense urge to satiate their hunger with baked potatoes may be evocative of the grotesque. But the narrator's acumen reaches the ultimate sense of the visceral realism for presenting with amazing credibility the speeches of Madhav and Gheesu, redolent with the taste and flavour of a delicious meal, and then dancing with the joy of good feast and country liquor, sought from the begged money, which was meant for the shroud of a young loving wife and caring daughter-in-law. The story invokes the coarse realities of extreme deprivation of the illiterate and landless in rural Uttar Pradesh. A writer of Premchand's magnitude by no means wants this story to be read as a piece of despicable greed. In letting the characters speak out about the joys of relishing good food that they desperately missed, he is goading his readers to comprehend the perspectives of those who have been famished for a long time. The reader is compelled to perceive the subtle balancing of rival consideration seeping through the narrative and it becomes difficult to pass judgement.

For the landless poor in rural India, the situation has not altered much. Hunger stalks those in particular, who are dispossessed. For them to slip into the state of starvation is easy; the pandemic lockdown in the recent months has demonstrated the appalling scenario of starving people in the villages and that also unfolded the mischievous ways through which they were denied food. The first two stories: Anant Kumar Singh's[4] 'Bhookh' (Hunger, 195–206) and Subhash Sharma's[5] 'Bhookh' (183–96) relate the excruciating suffering of the characters, whose bodily decrepitude has reduced their value in the rural labour market. In the case of the first story, Shibu, a *Dalit* worked in the company of his cousin, Charan. Though he received reduced payment, it somehow sustained his small family of one son. Sudden illness took the life of Shibu's wife some months ago. Those deprived generally suffer from the diseases caused by deficient nutrition or malnutrition. In a troubled household like Shibu's, women tend to be most vulnerable. The unseasonal heavy downpour and inundation stalled all farming work and resultantly blocked the earnings, the poor made through labour in the village. In the second story, aged and frail,

Jayakaran's family battled with a prolonged drought. Jaykaran's son died of a road accident, his daughter-in-law was severely afflicted with arthritis, and the onus of feeding the family with four children is upon him. Both Shibu and Jayakaran are the lone earning members of their families. Premkumar Mani's[6] 'Jugaad' (155–63), the third story, reveals another facet of how a landless labourer and his family of four somehow through clever tactics were able to feed themselves when the vagaries of weather stalled prospects of filling one's belly.

In the constant heavy downpour or drought conditions, the labourers are laid off indefinitely. It is worth noticing that the characters in the three stories, in spite of slight variations in their stature in the village society, are from the lowest castes and are landless. The endemic poverty of this class, *mahadalit musahars*,[7] to which the characters in the second and the third stories belong puts them always in a tight corner. If they have no land, they cannot produce their own food. Even if they were having land but no access to seed and fertilizer, their capacities as a farmer would be hampered and likely to face subsistence issues. If out of employment, they cannot lay claim to payment. Therefore, no job, no money to buy food; they starve. The stories give us an authentic graph of their settlements. They are generally crammed into less than four acres of land near the highway dotted with makeshift hutments. The majority of them from the SC and Dalit communities survive on the charity of their employers, because they historically are a 'landless' community. And even today they are treated as bonded labourers.

Disabled in Rural India: No Friendly Infrastructure

The landless disabled labourers whether middle-aged or too old, but could otherwise earn something with some manual work, whatever petty, to feed their family, find themselves totally helpless during hostile weather or drought conditions, when there is neither any work nor food. The physically able walk distances in search for work or manage to seek some alternative job, if not on the fields, then at the site of construction work. But what happens when a peasant is disabled? Sanjiv Phansalkar's (2018) article, 'People with Disabilities (PWD) Languish across Rural

India: Neglected Lives', reveals that there are 27 million people in India with disabilities, of whom more than 71 percent live in villages. They remain the most neglected segment of the population in spite of the promises by the central and state governments. Since there is no disabled friendly infrastructure in the rural area, they are generally invisible and are not seen in public. They also suffer from the burden of stigma and the insensitivity of the general population towards them. The study made by Cardona et al. (236) notes that the leading causes of injury—falls, road traffic crashes, and suicides—are all preventable. It is important that effective interventions are developed and implemented to minimize the impact of injury in the rural India. However, there are also high rates of falls in younger age groups and a high level of risk is encountered by women as they go about their usual household and agricultural tasks. Rural life is difficult and really accident prone. More such studies cite events of death or decrepitude due to accidents occurring during the miscellaneous onerous task of labouring, preparing the field, or meeting with an accident on the roads. One who faced the casualty at close quarters said: 'speeding trucks and cars do not differentiate between cattle and humans. We regularly lose livestock; we can't lose our children'.[8]

Hunger and an Injured, Disabled Body

Anant Kumar Singh's 'Bhookh' (195–206) opens with describing the mental anguish of Shibu during a very difficult time when for the last three days they had nothing to eat. Harsh winters of December, accompanying rains in the village, Kanchanpur, have brought about almost a halt to all farming works. The village had been gravely suffering for the last ten days. The west wind was slashing human flesh. The farmers owning lands were desperately watching, exhorting nature's fury to stop, waiting to harvest their rice crop, and for sowing the rabi (the crop sown in winter). Labourers rendered without farm work were done with whatever earning they had. They were now starving, pressing their belly, exhausted with borrowing money. All were waiting for the rains to stop, the unseasonal rain damaged them irrecoverably.

Shibu had suffered a grievous injury during a caste-specific task which as a *chamar*[9] he was obliged to perform. Shibu and his cousin Charan were summoned to the cattle shed of Ramshakal Pande for the task of lifting, dragging, and removing the dead animal away from the settlement of the upper caste of the village. Since Charan was running fever, his part of the weight of the animal was also upon Shibu's limbs. Unfortunately, the heavy weight of the dead animal fell on Shibu at an angle that grievously fractured his right leg. The owner of the ox, Panditji did not show any interest in helping Shibu. For not being able to avail proper treatment, the fractured leg could never regain the normal fitness. Shibu became lame for life. Earlier accompanying his cousin and neighbour, Shibu could manage to make some earning as a farming labourer, though on reduced rates, that helped him to subsist. Before meeting with an accident, he earned his living as a labourer in the fields of bigger peasants. Now Shibu has to fend for himself and his young son, Ganeshi. Watching his ten-year-old son Ganeshi silently sobbing is heart-rending to him.

> Hidden under a sheet, Ganeshi's face was not visible, sensing the sound of his muffled sobs made Shibu miserable. His helplessness made him cry bitterly. He thought of begging some food from his cousin, and neighbor, Charan, but when he heard some voices: 'First give me'/'Give me more, this is so less'/'no, yours is too much'/'no, Tilak's is more than mine'/'eat silently or you won't even get this'/'mine is finished'/'now what to do?'/'There are more people'/'give me a little more, I beg you'/'you're not the only one!'[10] (Singh, 199)

Shibu guessed that Charan's family was done with their meagre meals and his children were still hungry. That evening Ganeshi left home and he came back eating peas intently. Shibu guessed that Ganeshi must have stolen them from someone's field. There were too many peas lying on the cot. Beholding the satiated glow on Ganeshi's face made Shibu withhold himself from scolding him for stealing. He too picked a few of them and both began eating. The following evening, there was nothing to eat. At night Ganeshi was fast asleep, Shibu knew that the hefty cow of Dasrath Mahto died and was pushed into the ditch not very far from the settlement of chamars. He picked up his knife and went outside very scared thinking:

> Dying with hunger is right but defying the laws of Hindu religion is bad. This cow's flesh is not meant to be eaten. Hindus can't consume it even

if they are dying of hunger ... but after all, I am a human ... there is nothing wrong in eating a dead cow. Not much. After all, the dead flesh is fresh. (Singh, 203)

He brought home the meat of the dead cow and cooked it upon the fireplace. Both father and son had two sumptuous meals. The next day also, when he came to know that a calf had died, he thought that God was helping him. But this time, when he was about to insert the knife into the dead calf's flesh, Janardan Pandey saw him. His loud yelling summoned a large crowd and they pounced on Shibu, thrashing him mercilessly.

The Ritual of Punishment

The disabled Shibu was dragged to the door of Ramsakal Pandey, who is assigned the natural authority to pronounce the religion-sanctioned punishment over the sin of that scale. Heavy sticks were hitting Shibu's body. In the meanwhile, his son rushed to the scene crying:

'don't thrash babu', he pleaded with abject misery. 'Do you know that your father has committed a sin?' Ramsakal Pandey threatened 'Move from here or you too will become lame'. Shibu said moaning, 'kill me, but forgive Ganeshi'. In the meanwhile, a stone hit Ramshakal Pandey's head and the blood began dripping. The crowd watched shocked. His kinsmen rushed to attend to the injury and some dashed after Ganeshi who was seen running towards the field outside the village. (Singh, 206)

In narrating the humiliating struggle for food of a disabled peasant, the story raises a very crucial human issue: how can the bruised, accident victims whose ailment remain untreated, who live in anonymity, survive in difficult times when all means to earn and to avail food are blocked? People nurture natural prejudice against physically challenged individuals. With them is inexorably attached certain stigma and they are seen as a liability. The ending enacts a scene almost akin to the attempt of mob lynching of Shibu who had to be punished publicly for violating a religious norm since he dared to eat the flesh of a dead cow.

Starving in Parched Fields: Jayakaran's Ordeal

The pang of hunger and the efforts the poor and outcaste make to feed their families expose us to an abject and unfamiliar region of struggle and suffering. Another story, by Subhash Sharma, with the same title, 'Bhookh' relates the grim scenario in the village Jeevanpura, during the times of drought when employment was scarce. 'Several youths from the *musahar* community left for Panjab, Delhi, and Haryana for jobs, some could get some random work to sustain themselves and some could get something better so that their families could be helped' (187). For the aged, ill, or physically challenged rural population, it was even more challenging to subsist. Old and physically weak, Jayakaran wobbles while walking. His son died in a road accident. It is an unacknowledged truth that many villagers die of accidents. The state transport system has built inroads through the middle of the villages at the borders of the fields or in the close surrounding. The speeding buses and trucks kill with impunity. There is no record of how many villagers die of road accidents. Earlier, Jaykaran's daughter-in-law would earn some money by doing menial work in the household of the village elite, but now her arthritis grown worse and has almost incapacitated her. He hears his disabled daughter-in-law agonized weeping: 'O God, why do you make us live? If you cannot give us food. Why don't you take our lives!' (193).[11] Enduring the pain of arthritis and hunger has created a condition of severe crisis. Even walking some distance gives her excruciating pain. It is a known fact that the medicines for the ailment available in the cities are exorbitantly expensive and unaffordable. In the situations, Jaykaran was forced to sell five of his pigs, that helped in mustering resources for food, but the money was spent soon.

The Caste Tensions Polarized the Upper Caste, The RED Flag Instigated but Failed to Help

The narrative lets us into the social structure of village life. The three castes: brahmans, *yadavs*, and *musahars* lived in their respective tolas (localities) set at a marked distance from each other. The people from the same community flocked together. Brahmans, the landowners and moneylenders, *yadavas*, farmers and cattle keepers, were not very far from each other. In the other end corner of the village, lay a cluster of huts called labours' tola, where *musahars* lived. The atmosphere of the village was charged with political undercurrents. There existed a subdued prejudice and tension among castes. There were times when it would come to a boil and disturb the otherwise normal atmosphere of the village. The Red Flag Party[12] (a group advocating Communist ideology) vehemently claimed to side with the scheduled castes and was aligned with the ideology of liberating the outcaste from age-old oppression. One of the prime reasons for sporadically surfacing prejudice in the village society was the assumption that the chamars and *musahars* were being instigated against the upper castes and this suspicion never allowed the bigotry to neutralize. The condition deteriorates further. Jaykaran had not paid back the loan borrowed earlier, so none helped him. Despite being slow, Jaykaran kept getting some work in the fields even though he was not paid the accepted rates of payment, at least he got only that much which could buy for the family food grain for a day. But the conditions of work became more difficult since persuaded by the Red Flag Party; the *musahars* demanded raise in their wages and in retaliation, the outraged Brahman landowners and big farmers refused to employ them. The chose to employ labours from outside the village. Due to the dearth of employment, the likes of Jaykaran suffered more harshly.

Mango Kernel and Field Rats

Now Jaykaran is the lone provider to the widow of his son and three children. He worked as a labourer in the fields of a Brahman. In the wake of famine, most field jobs came to a halt and his means of livelihood was snatched. For three years, it had not rained. The wells were drying. The cattle could not be fed and many died. The blazing heat continued unabetted. It is being said that the climate has changed since the forests were destroyed and poisonous gases emanated. Jaykaran's family previously could survive by hunting and roasting rats. But since there is no crop, no rat. Sometimes the family would collect dry mango kernels scattered under the trees and cook them with salt to satiate hunger. He was forced to sell his goat and soon thought of selling the kids also but the filial attachment of his grandchildren with the kids did not let him go through the deal, in a few weeks, however, they too died due to the lack of any fodder. They were buried under the ground of the hovel.

On the condition of returning more than one and a half, a Brahman small landowner gave him a sack full of corn weighing 20 kilograms. 'The elated family's fireplace was lit, all sat around breathing in the aroma of baking corn and they had real good meals after a long time'. Jaykaran hoped that it would last at least for fifteen days. However, 'the scent of freshly baked grain was spreading in the neighboring hovels too' (191). The neighbour, Seetaram, famished for days could not restrain himself from taking the opportunity of stealing half of the corn. The discovery in the morning was distressing to everyone. But Jaykaran though worried, forgave him: 'There is no sin that a hungry man cannot commit. After all he too has to save his children's life!' (192). In less than two weeks, the rest of the corn was finished and they didn't know what to do.

The Famine Relief and the Intermediaries: The Red Card Was Withheld

The sad thing was that in the governmental relief activities, corruption grows rampant.[13] At the Block, Jaykaran's appeal to the village functionaries and the BDO for some work to earn was curtly dismissed on the ground of his age and frail health, 'A gravel road is to be made, but how can an old and lame be employed?' (192) The BDO advised him to obtain the red card (meant for poor relief in Annapurna Yojana) to receive grain for the family. After a great deal of running and pleading with the village servant, Pradhan, and BDO, the card was made. It was however not delivered to him but placed in the custody of the sahukar (a moneylender, generally a grocer), allotted the charge of the Sahkari Samiti (government grocery store), on the pretext that Jaykaran's crumbling hovel was unsafe for the security of the red card.

In the meanwhile, the village pradhan, village servant, and Block Development Officer (BDO) made a deceitful confidential deal with Jaykaran. In return, he was promised 10 kilograms of rice. Desperate Jaykaran willingly submitted to the condition of the village functionaries. Accordingly, he was supposed to lead the drive of obtaining the thumb impression of the entire musahar clan on the Panchayat's paper 'acknowledging that their children were fed with *halwa* and *khichadi* for six months' (192).

One could gather that the village administration in collusion sent a fabricated report to the government about the success in ensuring drought relief. In complicity, they made Jaykaran a scapegoat and used him to achieve their objective. But for how long with ten kilos rice, he could feed the family? Despite waiting for the grain from the red card, nothing happened. One day Jaykaran fell ill and died, vomiting blood. The family was left with nobody who could feed them. In acute desperation, the eldest child dug into the ground where the kids were holed, washed them, cooked, and fed the family. By midnight they suffered from vomiting and diarrhoea and by the following morning, all of them died. The four deaths made a news in the newspaper, underlining that the deaths occurred due to poisoned food and infection.

> A group of doctors gave the postmortem report that the cause of five deaths was definitely not hunger but poisoned food and infection. The government is committed to the all-round development of all citizens. According to the directives of the state government, it would be ensured that nobody dies of hunger. It is a clear order of the government that if in any Panchayat there occurs any death due to starvation, the head of the village Panchayat would be held responsible. In all government storages lakhs of ton of grain is available. The news of dying of hunger is totally false. (196)

The narrator unfolds that in the state-run storage, the grain was rotting but the brokers and representatives in charge did not allow the food to reach the needy. The narrator lastly adds that after the collective deaths, the leaders from different political parties kept visiting Jeevanpur frequently. Lies and rumours substituted for truths.

In the course of Jaykaran's search for the solution to hunger in his family, he gets respite sometimes, feels assured that the *sarkari* arrangement takes care of the deprived and the poor, the institutions like *anganwadi*[14] aspire to reach out to poor families and their children but not much substantively appears on the ground. The sinister design of the predators of drought is glaring, when Jaykaran is not allowed to keep the Red card in his possession on the pretext that his age and limping body incapacitate him from visiting the cooperative store, and that keeping it in his hovel was risky. One gathers that the implementation of whatever good schemes the government launches is generally in disarray. Sainath (1996, 369) in *Everybody Loves a good Drought* puts it astutely in the context of drought situation in Palamau, Bihar.

> Corruption at many levels punches holes in the relief than the development There is more money for relief efforts that follow a crisis. Often a senior official says, there is more money for relief than for development. That suits a lot of people than for It is one reason why people call here *teesra fasl* (the third crop). It reaps a good harvest for the rural elites.

At the subterranean level, however, all this could be traced to their founding spaces in the institutionalized feudal-castiest ideologies, which is further abetted by the politics of vote bank in Indian democracy. The relief fails to reach Jaykaran and the likes of him at the right time. The village environment is ruled by might is right. One finds in the process, the rapidly vanishing old folk culture of empathy, generosity, and justice.

Manoeuvring: Prem Kumar Mani 'Jugaad'

The opening pages of the story give a graphic description of Hirwa's family. His father, a landless peasant, was working as a ploughman employed to plough ten bigha land of a landowner. Since his daily wage was his source of subsistence, he had to wander at every door for work. Because of continuous rains and waterlogged fields, there was no work and no food at home. He and his family had to manoeuvre and invent new ways of obtaining food. Hirwa's mother also managed to earn some money by doing some household chores and oil-massaging women in the families of the privileged elite in the village.

The plight of the landless labours and small peasants grows vulnerable whose two meals rely on the daily wages. They are employed only when needed for the fieldwork, i.e. in the seasons of sowing and harvesting. During the rest of the year, they have to take recourse to a variety of manual jobs. The developing technology in the field of farming has further rendered several manual works unnecessary. The narrative proceeds to describe a day in the life of one such family, when they have nothing to eat and no work to earn money. The two children, Hirwa and Johni, were desperate with hunger. From the ashes of the earthen hearth, Hirwa groped for some potatoes. They discovered that there was no rice at home. Only a few days before, a relative overstayed and hosting him involved the consumption of 10 kilogram of rice. This caused arguments between Hirwa's parents. It seemed that the family might have to go famished that day also. The children in the company of two pups demand food. Binda, Hirwa's mother the forces her husband to step out and look for some work, earn something, and sends her son to the landowner Kisna's daughter-in-law who owes Binda the money for four days' massage. Hirwa readily agreed for he was aware of the generosity of the daughter-in-law of Kisna Malikar. 'She was not only beautiful like the fairy of Indra, but he knew that she could also give him jaggery and puffed rice. He thought of asking for two kilos of rice as well'[15] (Mani, 161). By late afternoon his father steps in, giving them a happy surprise; his search was successful, having found eight field rats. The hearth smells of cooking rice, and baking rats in the flame.

Facing hunger for the family of Hirwa in 'Jugaad' is a story of a day or two, and not for weeks. Jugaad brings about some solace to a famished family, but enduring hunger for weeks when the one in charge of arranging for meals is physically debilitated is tougher as in the stories, Bhookh-1 and Bhookh-2. The narratives let us into two different situations afflicting the peasantry, the sites worth looking into. Vijay Prashad (2020) puts it, 'hunger is a bitter reality. That modern civilization should have been expelled centuries ago. What did it mean for human beings to learn how to build a car or fly a plane and not at the same time abolish the indignity of hunger'? Acute food insecurity is experienced by acute hungers. Hunger is among the most urgent of human needs, and immediate steps need to be taken to get food to people in this crisis.

The stories under the same title 'Bhookh' severely indict the insensitivity of the village society towards very poor, aged, and disabled who in the tough times of drought have no means to garner employment for themselves or find any alternative means of subsistence.

Our experience testifies to the fact that disabled and very poor are invisible segments of our population despite the ameliorating schemes of the government for them. Since there is no disabled friendly infrastructure in the rural regions, they are generally invisible and are not seen in public. They also suffer from the burden of stigma and the insensitivity of the general population towards them. The much-desired urgency is to ensure living wages for agricultural workers, farmers, and others, regardless of whether they are able to work or not during any period of flood or famine or lockdown. This must be sustained according to the situation even after the crisis.

Notes

1. Arsenault's article appears in World Economic Forum's *Agenda Weekly*, https://www.weforum org> agenda> 2015/ 05> why-ar… Arsenault writes for *Thomson Reuter Foundation News* in which the same article is published on May 27, 2015.
2. In the *First Post*, 10 November 2020, Devaparna Acharya's findings tell us that the landless rural poor consider themselves lucky on days when they get two meals. If somehow get some vegetables in one meal, the second meal is just rice and some dal water. Unskilled and uneducated, these families don't have much choice as far as their livelihood is concerned. In the absence of steady jobs, the villagers are forced to either migrate to other states or depend on the good graces of the landowner big farmer or mill owners. In Bihar, landless endure modern-day 'slavery', and await promised lands. It is reported that despite a series of laws, acts, and yojanas, nothing appears on the ground to lift Bihar's landless out of pitiful indenture. Human Rights Watch Caste Violence Against India's "Untouchables" (https://www.hrw.org/report/1999/03/01/broken-people) finds that the distribution pattern of land and other resources is based on caste hierarchy. One-third of the upper castes has land worth more than Rs. 55,000 (US$1375), whereas two-thirds of the scheduled caste households are landless and approximately one-fifth hold land with a total value of less than Rs. 5000 (US$125). Sixty-six hierarchy throughout Bihar although the degree of relationship may differ in some districts.
3. Premchand's 'Kafan' is translated into English as 'The Shroud' by Frances W. Pritchett.
4. Anant Kumar Singh (1955–) hails from Aara, Bihar. Chourahe Par', 'Latur Gayab ho Gaya' 'Raag Bhairavi', 'Yeh Tumhari Tasveer nahi Hai' are his representative stories. He is also known for *Naya Saal Mubarak* (collection of stories) and *Azadi Ki Kahani* (collection of stories for children) and the novels, *Aur Hariyali Bachi Rahe, 1857 ki Kranti*. He has also edited the magazine *Janpath*.
5. Subhash Sharma (1959–) belongs to Sultanpur, UP. His collection of stories *Bhookh evam Anya Kahaniyan, Angare par Baitha Aadami,* and *Bezuban* received the acclaim of the readers. He has also published a collection of poems. For writing the book *Bharat me Manavaadhikar* (Human Rights in India), he was

given an award by the Human Rights Commission. He has also received awards from Bharat Rashtra Bhasha Parishad, and the department of Bihar Rajbhasha.
6. Premkumar Mani (1953) belongs to Patna, Bihar. Among his several collections of stories, the representative stories are 'Andhere me Akele', 'Ghas kre Gahane', 'Guldasta'. *Such yeh Nahin hai, Khuni Khel ke Irda Girda* are his published novels. His collection of articles is *Chintan ke Jan Sarokar*.
7. *Musahars* are the lowest in the Dalit category, known as *mahadalit*. They have been traditionally working as bonded labourer in the fields; the new machines for farming have also created job crisis in their lives. They raise pigs and are also known as eaters of mice.
8. Achchelal, a landless *musahar* labourer who worked in a nearby sugar mill, narrated to Devaparna Acharya (*Firstpost*, 10 November 2020) how his neighbour's son was crushed under a truck while crossing the road to go to school. Therefore, he decided not to send his children to the school. M. Cardona, R. Joshi's *Injury Prevention* (236) rightly observes that the immensely busy, fast, rushing trucks and heavy vehicles on alleyways and routes passing through the villages have caused many accidents if not deaths, damaged many bodies.
9. It is the obligation of Chamars (Harijans) to dispose of the dead animals as a Hindu traditional practice.
10. The references are from Anant Singh's 'Bhookh'.
11. The subsequent excerpts are from Sharma's 'Bhookh' (183–96).
12. Refers to the communist party of India. It has close alignment with the Naxal groups.
13. Sainath's (317–24) exposes how in rural India the drought relief measures happen to be a huge scam site. Often it is seen that there is no connection between the place where relief is demanded and the real drought conditions. The charm of this scam is that it is made to appear legal. Recently, in 2020, during the pandemic, it was found at several rural regions that the individuals in charge of cooperative shops or agencies were withholding the grain received in aid to sell them in the open market. *Jamakhori* (hoarding) was rampant specifically in the rural India.
14. Anganwadi is the Government of India's child caring center. Educating children has been a major part of its programme. Lately, it has been focusing more on protecting children from diseases, hunger, and malnutrition.
15. The references are from 'Jugaad'.

8
Farmers in Death Row: Farming—Risky, Sisyphean; Usury—Back Breaking

Yahan Darakhton ke saye me dhoop lagati hai chalo yahan se chalen aur Umra bhar ke liye
Let us depart for good. For here, even in sylvan shades, you feel searing heat.

—Dushyanta Kumar[1]

Much more effectively than the surveys and academic studies, the rural stories in Hindi and in vernacular discursively unravel that a farmer's planting and readying the fields for the produce could be a highly uncertain and frustrating endeavour and takes much more than what it ultimately yields. Not that the farmers were not ending their lives earlier as well, but that it has visibly catalysed in the recent decades is a sure indicator of a greater structural drawback that is allowed to remain entrenched in Indian agriculture, particularly over the last three decades. The farmers inevitably carry the burden of debt, since to coax their single crop out of the ground, they need to take credit to procure inputs like seed and fertilizer, sometimes even water. The stark fact cannot be countered that agriculture is a loss-making enterprise which does not even bring enough to eat, let alone any surplus. Relying on it however does not enable a farmer to fill his stomach or carry the burden of the family successfully. Even then a farmer is unable to quit farming. Let us accept that no segment of India has been as long battered by adversities as the peasantry, several times with no option but standing in the death row.

Suicides of farmers are generally the result of various factors and indebtedness has historically been a major cause leading to the increase in suicide since the 1990s. Since 1990s the farmers' suicide has been frequently in the news. Several studies[2] and surveys have engaged in understanding the causes. Of which the most pronounced cause identified is the loans from the banks. *Finance Express* (2017) reports that 80 percent farmers commit suicide due to loan from banks. Banks and registered micro-finance institutions have emerged as the prime reason behind India's farmer-suicide narratives, though the situation has been difficult in the preceding era as well.

Peasants Not Attuned to Alternative Modes of Subsistence

Let us understand the structural aspects of peasantry's survival in the state of Bihar. The survival in the agricultural sector[3] constituted the bulk of the rural poor whose family would join them in cultivating the land labour and also supply labour to other cultivating class. Some of them owned some cultivable land; quite a significant number leased land mostly on crop-sharing basis; a sizeable section has been that of landless agricultural labour. Almost all the peasant households were deficient ones in the sense that their bare minimum consumption expenditures exceeded their incomes. With the crises in farming, grossly inapt education facilities, neglected—unimplemented or indefinitely shelved development programmes created crises in job prospects for the rural poor; jobs have literally vanished in the rural sector and this has served to intensify the alienation of the peasants. The lives of average village youth in contemporary India are largely directionless. Our experience of having observed them confirms that they cannot afford any other alternative job opportunity since they do not have any alternative job skills. Traditionally working in the fields, and not being adequately educated or trained in any other technical work, they have no other option as they have no other work.

It implies that Indian farming people are generally not programmed to deal with the severe issues of subsistence, other than their total dependence on farming and agricultural production. They were thus forced to take consumption loans both in cash and in kind from the big landowning class. The stipulated rates of interest on these loans were very high and, leave aside the loan, even full payment of interest was beyond the means of the semi-proletariat. The big land-owning class or usurers however do not insist on full payment even in the long run. It often forces the debtors to sell their assets (mostly land) but rarely for complete release from the debt obligation. It uses the debt obligation to force upon the direct producers in agriculture a system of unequal exchanges, thereby deriving enormous economic benefits in such forms as cheap and assured labour and better terms for leasing out land. The situation however remained perpetuated in the following decades too. The facts unfold that the farmers, rich or poor, owning 32 acres or 2 acres or owning a piece of land through rent/lease, if they conceive of their field as a site of produce, suffer contingent situations that grow increasingly difficult to deal with (1305–08).

Relying for subsistence on farming alone renders a farmer in a state of insecurity and indebtedness, endemically spurred by miscellaneous reasons: investment required for a successful crop, fatal illness of someone in the family, demanding adequate treatment in the city hospitals, educating children, wedding or some rituals and celebration, death of a near or dear one, or of cattle. Besides, there are issues such as unpredictable weather, erratic or unseasonal rainfall, hailstorm,[4] rising temperatures due to climate change, degradation of soil, wilting crop threatening to relentlessly deplete whatever could have been enough for subsistence. Smallholders and marginal farmers are the worst-hit.[5] Recurring crop failures lead to depression which remains undiagnosed, and it has driven many farmers to end their lives. One hears of the same ill-fated story from most of such suicide affected families. If the crops turn out bad, it only adds up to the mounting debt—everything gets stalled and sometimes descends the realization: life is not worth living.

Rising inflation and the rise in the means of survival make it necessary that other than peasantry they have some source of income. While most farmers killed themselves because of debt, it is however not recognized that farmers have been committing suicide since ages. And the number of suicides keeps on mounting. Our retrospection of the history of Indian peasantry lets us know that they do not only end their lives because of crop failure but also because they are at the mercy of unresponsive political and social arrangements that aggravate their crisis. The government's initiatives such as the Pradhan Mantri Fasal Bima Yojana (Prime Minister

Crops Insurance Plan),[6] to alleviate the losses of the farmers due to uncertainties of weather, are yet to show results due to poor implementation. Only lately since 2020 it has been showing some results. To receive the compensation, the stipulated criteria are to be met, which is very often found caught up in muddled up norms and directions pre-empting it from reaching the really aggrieved or deserving. We hear, in quite a few cases, that the frustration of long wait leads to suicide.

The stories[7]: Omprakash Krityansh's 'Pret Chhaya' (The Ghost Shadow), Kailash Vanavasi's 'Prakop' (Calamity), Ram Kumar Aatreya's 'Tractor and Suhaga' (Icing on the Tractor), and Punni Singh's 'Mukti' (Deliverance) in the collection, *Katha me Kisan* (Peasant in the Story), compel us to enter into the very relatable world of men and women and experience the entire spectrum of emotional vicissitudes—the hurt and despondency suffered in the peasant families, driving them to take extreme action. Each of these stories, with respect to their individual contexts, invokes not only the vivid scenario of farming lives—the cultural mores and aspirations and difficult struggles of these people—but also the manner in which they show immense resilience, restrain in dealing with disappointments, selfishness, and deceit in precarious societal and domestic circumstances.

Drought, Debt, Daughter: 'Pret Chhaya'

Rajdhani Mahato hopes that after being done with his daughter's wedding, he would be able to gain good produce from the fields. Continued drought,[8] however, failed him, so did the disease[9] of his wife. A glimpse of his earlier life reveals that his reckless father, Collector Mahato, had taken to opium addiction.[10] Rajdhani's toiling mother struggled with raising her children and the pressure of loan. After Collector got his daughters married off by selling seven acres of land, the usurer stopped giving him loans. Even during his critical illness, the doctors refused to touch him for fear of not receiving the fees. Sugya, his wife, could not bear the pressure anymore and died a year after. Young Rajdhani however got the support of his maternal family at this stage. The loss of Rajdhani's parents in his early adolescence laid the responsibility of raising his siblings. Paying the burden his father's debts was on Rajdhani's young shoulders. His schooling was given up but the younger sibling went on to pass the ITI and got employment in the Tata Steel Plant at the behest of Rajho Babu scion of an influential family in the village, who was then luckily the manager at Tata Plant in Jamshedpur. While all appeared modestly enough for the subsistence of the family, his wife, Devki's fatal illness and the onset of famine turned things upside down.

The narrative opens with Devki's moaning with acute pain in a state of delirium breaking the ominous silence in the house. The moment Rajdhani steps in, hears his daughter, Kabutari's anxious voice: At the door Kabutari was standing imploringly, eyes brimming with tears, 'Babujee, come hurrying, Mai must be shown to a doctor! In extreme pain Devki was muttering, 'I cant be saved now'[11] (174). Rajdhani feels guilty about not being able to move Devki to the city hospital for treatment as advised by the doctor.

The younger siblings arrive at the earnest call of Rajdhani. Kabutari obediently cooked delicacies her father could afford to feed lovingly his younger siblings. Their cold and aloof manners however were not softening in spite of the feast of fish and *litti chokha* (A rustic dish made of lentils and flour) served to them. It was difficult for Rajdhani to muster the courage to appeal to them for monetary help for the treatment of his wife. 'Today is the fourth day, ... whatever you have to say, say!' Chhotelal's voice sounded annoyed (175). The siblings' impatience hurts Rajdhani who desperately craved for some empathy. Feeling a little shy of begging for some financial help, he conveys the matter-of-fact conditions:

'Nothing worth relating; there is no promise in farming. The peasant in this country is to be pitied. Our elders in the past are proven wrong, who held that compared to farming on one's own land, all other vocations were like begging. Now the situation is contrary'. Spitting tobacco, he sat squatting. 'Drought has been persisting, peasants are dying. This time it seems that even animals won't survive. The scheme of loan sought from the bank also failed. The monster of debt and the mounting interest of loan forced several neighbouring farmers to sell off their substantive portions of land. One of them tried to commit suicide; several chose to join the scores of other rural migrants in the cities'. (175–76)

The siblings could perceive that Rajdhani's illustration of the peasant's misery is intended to seek sympathy, to procure urgent financial help for the treatment of his wife in the city. But, obviously, the burden of getting along with their own households in the city has hardened their hearts. So distanced are they that the gravely ill wife of the elder brother, who too contributed to their upbringing, is not of much concern to them. The family get together ending on a note of impatient, acerbic retorts trivialize the agony of Rajdhani, that unfold the changing equations in a village family. While leaving, the younger of the two relents a little.

Devki's condition worsens. She is conscious of the disappointment that secretly devoured everyone. Even in her despairing state, she tries to lift the spirit of Rajdhani and Kabutari: 'Kabutari's Babu! 'I have to welcome a son-in-law, I'll not die now. Trust my words, go and eat something and then do your work' (179–80). In the following five days, Rajdhani finds some hope in the news that the report of a central team of the government visiting the region recommended aid of 35 crores to the farmers. His hope is raised; besides the expectation that some help from Chhotey (the younger sibling) could arrive, also made him take a sigh of relief.

On reaching home, the moment he steps in, Devaki's dead body hanging by her saree's noose, and close by, the daughter Kabutari's lifeless body horrifies him. The elder sibling receives Rajdhani's call:

> 'Your sister-in-law is no more. She deceived me. She was lying when she said that she would die only after getting Kabutari married. Kabutari could not face her mother's dead face; with the noose of her mother's saree, hung herself. I regret that I had deposited some money in the post office for her wedding. I did not withdraw it even in dire need. If you people had given something, I could've made payment of the bank loan. Kabutari had some money and I was going to take her mother for treatment in Patna. The money for Kabutari's marriage is still in the deposit'. His voice was distraught, hoarse with sobbing: 'Now you people don't have to worry. I'll pay the bank loan with the money, I ought to have used to admit her to the city hospital'. (180–81)

Mostly the people from the farming community find themselves in a similar dilemma. The choice regarding where to invest the funds, turns out to be at cross purposes. Rajdhani is compromised by his financial entanglement. His wife and daughter sought death as solution. It is a serious blow to him. Suffering from a sense of guilt for not investing in his wife's treatment as a first priority, he cannot escape the feeling of having lost his foothold on life, doomed to the life in death—a ghostly life—haunted inexorably by a sense of irredeemable remorse. One can guess that the lingering effect of trauma in the aftermath would be equally wrenching.

Farming on Lease, Vagaries of Weather, and Predators of Drought: 'Prakop'

Agriculture in India is primarily rain fed and heavily relies on nature. Excessive monsoon or deficient rainfall, extremely hot and dry weather, droughts have direct effect on the performance of the crop. The outbreak of famine destroys the lives of farmers pushing them to take recourse to extreme steps like suicide.

The opening of Kailash Banvasi's story 'Prakop' Calamity) announces the news of Itwari's suicide. The news is shocking to the villagers.

> 'Nobody believes that a gentle, timid, forthright simpleton like Itwari could think of ending his life! How come that timid fellow dared to end his life; was he not scared! Lately, his faraway, distracted look hinted at something wrong. His body had shrunken like dead wood; must have been 45–50'. Kachru Mandal said in a gathering, spitting the gutka.[12] (261)

Itwari acquired four acres of land on lease[13] for a year, borrowing money from a local moneylender nurturing the dreams of sowing, planting, and harvesting, and looking forward to the yield. The outbreak of famine however devastated the peasantry's hopes and drove the villagers to take resort to folk customs of appeasing the rain gods.

> The wedding of a male and a female frog caught from the mossy water of the old well was performed to propitiate the wrath of Gods. 'May the God Indra be appeased.' Akhand Ramayan[14] was recited in the temple of Lord Shiva under the peepal[15] tree continuously for three days

without stopping even for a moment. May gods bring rains. Bring rains! Don't snatch the morsel from our mouth. (268)

In spite of the drought, like other fellow peasants, Itwari musters the courage to arrange for irrigating his field by the pumping set for which he pays Rs. 80 per hour. The sprouting paddy crop, watching it grow taller, exuding a familiar fragrance exults him. The doom however continues to chase him when his ready for harvest crop gets fatally pest infested. 'As if taken hostage by the brown insect from all sides. Multiple holes broke out on the wilted leaves. The shock penetrates into his chest; he shivers like a patient of epilepsy, crying inconsolably. It is back breaking.' (269) People were citing the report by Rural Agriculture Expansion Official that 'the entire region is in the grip of that pest. There is no definite control measure, since no known pesticide is of help; the pest multiplies fast' (270).

Inevitably farming is not only prone to the problems of no rain at all, or torrential rain or cyclone but also to fungus disease that destroy the crop. The narrative moves forward to describe how the widespread drought draws the attention of the state and the visit of a local member of the legislative assembly is hailed as a much-needed assurance; his concern and queries raise hopes of the villagers. However, we come to understand that 'The Relief fund is announced but remains promises on paper.[16] The moneylenders are closing in on the hapless farmers (271). Being illiterate, peasants are duped into paying exorbitant interests. Itwari is in for a massive jolt when Hira Seth lets him know that the loan amount noted in the ledger was Rs. 286: 'Itvari writhed helplessly. He felt like picking the 1kg weight lying near, and thrashing Hira Seth's smug face. In the coils of debt, his condition was like one caught up in the stranglehold of a python … A wrenching terror was gashing the veins of his head' (271). He had rented this land—four acres each at Rs. 700, on the condition that in the coming harvest, the debt would be paid but the debt went on increasing. For all this, he had pawned the jewellery of Janaki, his wife. Aaju, his son, who had recently passed class VIII, goes to the road building programme that started under the government scheme for famine relief. To deal with subsistence, Janaki too worked as a labourer in the company of her son. Some news of the government relief in terms of financial assistance is announced but it still seems far away.

Drowned in Suffering, None Could Understand

The pressure, growing immense, totally shattered Itwari. Barely two months passed since the news spread among the villagers that something seemed gravely wrong with him. The signs of mental derangement were noticeable. He was seen wandering aimlessly, frequently performing devotional rituals to propitiate Gods under a banyan tree and making small offerings to gods, goddess, the tree deities, and the snake deity—dreaming of the certainty of God's grace—some divine mercy. People in the village locality would ask for some Prasad and make fun of him: 'Which God have you contacted today, let us know …' (262). Nothing yielded any results. The anxiety of his family was difficult to contain. Watching him making either odd, rambling conversation or brooding would unnerve his young daughter Gita, and make her cry. He was even taken to an occult practitioner for treatment. None could imagine the magnitude of his suffering.

While returning, close to his home, Aaju sensed the presence of a gathering, muffled melancholic cries of his mother and 13-year-old sister at the door, some women whispering, and men talking about a body found somewhere.

The story points to the fact, very often overlooked, that anyone apparently incapable of committing suicide could be drowned in inconsolable suffering. Unaided loneliness, fear, and hopelessness can drive a simple person like Itwari to derangement and suicide.

Peasant's Death Is a Commodity: Police Extortion

What follows Itwari's suicide is, however, a telling illustration of how the village administration and the police deal with the event; they do not even hesitate to bargain over the dead. The police extort money from Aaju, Itwari's son in handing over the body to the deceased's family. The usual police inquiry takes place when a body is found. The rest of the narrative predictably reveals the brazen greed of the officials who are to be paid a bribe of Rs. 300. The Indian peasantry that supplies food for the entire nation is left without bare means of survival, and their lives are forced to become what Giorgio Agamben would call 'bare life' (Edkins, 74–75).

But that is not all—the corpse of the farmer who commits suicide is commodified by the indifferent state machinery in such absolute terms as to ensure the total desacralization of the agency of the self-killer.

Wrath of God and Ludicrous Relief: 'Tractor and Suhaga'

It is not just the banks but the agents of the big companies too, who target the relatively middle-level or well-off farmers and lure them into making an expensive purchase of an agricultural equipment, and the deal is at exorbitant rate of interest. Devinder Sharma (2018, 3) puts it:

> Farmer buy a tractor at an interest rate of 12%. Big entrepreneurs can buy a luxury car at an interest rate of 7%. For a farmer, a tractor is necessary to improve crop production, which directly contributes to an increase in his income. The role of mechanisation to improve farming has never been in question, but for the rich, luxury cars are more of a status symbol.

Hari Singh, the owner of three acres of land is known to the people from a Tractor Agency who visit the village one morning. Their clever talks and elaborate mathematical explanations make Hari Singh believe that the agency was giving away the tractor free of cost. It was at 199,999. He was asked to pay only Rs. 20,000 in advance and the rest along with easy interest was to be paid in six instalments, that is, Rs. 40,000 every six months. The only condition was that if the money of the interest was not paid in due instalment consecutively, for three times, Hari Singh would be obliged to give away his three acres of land. They however assure him soothingly that it is only a precautionary measure since there is no reason why the owner of a tractor could not pay the interest in due course. Hari Sigh was not unaware of the methods of extorting dues from a farmer. They had even barged into a farmer's cane fields accompanied by the police, where the latter was hiding from being caught. The sharp cane leaves lacerated his body, and mosquitos bite had swollen him. They had nonetheless used force and forcibly exacted the full price with interest on their terms. Even the government bank officials bring police for loan recovery. If the farmer is unable to pay, they never hesitate to auction his lands.

But the thought of owning a tractor could not dissuade him. After accepting the deal by paying the initial amount of 20,000 that he had saved for his daughter's wedding, he is tempted to procure a thrasher and a trolley at 70,000 by raising money through loan. He also buys pesticide for paddy farming. The tractor at his door is the owner's pride and the neighbours' envy. As if the tractor arrived with the promise of good fortune. It was expected that with his elevated status, his daughter would be wedded decently. The demand for the gift of a motorcycle and other items in marriage called for further borrowing. He and his wife sweated hard in the fields, applying all their might to ensure things go right.

> One evening, the dark clouds began enveloping the sky and in minutes the hailstorm began pouring, small and then bigger. Rain stopped and a sheet of snow was spread on the fields, as if the dead crops were covered with white cold coffin. Not a single plant of Basmati could remain erect. The paddy of thicker variety and inferior variety was already sold off in the market. For those who planted Basmati, it was famine—poured from the clouds. Watching his field Hari Singh fainted, the people around brought him home.[17] (49)

After several days he could rise from the bed. The hailstorm had totally damaged the paddy crops. They heard of the relief camp sponsored by the government.

> The government had sent its agents to peruse the condition of those who suffered loss due to the hailstorm. Hari Singh had hoped that the government would surely give the aid as promised to the peasants, hit by natural calamity. But 'some received 300, some a 100, Hari Singh received 153. He refused to take it. The state's blinkered sense of justice to the farmers was cited in the newspapers as some kind of outrageous joke'. (50)

The people from the agency arrived. He tried to convince them that he would surely make the payment, promising that once the wheat crop was ready, he would make payment with penalty. They were happier with the thought of money growing more in the process and agreed. The pressure to get his daughter married was mounting and by borrowing money, he raised more funds (which burdened him with more loan), and was able to host the *baraat*[18] and the daughter's wedding could be performed decently. The financial crunch now reached a level that forced both Hari Singh and his wife to work as labourers in the fields of neighbouring farmers. In the meanwhile, a new machine, Combine Harvester purchased from Punjab by the biggest landholder of the village resulted in rendering the labourers in general, deprived of employment in the fields, hopelessly jobless. It was hitting the belly of those who survived on earning wages through labouring. Hari Singh's tractor unfortunately developed some defect and could not work. The village mechanic could do nothing. It needed to be sent to the city for repair.

In the meanwhile, he heard from his daughter about the vicious brutalities she faced in the house of her in-laws, and very soon she returned for good. Hari Singh at this point comes to realize that he was cheated by the middlemen who settled this marriage with a depraved alcoholic.

The agency people began visiting for the due payment otherwise, as was the precondition, Hari Singh would have to surrender his field. He requested for more respite, which meant paying the penalty amount of Rs. 5000. They were no longer polite salesmen. It was now certain: the men from the agency would confiscate his field the next morning. He stayed in his field that night, reflecting:

> His wife must be worried; he's not been home the entire day and night! His sons may not, but the daughter must be waiting for him, hoping, her father would assuage her misery, sort out the terrible mess in her life. His land is to be seized. Profound sense of helplessness and regret for being responsible for the ruin of his family overwhelms him .... He feels ashamed, let down ... 'Now what's to be done! Where to Go!' In the early hour of morning, the loudspeaker was echoing from the village temple, 'Om jai Jagadish Hare'.... He stood upon the tractor and gathered the rope, tossed it into a noose, threw it across the Peepal branch and hanged himself. His body was swaying back and forth; the rising sun watched mutely. (54) It is a characteristic story of the farmer, post-liberalization. The aspirations that the television and the technology of mass culture promote—fueled Hari Singh's ambition and he dreamed

of making money to compete with those displaying high standards in farming. The title ironically suggests the illusion Hari Singh harboured and the grim consequences he faced. The purchase of the tractor and the dream that it would bring fortune to him was like 'Sone pe Suhaga', a maxim which means hoping for the shower of good luck. The vagaries of weather however play pranks with him. At his home front, fate too grows hostile when he is duped in the wedding of his daughter. Like all human beings, he made mistakes. A *post facto* analysis of what happens makes him realize that he could have saved the situation and done better. More significantly, however, the story could be read as a severe indictment of the persuasive tactics of marketing and profiteering of companies who deploy their agents to flatter and inveigle a middle-level farmer into a deal that he fails to handle.

'Mukti': The Promise of Quick Money

Punni Singh's 'Mukti' probes the issues involved in the ambitious projects of planning and experimenting with crops which promise quick money. In India, most youngsters refuse to take up farming and the few who are immensely aspirational want to make a difference. The narrative draws us into a scenario where the foreign companies lure Indian farmers. Their advertisements, marketing machinery guarantee rich produce and prosperity overnight. Taken in by the tempting prospects, a farmer risks heavy loan to invest in the crop. When ultimately no investment works as expected, the irreparable financial distress brings hopelessness. The frustration turns into loss of self-esteem, shame—deep depression takes over—and one is likely to harbour suicidal thoughts. It is not that only the aged, ill, or uneducated farmers end their lives. The state data[19] tell us that one in four farmers driven to suicide has been under thirty, indeed a grim statistic in a country where 65 percent of the population is under thirty-five.

Studies probing the issue of farmer's suicide attribute the causes to: (i) the shift from traditional farming to the farming of high yielding commercial crops without adequate technical support. The state's withdrawal from activating the agricultural extension services, in providing counselling on farm technologies, problems faced, immediate remedial steps and lack of timely advice to farmers; (ii) decline in public investment in agriculture in the last two decades; (iii) low rates of germination of seeds provided by large global firms, spurious seeds and pesticides by private agents; (iv) crop failure, pest attack, and drought; (v) debt at very high interest rate of 36 percent to 120 percent from private money lenders; (vi) cheap imports leading to decline in pricing and profits; (vii) lack of access to water for crops which forced the farmers to borrow money at exorbitant rates of interest to sink borewells, and that failed. (As mentioned in Mehta and Ghosh and in Sainath, 'Swelling Register of Deaths'.)[20]

Some of these findings lend us the clues to comprehend the contingencies an educated, ambitious farmer undergoes when he ventures into an innovative field of farming in 'Mukti'. Ravinder, a young man belongs to a well-to-do peasant family which owns substantial lands. Unlike many other farmers who are uneducated and who do not have other options of livelihood, Ravinder has a master's degree in Agriculture and could easily get a job but he decides to join farming of cash and exotic crops using his knowledge. His meeting with an agent of an American firm promises the fulfilment of his dream of making quick money. His enthusiasm about the huge profit it would yield does not let him listen to his wife Nalini's vehement resistance:

> There won't be much space left in our house to stack all the money we're going to make. You'll go crazy, counting!
>
> We have lost twenty acres of land! Now only half is left, that also will be sacrificed in the name of a new kind of farming....
>
> Oh no! Don't you worry! The manager of the company promised that only if I could arrange for one lakh twenty-five thousand, we could earn from our fields fifteen to twenty lakhs. White muesli[21] is in huge demand in the herb market, the price is also very high.[22] (31)

The offer of the multinational company of a whole package: seeds, manure, and pesticides to cultivate medicinal plants and even a promise to buy the produce at hefty price sounded reassuring. Their agents went around the villages carrying smart imported bags, armed with colourful charts and figures indicating huge profit by such plantations and were effectively persuasive; the data sheets of immense profit and gain were convincing.

The narrative unfolding the background of Ravinder's life lets us know that his family possessed forty-acre land deemed as an enviable expanse of farmland. His father's prolonged illness with cancer compelled the family to sell off household resources preserved for generations to raise money for medical expenses. They were unable to pay the loan borrowed from the bank for a tractor purchased by his father and lost ten acres of farmland. Clearly, the interest in progressive farming had further made the family finances precarious. Despite costly treatment Ravinder's father could not be saved. The enormous faith in his own abilities makes Ravinder seek the loan of 1 lakh. He meets Seth, a prosperous moneylender, an old acquaintance of his father, to borrow Rs. 1 lakh.

> Sensing the thrill infusing Ravinder's demeanor, Seth however tries to talk sense into him: 'Doing farming by taking the burden of loan is not sensible today ... The interest could be oppressive. I won't advice you to invest money in the raw vocation of farming'. Ravinder retorted with great self-confidence: 'Now a days it is no longer a vocation of risk. You'll see; the crop I'm going to plant will yield gold. All I seek from you is one lakh. In about ten months I'll pay back your loan with interest, whatever it be'. (34)

But Seth being a businessman, a usurer, was not assured and he sought from him something substantial as mortgage. Nothing less than a heavy ancestral jewellery—the waist band—could make Seth agree to give the sought-after loan to Ravinder. Seth knew that the several American Multinational Companies had aroused in educated young men like Ravinder the craving to become wealthy as quickly as possible.

Ravinder collects the seeds and other necessary things from the company people. As instructed, he sows muesli but when he reads the manual for cultivating the white muesli, he discovers that the crop plantation is already delayed by more than one and a half months. He visits the company to seek explanation for this mistake. The company representative, keen on ongoing business and profit, inveigles him into believing that in spite of the delay the seeds could still be planted and that the weather department has forecast the late arrival of monsoon. Plantation is done rather late. 'When the first watering began unluckily, Ravinder's tube well breaks down and the blazing heat scorches many saplings. When monsoon rains fall, numerous roots get rotted with the heavy outpour. Many more saplings die with the onset of sudden torrential downpour. Ravinder is desolate and the whole household goes in mourning' (Mukti, 38).

The harvest however awakens his hopes when he manages to dig out one trolley of roots. He takes it to the company office but seeing the quality of the produce, the company refuses to buy it. He feels cheated and let down. His pleading, begging, and reminding them of their promise fail to be of any consequence. He roams about in the market looking for vendors who specialized in herbs, but nobody agrees to buy the poor-quality roots. Finally, a vendor agrees to buy these but at a meagre sum of Rs. 5000. 'Listening to the vendor he lost all his senses. He felt like holding him by his throat and shaking him violently. But he wistfully smiled and took what was offered and gave the stuff' (Mukti 38). Holding the sacks of notes in his palm, he walks through the wide roads of the main market, and a miasma of images inundates his mind. He has the vision:

> 'Nalini laden with ornaments, his daughters chirping and playing like birds in the courtyard and his father wearing the 22 *tola* waistband....'... A feeling of hopelessness engulfs him. He stops by a shop where he used to buy sulfas[23] tablets to keep away pests in wheat grains. Buying some, he walks further. Avoiding the gaze of onlookers, he gulps down all the tablets. When swallowing becomes difficult, he goes near a tap and drinks some water. He falls down groaning; people passing by ignore him, assuming he was a young man returning from the liquor store. He wriggles, mutters and gets up, staggers back towards his house with dwindling steps and collapses. (39)

The stories reveal that the investment made in sowing, planting, and readying the fields for the produce could be a highly uncertain endeavour and turns out to be much more than what it ultimately yields. Even then a farmer is unable to quit farming. Relying on it however does not enable him to fill his stomach; carrying the burden of the family is indeed insurmountably difficult. He sees no other option; standing in the dark, groping for a safe pathway, he finds no helping hand extended to him. And eventually he has to quit: reluctant to block anybody else's path, he departs from this world silently. One finds many more peasants standing in the death row. They all have their ways and means of dying. Another kind of response to the disappointment and hopelessness is to run away from farming but not from life. Now what is worth noticing is that in the present days, the peasant has to wrestle with not only the vagaries of weather but also the mind-boggling world of multinationals with packaged lies and tall tales of profit. In spite of being so educated, Ravinder is gullible; he finds himself at the site of bargaining that brings him on the brink of inconsolable loss, shame, and breakdown. He is finally completely overtaken by the death drive—the demoralizing impact of trauma. In diverse settings, Rajdhani, Itwari, Harisingh, and Ravinder are driven to stress and humiliating shame, traumatized[24] self-berating, locked in a sense of guilt, haunted by an ignominious past, and face a future of impasse. No matter what, alone and despairing, they cannot shake their demons. Itwari, Harisingh, and Ravinder embrace death. For Rajdhani, however, it is life in death. The idiom of La Capra (2001, 712–13) uncannily corresponds with their 'condition of incomprehensible pain, experienced as if it were actually being inflicted for the first time'. It is so consuming that the possibility of gaining some time to distance oneself and let the healing process begin remains pre-empted. Their crisis holds up a mirror to our own ugly middle-class, urban indifference towards the peasantry and rural life in general. We come to understand that this crisis cries out to be acknowledged as a crisis. Their deaths, narrativized in such specimens of vernacular fiction, teach us that peasant lives matter, that belittling or ignoring the rural population of India, which has become the casual cultural idiom of our urban everydayness, has something criminal about it. Their deaths need to be read symbolically, as a cultural semiotics of excluded *bios* (a la Agamben [Durantaye 205]), as a history of the deaths of those who sustained our lives by producing food, the basic source of our survival. The mainstream urban morality of India, which sustains itself on the diet of news items of film stars and other kinds of celebrities, finds it convenient to exclude the unglamorous stories of peasantry beyond the contours of its conscience. Our urbanity conjures up a bauble-world which creates the illusion of non-existence of rural scenarios except as sites of romantic excursion. That we do not think of the corpses of the farmers while enjoying our everyday platters of food indicates that we have become too insensitive to understand how unethical it is to refuse to be haunted by the spectres of those whose labour got translated into our subsistence.

These stories and many more not discussed here that depict the humiliation of our farmer in the existing conditions, let several facts descend upon our consciousness. It could be noted that while previously, the political, economic, and cultural crisis created by the imperialist powers were exclusively troubling the interest of the elite and privileged class, the distant villages, rustic-rural zones sustained their separate autonomy and structural entity and would get away from being beset by any major international/global change. Now since the much-applauded globalization has spread its tentacles overwhelmingly to influence and determine India's agricultural sector, rural world is rendered in a state of confusion. Previously, except for the vagaries of weather, a peasant remained unruffled by the outside forces unexpectedly taking control, grabbing him to direct and decide the course of his existence. Today, a common peasant is the target of the powers sitting thousands of miles away. Before the policymakers in our country could figure out the implications, the petty peasant's life is sacrificed by this onslaught. It has hurt the age-old values of our culture; the dignity of kinship is destroyed; petty slit throat competition is promoted. The family structure however strong and secure it seemed fails to defend itself. Along with economic hiatus, the emotional hiatus has doubly increased. In the game of achieving the goals set by the idea of globalization, the speech, thoughts, language, dress, eating habits would be influenced and dictated, so that the leaders of globalization could remain ever invincible. The prose in all the stories shows mastery at the kind of direct unadorned narratives that bring the events alive in all their visceral power.

Notes

1. The lines are from Dushyanta Kumar, a Hindi and Urdu poet who died young. He is remembered for several of his poignant and deeply reflective melancholic poems. The opening lines in the chapter, translated by me are from the second stanza of the poem, 'Kahan to taye tha charanga ek ghar ke Liye'.
2. Sanjeev's novel, *Phans* (Noose) provides an astute study of the repercussions of farmers' suicide, underlining its exacerbated state in the wake of globalization. Suman Sahai (2020) probes the increasing sense of insecurity pervading the farming sector and attributes it to the role of World Trade Organization (WTO). She holds it a suspect for the mayhems occurring; the consequence of which is

the race for promoting high-cost farming and corporate monopolization of the sector to ensure the interest of agree business multinationals at the expense of small and marginal farmers. Multinational companies have given a jolt to the marginal farmer. Farmers are growing bankrupt because of the production expenditure, costly seeds on one hand, reduced price of goods on the other. Agri contracts are hitting him.
3. Prasad, H. Pradhan's studies (1305–08) of the cultural mores existing in the agricultural sectors provide an analysis of the escalating crisis in agriculture which has close correspondence with my fieldwork as well.
4. The news report (4 November 2019) that a 58-year-old woman farmer in a village under Modasa region of Aravalli, rural Gujrat, committed suicide after her farm suffered crop failure due to unseasonal rainfall in Gujarat is one of many such events reported or unreported across India.
5. With reference to the NCRB report, Sayantan Bera (*Mint*) refers to agricultural crisis affecting farmers and labourers. 2014, the year when more suicides occurred. He observes that the crisis peaks when there is poor monsoon, loss of crops such as rice, wheat, and cotton and slower growth in rural wages. In these conditions, the small- or medium-sized fields taken on lease or rent cause severe disappointment to the farmers. He adds that the government's Employment Guarantee Scheme also fails to provide any relief to many for varied reasons. One surmises however that the farmers end their lives not only because of crop failure but also because they are at the mercy of unresponsive political and social arrangements that let them down in times of acute crisis.
6. The Prime Minister Crops Insurance Plan has only lately since 2020 shown some results. The individuals/officials at the district level and the local village level until recent years were seen as failing in making fair judgement of identifying the needy. The *scheme* also covers pre-sowing losses and post-harvest losses due to cyclonic rains and losses due to unseasonal rainfall in India. One gets to know that in the regions beset by flood or famine the promises of relief remained on paper for a long time; by the time the relief reached the farmer, it was generally too late. Besides, delayed or wrong assessment of loss and settlement of claims by insurers have also led the farmers to lose faith in such schemes.
7. Omprakash Kratyansh (1959-) hails from a rural region of Bihar. His 'Pretchchaya' (171–82), and more than hundred stories, illuminate the emotional turmoil in the lives of peasants. He was given the National Sahitya Academy Award from Ujjain. He also edited a magazine, '*Avantar*.' Kailash Vanavasi (1965-), the narrator of 'Prakop' (259–74), has written many short stories which appeared in several collections. He is the recipient of Yuva Lekhan Puraskar in 1987, Shyam Vyas Puraskar in 1997 and in 2010, he was awarded Premchand Smriti Katha Award for the collection, *Peele Kagaz ki Ujali Ibadat*. Ramkumar Atreya (1944) is the writer of 'Tractor aur Suhaga' (41–54). He hails from the village Karoda in Haryana. He is the recipient of Haryana Sahitya Akademi Award and Balmukund Sahitya Award. His short stories have appeared in Magazines

and anthologies. Punni Singh (1939–) belongs to the village Milavali in UP. He served as a professor in Madhya Pradesh, higher education. His 'Mukti' (29–40) is anthologized in several collections. His novel, *Mandali*, and many short stories deal with the intricacies of farming life. He received Madhya Pradesh Sahitya Akademi Award, National Muktibodh Award, and Bhavabhuti Award from the government of Madhya Pradesh. All excerpts are translated by Vanashree. All these stories are in the collection, *Katha Me Kisan*-II; the introduction of these writers is drawn from the same anthology.

8. Drought plays havoc in the farming community. Small peasants and median farmers generally do not own personal irrigation facility and depend on the rains for irrigation. Rahul Tongia's 'India's Biggest Challenge: The Future of Farming' exhorts the government of India to find means and ways of increasing the income of farmers. Less than 10 percent own any irrigational equipment. A very small faction avails themselves of the canal-based irrigation. Almost 30 percent depend on rains. Many who afford irrigation facility sell water to their neighbours. He reveals that 5 percent of rural homes have no land and they work as labourers; they are not beneficiaries of free electricity.

9. The rural health system is seldom accountable. The determinant of health is social and economic rather than purely medical. Malnutrition and lack of awareness cause several life-threatening diseases among the rural population. The deaths remain unreported and the diseased go to the city hospitals only when they are about to collapse. Many villagers die at home. Illness and its treatment generally wipe out all savings and are common reason for indebtedness. Farmers have to spend a chunk of their earning on health issues including cancer which is common in some parts of India and it has been found that in several regions the groundwater is highly contaminated. The availability of healthcare facility has revealed an appalling scenario. This needs urgent attention. While the government health facilities generally languish in the rural India, availing services of the private medical service is totally beyond the reach of the rural poor. And even those middle poor or middle-level peasantry has to deal with medical issues like cancer by selling their lands or other family assets. Facing serious illness is an ordeal for the farming community. Many lives are terminated, without availing formal treatment. Medical issues happen to be one of the causes of taking loan again and again. And thus, getting pushed into debt/death trap. The high expense of medical treatment of availing family member could be traced as the biggest factor driving people to poverty.

10. Arrack and opium are the commonest addiction the villagers take to. It could be their way of coping with frustration, hard labour, deprivation.

11. The subsequent references are to the story, 'Pret Chchaya'.

12. Subsequent excerpts are from the story, 'Prakop'.

13. *The Hindu*, 15 June, 2018, reports that most farmers who ended their lives were cultivating on tenancy. While at the behest of the state, the landowners were directed to pass on the benefit of the Ritu Bandhu scheme to the lessees, at the ground level the landowners increased the lease rates.

14. Performing ceaseless recitation of the *Ramayana* is a popular religious practice in India. The story of kindness and love of God is sung by a group of singers.
15. Peepal (Ficus Religiosa), considered a sacred tree in which Gods reside, is also considered a place for some kind of occult worship.
16. In spite of the propagated announcements, the state's methods of implementing relief have disappointment to the peasants. In the bureaucratic process, it is either granted too late, or ridiculously too little in comparison to the loss incurred. It is but a given fact that the local and state bureaucracy demand their share. The scheme becomes an exercise in profiteering.
17. The references are drawn from 'Tractor aur Suhaga'.
18. In the Hindu weddings, a large crowd of relatives and the community accompanies the groom as guests. It is the obligation of the bride's father to extend decent hosting and feasting to them; it turns out an expensive affair.
19. See https://www.livemint.com/Opinion/zR8V3yKF7wENz14OYBdpMN/Understanding-farmer-suicides.html.
20. I have given a gist of the findings of Mehta and Ghosh in *Globalisation, Loss of Livelihoods and Entry into Poverty*, and also drawn on P. Sainath in 'Swelling Register of Death'.
21. Safed muesli is a tuber said to possess aphrodisiac qualities. It is also known for several other medicinal properties. Its cultivation was done at an investment of Rs. 3 lakh per acre. Another Rs. 1 lakh was to be spent on other agricultural operations in the field (the actual field expenses were much more than this according to the growers). Through its local franchisee Herbs India, the company took up the cultivation of *safed* (white) muesli in 100 acres in the state. For this, a tripartite agreement was entered between the company, the franchisee, and the farmers. However, at the end of the crop cycle, when the crops matured, the farmers and the local franchisee discovered that the company had no intention of procuring the produce. Says Vinay James Kynadi, CEO, Herbz India. After having invested Rs. 3–4 crores, the farmers in the state were left in the lurch as the company said they would buy only dry muesli. See 'Safed muesli farmers cry foul as company breaks promise' (1 October 2005). economictimes.indiatimes.com/articleshow/1248766.cms?from=mdr&utm_source=contentofinterest&utm_medium=text&utm_campaign=cppst? (Accessed 16 November 2020).
22. The excerpts are from 'Mukti'.
23. M. Cardona, R. Joshi, et al. write in *Injury Prevention* (235) that it is not surprising that the ingestion of pesticides and insecticides for self-poisoning is often the most common suicide method. This population is largely rural, with agriculture as the main occupation. Therefore, there is easy access to agricultural chemicals, and these are a readily available method of suicide.
24. The characters in the three narratives reveal distinct traits of traumatized selves as La Capra perceives.

9
Despoiled Environment: In the Politics of Integrated Development, Money Grows on Trees

> The same silence falls. The trees, their stemmed, bruised branches, as if so many shriveled fingers, seem to point at us accusingly. Thousands of acres of prime teak and other rich produce were destroyed here forever.
>
> —P. Sainath[1]

Shrilal Shukla's (2020) 'Umraonagar me Kuchch Din'[2] (Several Days in Umraonagar), first published in 1986, also appeared in the collection, *Jahalat ke Pachchas Saal* (Fifty Years of Stupidity). It explores with shrewd insight, the historical and structural conditions of a rural township, Umraonagar in the democratic state of India and draws the chaos of plans and programmes of development which instead of serving the purpose of uplifting the conditions of the village society, opened a free space for plunder that made many lower middle poor rich and the middle class amass a lot of wealth. While it was not uncommon to see that development projects were traditionally hijacked and manipulated by local landed gentry possessed with clout but here the new set of hijackers emerge from the section of a middle-poor and middle-middle class who have garnered political and economic influence without any accountability. Ironically, the resources the new biggies in charge applied to raise the village to the level of an urban township reduced it to emerge as neither rural nor urban.

The narrator, a keen researcher in the rural economy and an independent journalist, undertakes a journey to Umraonagar, a village

Rural India and Peasantry in Hindi Stories. Vanashree, Oxford University Press. © Vanashree 2023.
DOI: 10.1093/oso/9780192871572.003.0010

known for its fast pace of development. The meandering narrative of 'Umraonagar me Kuchch Din' traverses through various histories in vignettes, that in interconnected digressions, acquaint the reader with a rich conglomeration of people in a complex village society. The reader, drawn into the cultural and political configurations developing in the 1960s–1980s in UP, India, makes sense of the undercurrents prodding rural–urban politics in the service of augmenting the mercenary designs of men from different spheres of society. In the tone of casual mockery, but subtle pathos, the story subtly ferrets out the fault lines in the claims of development in every sphere.

In the pattern of a documentary, the story navigates the readers to every facet of the village Umraonagar; its principal focus however enlarges upon the grim aspects of the speedier destruction of the environment in those several decades. One gathers how the plans initiated by the Ministries, experts, and the outsourced think tanks contributed to the process of deforestation. Being in the administrative service, posted in remote towns, in the vicinity of suburban forest villages, enabled Shukla to understand the insidious goings-on of mammoth-scale operations in logging which he knew occurred as a major fallout of ill-conceived plans.[3] It created vast spaces of wasteland and concurrently involved embezzlement and smuggling, but were ironically foregrounded as the major contributor to the development. Much before P. Sainath pointed[4] his finger at the game of plunder played in the name of development, with astute insight, Shukla registers its mechanics. Umraonagar, known for adjoining a dense forest from all sides, is talked about for its implementation of government-sanctioned planning towards an ideal Indian village. The kaleidoscope of the village, Umraonagar, exhibits how urgently the Indian village was ushering into a different level of advancement that we conveniently describe as rural–urban.

Nepotism, Bribery, Complicity in Corruption, Cut/Commission

Visiting places and people of the village exposes avenues of loot, nepotism, bribery, complicity in corruption, the narrator to the varied and exploitation of women under the precincts of an Ashram. The story opens with the narrator's account of a journey in a private bus, stuffed with passengers in the company of goats and hens.

> In the lap of my seatmate, there was a chicken. The goats were in the back. Back there if a baby goat happened to be on someone's lap, or if a goat was resting on someone's knee, there were also people resting their feet underneath a goat's belly or on top of a goat's back, as they leaned against the back of the bus. In that mess, it was difficult to say where any one person's head was: it was heads upon heads upon heads. (Shukla)[5]

The scene of alighting from the bus becomes chaotic:

> But my chicken friendly seat mate was more energetic than me. Like Abhimanyu, he broke through the throng of passengers, and I grabbed on to his kurta's hem. We arrived where in theory the door should have been and, without being able to confirm this fact we jumped down, landing face first on the ground. The brief case that had been dangling from my hand must have got caught on someone's leg because the traveller behind me pushed from the bus with a stout thrust had one leg in the air. (Shukla)

The experience reveals the state of private buses running up and down in the rural regions. The later snatches of conversations, let us know that to acquire maximum profit, the wealthy private bus owners had used their influence to clamp down the state-run buses and the daytime railway service. Their private buses would ruthlessly stuff as many passengers as they could. In the scenario, the reader is made conscious of the languor characterizing the larger populace of the rural region, sickly, living in filth and squalor, unconcerned with their servile, sloven misery, accepting their status as sheep and goats, habitually regulated by a few principal players.

Alongside the street, where the bus stops, there was a pharmacy, bearing the name of Dr Ansari. The signboard announced the doctor's degrees such as AAUP, PMP, and MD. The narrator is impressed that a highly qualified doctor was serving a village. In the company of his friend, a teacher in the locality, the narrator meets the BDO (Block Development Officer) who lets the curious narrator know the history of Umraonagar's inhabitants, and their antecedents in the order of timeline. It is disclosed that AAUP meant 'Allopathic, Ayurvedic, Unani physician' and MD meant what was in parenthesis in Urdu, 'Managing Director, Ansari Clinic' (Shukla). Clearly, it was a trick to cheat the credulous patients since the prevailing sway of ignorance and stupidity allowed the fraudulent medical practices to make money. The BDO explained further that

> a dispensary faced the pharmacy of Dr Amjad Ansari. In the pharmacy there was a yawning octogenarian, foul odour and a thousand flies. The pharmacy stole the drugs from the dispensary to sell for itself. It was the compounder's nephew's store. The medical practice was supported by the store, and his store was supported by the government dispensary. Dr Ansari and the government doctor had no dispute. Actually, thanks to Dr Ansari, the government doctor was able to run the clinic while living in the city. The first of every month, he showed up right on time to collect his salary, a fourth of the cut from the compounder's private practice, and half of the proceeds that Dr Ansari earned from selling the government drugs. Then he scurried back to the city. (Shukla)

Sainath's (1996, 21–45) extensive surveys of village health services confirm that the villages death toll grows more rapidly because of the absence of a permanent doctor. In the case of an epidemic, a temporary appointee doctor visits but leaves soon. There are no longer *jholachchap* (quacks) medicine men, but the recent one appear in an outfit which gives them a convincing modern-day aura. It has been observed that several village hospitals house cattles and are also used as venue for *baratis* in the wedding season.

The Rise of Swami/Guru

The narrator is distracted by the amplified sounds of *bhajans* coming from the Ashrama, run by a Godman, Swami Raghubardas, who declared himself, *Bhagwan*. The BDO proceeds to tell the journalist the stories pertaining to Siyadulari, one of the shishyas (disciple) of the Swami. She heads the Bhajan *Mandali* at the Ashrama. She is an illegitimate offspring of a revenue collector in the designated area and his alleged romantic relation with a widowed daughter of a *mallah* (fishermen). The presence of the community of fishermen (*mallah*) at the river bank, who dealt with fish as well as illegal country liquor (*tharra*),[6] brings into play the background of the story further. 'Underneath a red velvet canopy decorated with strings of sparkling silver stars, the Raghuvanshi court announced its glory while Raghubardas and Siyadurali sat together on the throne. Lord Ram (Raghubardas) had noticed her when the Ziledar Sahib had sent her to study in his high school. Siyadurali sat as motionless as a statue, and her big, intoxicating eyes that moved were the only things on her dark and attractive face' (Shukla). Siyadulari being poor could not grant herself the freedom to escape from a compromised relationship with Raghubardas. His antecedents as a former schoolmaster who was absconding due to being chased by a girl's family for trying to molest her and some anecdotes of his former misconduct make his posture of an ascetic life dubious. After having returned from Himalaya, however, he declared himself a true Godman and was able to cultivate a *Kirtan Bhajan* gathering of rural devotees in his Ashrama. The devotees routinely thronging the adjacent temple with offerings contributed to the material well-being of Raghubardas. It was a period when the rise and celebration of Gurus[7] had already begun to take root in the free India. 'Bhagvan Rajneesh, Maharishi Yogi, Swami Sadachari, Asaram Bapu', these and other men, the narrator describes, are 'the fruits of a scientific and technological age. Swami Raghubardasji is another link in this chain. The rumbling of his jet has not yet been heard on the international stage, but from the speed at which he rose into the sky of Umraonagar, it seemed as though he had been transformed from a man into a god and from a god into a jet plane' (Shukla). The satiric innuendoes amply hint at the acquisitive goals involving the activities of Gurus and Swamis. In Shukla's vision, their ever-growing influence is responsible for injecting lethargy into the masses blinding them to their own as well as their society's well-being.

Village, a True Model of Communal Amity or Business Interest!

In the vicinity of the temple, the presence of a masjid made the narrator wonder whether the appearance of amity between the two traditionally rioting communities, Hindus and Muslims, was actually maintained by Thakur Sahib and Iqbal Miya, the successful mercenaries, respective patrons of mandir and masjid. As part of the custom of Umraonagar, in the evening right after the *azan* ended, the bhajans and the kirtans would start up. Calling this communal harmony and unity in diversity, 'the politicians pushed forward the example of the village. The ironic narrator puts it: 'The situation was predictable, communal violence could break out at any moment. But it hadn't. Why? Each side was still busy counting its own money, and it was their good luck that they hadn't yet achieved the status of being able to waste it' (Shukla).

Each side—Thakur Sahib's and Iqbal Miya's—is deep in the business of contract logging and auctioneering with the mutual cooperation of government agencies and the blessings of the local legislature. The latter has now raised his rates of bribe after being appointed a minister. He has initiated some bogus programmes with some fanfare which have flopped, for example, establishing a sugarcane mill or a fishery department. All in all, a glimpse of Umraonagar figures in the following, similar to a period film:

> noises behind him acted as the soundtrack. Below on the street, there was the hueing and hawing of donkeys wandering around grazing, the cacophony of trucks blaring their horns, the sound of flour hand mills whirring around, the sound of transistor radios from several stores, and from another store, amplified to top volume, a folk tune that was almost obscene. A little while before this aural background was audible, the call to prayer had drowned everything out with its echo-heavy loudspeaker, but the azan's glory lasts only several minutes. Then the devotionals from Swami Raghubardas's ashram swamped out all other sounds. (Shukla)

Discourse of Progress Overawe the Common People

Proudly of being possessed with a storehouse of knowledge, BDO found in the narrator journalist a good audience. He yielded information not only about tantric practices, astrology, archaeology, meteorology, sociology, novels, and poetry but also 'the local development projects in the forest region affecting the thirty or thirty-five villages where he had family members—schemes bearing the titles of "self-generating," "self-propagating," "infrastructure," "orchestration," and "take-off stage" in the language of the "Planning Commission" in one breath' (Shukla). All this is another illustration of the governmentality[8] intended to confuse people with jargons and gossips. The BDO's pride now rests on being in charge of the computer training Program. 'The fondness of the trainer-officials from the city for cashew and pastries, for which their junior employee is sent to the city 150 kilometres away', (Shukla) says a lot more about the waste incurred in these programmes.

Appropriation of Land, Deforestation

It is believed that the way a civilization uses its land indicates its future. The conversations with the people around let the narrator infer how nepotism helped the new versions of imperialism to thrive. The small princely state, Umraonagar was a forest village. After the demise of Raja Umrao Singh, his successors, educated and aspirational, settled down in the metropolitan cities or joined high places; one of them was an ambassador to a country. The huge mansion with many chambers was now emptied since long. The new land sharks in the form of on-sight managers, 'started racking their brains about how to sell off Umraonagar's fields, forests, and state property. Everything was for sale. But there was no buyer' (Shukla). Hence followed litigations. Several people claimed their ownership of some land or the field.

> One of the minor retinues and a distant relation of the Raja however appeared on the scene, lent five segments from the mansion on rent to house the cooperative federation which soon displayed the signs of progress: Fair price shops, ration, clothes kerosene and cement expanded the development further. (Shukla)

This move forward paralleled a series of uninterrupted cases of corruption. In the programme, a chairman of the district cooperative federation misused his position, made fast bucks, and also built a mansion. He gave up the post after corruption charges were levelled against him. But he retained the house. Subsequently after him, five more chairpersons joined, made money, built houses, were saddled with corruption charges, and transferred. The first rented the ground floor of his house to a government hospital on lease. The second too built a house for himself and squeezed as much rent from it as he could; he would claim that that the house had been built from his own sweat and blood, though he had actually spent not a single penny in its construction. His nephew was a ranger in the Forestry Department. Through covert sources and influence, he made it happen: In only a few weeks, a branch office of the state Forestry Department opened up in the house. Not only that but also the backyard was rented out to become a state-level public park where in no time at all, forest timbre from the Forestry Department's branch office was used to put up a huge depot. The third gave the mansion to the computer training of the development officials of the village; the fourth one rented his house to the office of fishery development, since the elected member to the legislative assembly decided to promote fishery in the region and upon the door was adorned the nameplate: Fishery Department. 'When some villagers filled in a puddle or a pond and started planting grain on the new land, then the "pissing" officers came, dug up the fields, and started a fish husbandry scheme there' (Shukla). One finds the random ways the projects of development were planned; most flopped, but the whereabouts of the funds received for the same was nobody's business.

The fifth one (the director) arrived in a broken-down truck, on the back of it was marked, 'Buri Nazar vale Tera Muh Kala' (May, Those of Evil Eye, Be Struck by Misfortune). Its owner brought a bunch of things from the city and set up a shop right there. 'I'm staying right here for good. I'm going to get creative' (Shukla). And that is where Ramesar Bhai has stayed since when the scheme of logging of forests began gaining momentum. The narrator infers from the BDO's talk that the dense forests were secretly coveted by the sharper and more intelligent of these creative directors. Very soon Ramesar Bhai now known as Thakur Sahib and Iqbal Miya, a contractor, became the champions of development.

Trees Are Withered Skeletons: When Corruption Infects the Sovereign Segment of a Society, Every Individual Becomes a Predator

Thakur Sahib dedicated his broken-down truck to these trees. The narrator gets to know that every night, one tree or another was cut down, and the timbre was sent off to the city while its leaves, twigs, branches, and extras went on to some nearby village. This work went along without a hitch for several months because the road's junior engineer then was one of Thakur Sahib's old classmates. But Thakur Sahib didn't do this business for long. After having sold the old truck, Thakur Sahib purchased three new trucks. He would get the logging done of the roadside sarkari (government-owned) trees to be dispatched to the city. 'But that was done with a proper licence that meant the trees along the road belonged to the government. And so, through a method of cutting them up "without cutting them down," they were turned into stump' (Shukla).

The strategy was to show that it was like the method of taxing without an actual tax. The BDO's narrative was uninterrupted, but the narrator's attention is drawn to a scene just some distance away.

> a dried-out but thick branch rose from a mango tree stump, stretching toward the heavens as though in supplication. Nearby, there was a house. It was Umraonagar's first proper house. Based upon the mango tree stump, you can guess—and would correctly guess—that this was once a mango orchard. The trees back from the road were the first to get cut for the townspeople's stoves and fires. The trees along the road belonged to the government. And so, *through a method of cutting them up without cutting them down*, they were turned into stumps. (Shukla)

The felling increased with more speed. The description reminds one of dismembering a live creature. The images, darkly mysterious and foreboding, disturb the conscience of the beholder.

> All the branches were cut off the trees, and only the freshest shoots were left. Then the trunk was attacked. First, the bark was stripped. Then the trunk was cut into to extract bits of wood. And this went on. Afterwards, all that was left was a misshapen trunk and one branch

like an arm reaching up to the heavens. In the end—meaning, the tree's end—it was a withered skeleton, and its leaves disappeared. The tree's shape was ruined without the use of power tools, and, all in all, it looked like the oval of India on the map. In this way, the tree was all cut up, without being cut down, and the number painted onto the tree in tar by the government would stay there forever! These skeletons lined the road for quite a way into the distance. As for the trees of the mango orchard that lay behind these skeletons, there was no need for such decorum. That was because they had already been laid to waste. That's where the house now used for the government dispensary was built. (Shukla)

One understands that it was but natural that 'the villagers took the government's lead. The trees back from the road were the first to get cut for the townspeople's stoves and fires' (Shukla). The village householder would cut some wood from the tree along the road. True, when corruption infects the sovereign segment of a society, every individual becomes a predator. The local tribes for the dearth of resources pilfer whatever is left of the roadside trees.

The Destiny of an Ancient Forest: Instead of the Trees, Trucks Line Up: Logging, Stealing, and Auctioning

There is however an underhand method that guarantees great success. The mutual compatibility between Iqbal Miya and Thakur Sahib made them respect each other's territories. Poaching from the forest part was the monopoly of Iqbal and cutting from the roadside was 'the jurisdictionally acquired prerogative of Thakur Sahib' (Shukla). His clout could put a permanent halt to the government-run transport; only his private buses moved on the roads. In recent days, he constructed some good shops in the building. His counterpart, Iqbal Miya, was seen respectfully as a type of specialist in village economics. None could touch his knowledge about the cutting down of forest timbre and its uses, the protection of the environment, and forestry. Iqbal Miya began auctioning timbre at the forest depot by offering gratification to the forest officials under the label: Messer's Iqbal and Bros, government contractor and timbre merchant using his clout, as he had become the local President of the ruling party. In the same series of progress, sawmills were established for logging forest timbre and a house was built close to it in the compound of sawmill. With the installation of electricity, workshops and small factories too opened to carry them to the city for auction, big, transport multiplied, trucks were lined up, and their numbers increased as more development was showing. At the factory, timbre was transformed into planks, platforms, doors, windows, and so on. In other words, his skill in logging, stealing, and auctioning illegally but making these exercises legal has been noteworthy. He is a model of acute business acumen and expertise in the art and craft of contributing to the development by expanding the business of chopping and selling rosewood and timbre.

Corruption and the Politics and Economics of Development

On the occasion of a lavish feasting and drinking programme to celebrate the completion of the village computer training programme, the Finance Minister, praises the transformation of Umraonagar, wants the journalist-narrator to publish its achievements: 'Just think, how much constructions took place in the city with the rosewood lumber shipped there; just think how many new neighbourhoods and houses were built—this could be written about as well' (Shukla). The narrator's reply however opens Pandora's box. He says that the government's war on the players who indulge in the double economy, black money, tax evasion, embezzlement, fraud, and so on, sounds noble. But the fact is that the government is hand in hand in all these nefarious dealings. Corruption made development possible:

> Yet if stealing and skimming did not take place in public works projects, then I'm convinced that despite a handful of government agencies having opened branches here, it would still be a thatched-roof village, and the healthy middle class today would be living under the poverty line. These houses, these factories, these busy stores. (Shukla)

The narrator's acerbic analysis of rural development however unpleasant drives home the crux of the economics of Umraonagar's development.

The 'Finished' Job of Transporting the Stolen Goods

The dexterity with which the finished product of the stolen wood is loaded onto Thakur Sahib's truck was worth watching:

> Just like it is impossible to recognize how there's old horse fodder inside ground coriander, so too it was impossible to know which wood was stolen and which was bought at government auction. You could stop and inspect timber before it was loaded onto a truck, but after the product was made it was impossible to know what was what. (Shukla)

The curious narrator could make out that Thakur Sahib and Iqbal were experts in poaching timbre with the connivance of forest officials and patronage of the stakeholders. In the context, connections mattered, distance or close. The Engineer turned out to be a friend of Thakur Sahib's brother-in-law. Since, the road's junior engineer was then one of Thakur Sahib's old classmates, the work continued without obstruction. The timbre laid upon the truck, lined by the sides of the road, testifies to the mafia functioning as an organization. As a reader one understands however that the narrator refrains from using the term mafia.

The Sinister Sound and Sights of Logging

The narrative voice noticeably changes from being all along sarcastic to reflective, melancholic, acutely conscious of the sound and sights of relentless logging in this forest village. The frantic indulgence in eco-sadism rakes one's consciousness; the yearning to lose oneself in the expanse of deep dense forest is lost forever.

> The road went in one direction to the city and in the other direction, passed through the forest. An old folk story reverentially treats it as

an ancient forest, almost belonging to the hoary past of Treta Yuga[9] (epoch), when Lord Rama in the company of Janaki and his brother Lakshman walked into the untrammelled wood. Imagine! how ancient must have been the woods on either side of the road. The hardened wood almost took the weight, shape and texture of Ashta Dhatu (amalgamation of eight heavy metals, generally used in Hindu religious tradition to carve statues). They were laid on the truck now. Machines would skilfully cut some tree, routinely. Every night one tree or another was being cut down, and the timber was being sent off to the city while its leaves, twigs, branches, body—leaves, twigs, logs, branches, barks, intestine were carried to the other villages or for local consumption or the city. This work went on without a hitch for several months because the road's junior engineer was one of Thakur Sahib's old classmates. (Shukla)

The illustration tellingly reminds one of dismembering of a live body, a sense of bereavement saturates the description at the end, as the narrator watches the heavy ramshackle truck carrying loads and loads of rosewood logs from the forest to the city. So you can imagine how old the rosewood trees along it must have been. Its lumber was practically as heavy as iron (the hardened wood almost took the shape and texture of Ashta dhatu) (Amalgamation of eight heavy metals). Thakur sahab dedicated his broken down truck to these trees. Every night one tree or another was being cut down and the timber was being sent off to the city while its leaves, twigs, branches, and extras went on to some nearby village.

The Seed Capital and More Network

The profit earned, helped Thakur Sahib build a line of trucks. To the chart of his multiplying prosperity, another network was added with the seed capital gained from selling the rosewood trees. The tile-roof buildings were torn down; the modern stores were set up for selling everything from Ayurvedic remedies for impotence to diesel engine pumping equipment. This business helped him invest in the national banks—a subterfuge to refashioning the art of money laundering. 'The bank down the road was of the same sort. When nowadays it seems like new bank branches are opening everywhere, even on the back of a mule grazing in a field, there should have been banks opening up in Umraonagar. Thakur Sahib took out loans from banks in order to build his bank' (Shukla). But it was said that he lent this loan money out to others at an interest rate three times what a real bank charged. The type of work for which he loaned money was the type of work that banks shied away from. 'He had found a market where others feared to go' (Shukla). In Sainath's calculation, timbre smuggling has been a big business. If you fell just four good trees and smuggle out the timbre, you can make over 1.2 lakh, on that deal alone. 'The money grows on trees; the capitalist perspective would hold it righteous. Evidently, the quantum of money siphoned off from the sale of rose wood, is likely to be more than adequate to eliminate the poverty of lakhs of deprived (393)'. Shukla's description of poaching with mutual understanding reveals how it serves as a catalytic converter for Umraonagar's development.

The Land Utilization Act and the Project: Slaughter Trees

Shrilal Shukla's personal reminiscences recorded in *Jeevan Hi Jeevan* invoke how an echo system in his native village was destroyed with the extinction of both animals and trees. His accounts give us glimpses of how grievously his generation experienced—the loss of huge land tuning into wastelands—lands of stumped barren landscape. The nostalgic memories of the rich plantations, wilderness, existing in rural India make us understand how and why villages were earlier seen as the environment-friendly role model. He recalls (2005) the days of his adolescence when:

> in the three directions of his village was a thick rich forest of densely growing palash, karonda, berries and numerous vegetations, where rabbits, foxes, jackals, monkeys, nilgai,[10] wolves, wild boars moved. It was the dwelling of many species of colorful birds, though not many peacocks. In the midst of the forest, at some places were old wells, some small lakes, in which lotus bloomed and there were orchards of plums, mulberry, honey tree and mango. Such was our curiosity, he relates, that forgetting the lurking presence of wild boars and wolves, we would

wander into the forests for hours, craving to eat sweet berries during Diwali. ('Jeevan Hi Jeevan', 521-22)[11]

It was cherished as dense teakwood forests. With the onset of the 'Land Utilization Act',[12] by the end of 1948, forests and gardens were in the process of being axed. Presumably, it was enacted as a consequence of the supposed starvation in the wake of the Second World War. Accordingly, the lands, barren or forest, or the private property of someone, must be given away to the farmers on lease for farming. In case the owners failed to surrender the land property, the state was entitled to confiscate those spaces for the purpose of growing edible grain. 'Subsequently, most pastures, jungles, orchards, and barren lands were surrendered to the cause of "Grow more food"' (Shukla, *Jeevan Hi Jeevan*, 501). Wherever there were barren lands and private forests, it was mandatory for the landowners to assign them in parts to peasants for farming. In the process, the plum, honey tree, mango, and rosewood trees were also chopped off successively. The landowners knew that very soon, the law for the abolition of zamindari was to be implemented. The uncertainty of whether by that time the gardens would still belong to them made many indulge in selling spree, and vast tracts of lands were thus converted into money.

> Today there are all kinds of modern facilities in my village and a narrow-paved road runs through the region which once was a forest. Those gardens, lakes and spaces splashed with palash are no more. With the depletion of their habitat, birds and bats also disappeared. All around, one beholds, a vast stretch of barren land, where dust is raised by the passing buses. In the evenings, one does not hear jackals. Even the spirits and phantoms refused to appear for dearth of forests and mango groves. In all four directions there remains a grey sinister silence. All around, one beholds, a vast stretch of barren land, dust raised by the passing buses; the regions known for their 90 percent forest cover were now reduced to 70 percent only. I hardly visit my village. (*Jeevan Hi Jeevan*, 522)

The forest cover which was 70 percent now gone. The landscape changed. Shukla could understand retrospectively what was happening in the guise of development. He sensed fully well the harmful impact of deforestation on air and water pollution, climate change soil erosion, loss of biodiversity.

State's Ownership of Forest

One gathers that the government's proclaimed ownership of the trees too alienated the local populace from the flora and fauna. Traditionally, it has been the villagers who have shown concern for reviving the dying forests. Sainath's (1996, 396) survey in Latehar, Palamu (now in Jharkhand), finds that by 1992, the experiment was a great success. The locals had nurtured forest across 140 acres of land, with may have half a million trees on it. The state department came and claimed the forests. Others too started acting as if they owned the place. The fact was that if it were not for the villagers, not a single tree would have grown here. The forest department seeing how good it was simply appointed a guard here. It was really not about taking credit for the forest but for more sordid reason: the sheer commercial values of the trees. Basically, these people want to sell the trees. That is what these forest department people do anyway: sell the timbre, they are supposed to protect. Forest Department people though admit that if the forest is alive, it is due to the villagers. But it belongs to the government not to the people. Whose land it stands? In the case of the narrative of Umraonagar, the villagers are faceless people, languishing under the shadow of the intimidating local elite, politically empowered. Little do they know about the ways of betterment. No wonder Shukla's anthology is titled *Jahalat ke Pachchas Saal* (Fifty Years of Stupidity).

What Are the Implications of Despoiled Environment?

'Umraonagar me Kuchch Din' tells us that in the development programme, several are the surreptitiously operating stakeholders. What is worth noticing is that real development should involve the evolution of the human state to a higher level of being and living. Almost all versions of development accept this. The participation and consent of those who are supposed to be affected by the plans and projects seem missing.

They do not even have any say in the decision-making process. The intrusion in their environment, culture, livelihood, and tradition nonetheless continues uninterrupted, while it should be minimal. Those who loudly claim to be the champions of change are the ones who have done the least for it. One's attention is drawn to the scenario where a few resourceful people sitting at a distance, plan and plot the development of the underdeveloped. The appearance of growth and development craftily concealed the thick plot of cunning arrangements that involved the relatively educated, local men, the newly settled stakeholders, the political parties, bureaucrats, facilitators, and handlers. People were being sidetracked as a slew of development schemes was out to turn the village into a rural township and had smoothly opened floodgate of corruption, giving free permits to mint money. Life in the village goes on without complaint. Masjid, Mandir, and Ashrama alternately bellowed sounds of faith. The poor, downtrodden, exploited Siyadulari however stands nowhere in these transactions.

Slow Violence: Calamities That Are Slow but Long Lasting

The most significant character in the narrative is the environment—assaulted and dying—the images suffused in the narrative lend a grim elegiac resonance. Dense forests were made to become the playground of rogues. Cutting down the trees without approval and selling them elsewhere or in black markets as timbre were prohibited by law. Ironically, they were treated respectfully as a specialist in the matters of forest and in all nitty gritty of rural affairs. Several pieces of conversations and the glib speeches sound skilled in defending or evading any culpability. Though there is nothing uncommon about the images of torture and dismemberment evoked in the depiction of the trees lacerated and wounded, we are used to seeing them. The black print however in defamiliarizing the experience makes us conscious of our inadvertent communal participation in assaulting the trees and makes us sense the disturbing, repugnant aspects of incorrigible avarice. One is reminded of the movement, 'Chipko',[13] but sadly finds that the deforestation still continues. Vijay Prashad rightly puts it, 'What is important, at this moment in history is not so much to place blame or to vent our indignation and collective guilt over these grim facts. Certainly, any actions that slow or even reverse the destructive processes currently in motion are welcome and needed. But this emphasizes the psychological dimension of our relationship with the planet. The village Umraonagar is the scarred victim of slow violence perpetrated upon it. The process of development in Umraonagar is like 'slow violence' as Rob Nixon defines it early in his book as a term to describe 'calamities that are slow and long lasting, calamities that patiently dispense their devastation while remaining outside our flickering attention spans—and outside the purview of a spectacle-driven corporate media' (6).

Most significantly, the narrative of 'Umraonagar me Kuchch Din' attains a semblance of history in recording the insidious techniques with which the contractors, forest officials, development agents, specialists (local and the city-bred), and stakeholders in connivance, employ their might and skill to deprive the centuries-old forest village of all its resources. We are confronted with the images of the now denuded, wounded forest; most wildlife has disappeared, rivers and waterways polluted beyond recognition. The haze of dust raised by the lined buses, and ramshackle trucks carrying the slaughtered timbre, has engulfed all life around in the air, and on the ground. And it still does not seem to matter to most. But Siyadulari's future looks bleak, whom the journalist beholds getting off the Ikka to board a bus to the city.

The story drives home what the environment historian Donald Worster posits: 'the cause of ecological crisis is not a result of "how the ecosystem works but rather because of how our ethical system functions"' (27).

Notes

1. P. Sainath's 'And Silent Trees Speak' (126–32, 131) resonates with the tone, tenor, and timbre of Shrilal Shukla's narrative in 'Umraonagar me Kuchch Din'.
2. Shukla, Shrilal, 'Umraonagar me Kuchch Din', first published in 1986, eighteen years after *Raag Darbari*. It was also translated into English by Matt Reek in 2020 as 'Several days in Umraonagar'. It is the last story, in Shrilal Shukla's collection, *Jahalat ke Pachchas Saal*. I have drawn excerpts from Matt Reek's translation of the story, as 'Several Days in Umraonagar'. The narrative is a harsh critique of the disarray, the state's plans generated and their failure to raise every citizen's

life specifically in the countryside. It is the cunning inventiveness, nepotism, and greed that enable some characters to plunder a dense forest.

3. The character of the journalist-narrator in the story draws on the personal experiences of Shukla. The administrative officers like him were reminded of the doctrine: 'the need for development never ends, that is what the Planning Commission has said' (Shukla, 'Several Days in Umraonagar').

4. Sainath in 'Van Samitis and Vanishing Trees' (393–96), 'Whose Forest Is This Any Way' (397–400), and 'Who Says Money Does Not Grow on Trees' (401–404) details the short-sightedness and the mercenary and political interest involved in deforestation. He gives an account of how in Latehar, Palamau, now Jharkhand, formerly in Bihar, a forest officer's van carrying stolen timbre was waylaid by a group of villagers who belonged to the local Van Samiti (committee). The timbre worth lakhs of rupees was found. Large-scale illegal felling and timbre smuggling has devastated the resource of forests. Relentless felling has killed not just large forests but also the streams and rivers (396). He observes that though the forests are naturally degenerating, they need to be protected and allowed to grow. But what is being watched is that not a single hectare came under afforestation (392–96, 423).

5. The excerpts are drawn from Matt Reeck's translation of Shrilal Shukla's 'Umraonagar me Kuchch Din' into English as 'Several Days in Umraonagar'.

6. In the countryside, liquor making (*tharra*) is one of the unlicenced practice. The poor concoct it surreptitiously and generally they operate with immunity. It is a source of livelihood for the poor. During the election times, its nocturnal transport becomes frequent to woo the voters.

7. 1970s and 1980s were the time when Mahesh Yogi and Bhagwan Rajneesh had gained immense popularity. Heading an Ashrama and a team of retinues displayed their assets and were supposed to lend dignity and glamor to such people. Such self-declared Godmen were subjected to controversies and often implicated in shady deals. Several such *Babas/Gurus* were on the rise during these decades.

8. With the rise of the state, it had been the aptitude of the political class to fix meaning and political intentions in the discourse. (Clare O', www.michel-foucault.com). This is how a discourse appears in the facade of historical, universal, and scientific knowledge, that is, seeming objective and stable. It embraces the techniques and procedures designed to govern the conduct of both individuals and the populations at every level not just at the administrative or political level Parth Chatterji in *Omnibus: Impossible India* (253) and Barbara Harriss-White in *India Working* draw upon Foucault's notion of the dispersed practices of the government as 'governmentality' to understand the operations of the Indian state functioning as a 'bundle of everyday institutions and forms of rules, devices and technologies invisible to the common observer assembled into an apparatus having neither unity nor the functionality often ascribed to them' (1). Shukla comprehends the phenomenon shrewdly.

9. Treta Yug: *the age of three or Triads.* By virtue of external and linguistic evidence, the period of Ramayana's composition is believed to be a few hundred years between 200 BC and AD 200. The world ages are named after the four throws recognized in the Indian dice game: Kritayuga, Devaparayug, Tretayug, Kaliyug. The Ramayana takes place in the Treta Yug. Find more details in Nooten's Introduction to William Buck's *Ramayana*, xxi. This small segment of 'Umraonagar me Kuchch Din' is my translation since in Reeck's translation the exact transcription of *Treta Yug* and *Ashta Dhatu* was missing. My translation of the same story is not yet published.
10. We hear reports of how licensed gunmen from distant parts of India are summoned to UP and Bihar to gun down Nilgai. More and more fields replacing forests created crisis for the survival of Nilgai. For lack of their natural habitation, their only resort to satiate hunger is the fields and ready crops of the farms. *Economic Times* reports, 30 January 2022, 32 AMIST that the forest departments are backing the killing of nilgai. *Indian Express*, 6 September 2019, reports that the forest department has claimed to have killed over 300 nilgai in the last four days. A video of an alive, injured nilgai being buried alive with the help of a JCB in Bihar's Vaishali district went viral. In Damodar Dutta Dikshit's story, 'Samay Samrajyavadi' (118–23, Times Imperialist), the protagonist, a Nilgai bull's moving lamentation over his bleeding, dying pregnant companion indicts the human civilization of seizing hold of the lands where the animal world lived. I cite a few lines here: 'You chopped off trees, built fields, expanded them farther; our habitation gradually shrank. If we enter into the fields, you hunt and kill us, sometimes for merry making, or for our flesh. You call us intruders! The real intruder calling the elemental owner an intruder!' (119).
11. Shrilal Shukla writes in 'Is Uhapoha ka koi Ant Nahin' (There is no end to this dilemma) in *Jeevan Hi Jeevan*. I have drawn on his reminiscences. The excerpts are translated by me.
12. Land Utilization Act of 1947–49 empowered the state to take possession of uncultivated land which is not a grove land or land let to or held by tenant for farming with a view to increasing the production of food grains.
13. Paying tribute to Shri Sundarlal Bahuguna, Vijay Prasad notes that during Bahuguna's last years, he watched India's current government actively allow deforestation and land degradation. According to Global Forest Watch between 2019 and 2020, India lost 14 percent of its tree cover, with 36 percent of its forests severely vulnerable to fires. It is almost as if the forests are calling for another Chipko movement. This time not just in Chamoli or in India, but from one end of the planet to the other (7 June 2021).

References

Acharya, Devaparna. 2020. 'Bihar Elections State's Landless Endure Modern Day Slavery'. *Firstpost* (10 November 2020). Accessed 10 November 2021. www.firstpost.com/politics/bihar-elections-states-landless-endure-modern-day-slavery-await-promised-lands-8997051.html.

Anand, Shailendra. 1991. 'Uttha Puttar'. In *Kosi ke Us Paar*, edited by Ramesh Neelkamal, 141–43. Patna: Sanjay Prakashan.

Arsenault, Chris. 2015. 'Why Are Most of the World's Hungry People Farmers?' *The Agenda Weekly* (Wednesday, 28 May 2015). World Economic Forum.Accessed 14 July 2020. https:// www.weforum org> agenda> 2015/ 05> why-ar …

Atreya, Ramkumar. 2018. 'Tractor and Suhaga'. In *Katha me Kisan*, Part 2, edited by Amit Manoj, 41–54. Mumbai and Meerut: Samvad Prakashan.

Balani, Khushboo. 2017. 'Uttar Pradesh Has India's Largest Population of Children, but Least Teachers per Student'. *Indiaspend* (7 January 2017, 9:30). Accessed 18 August 2020. https://scroll.in/article/825966/uttar-pradesh-has-indias-largest-population-of-children-but-least-teachers-per-student.

Balani, Khushboo. 2017. 'Bihar Short Of 280,000 Teachers; Lowest Per Elementary School Student'. (4 January 2017). Accessed 18 August 2020. www.businessstandard.com.

Baviskar, Amita. 1995. *In the Belly of the River: Tribal Conflicts over Development in the Narmada Valley*. New Delhi: Oxford University Press.

Benjamin, Walter. 1969. *Illuminations*. New York: Schoken Books.

Bera, Sayantan. 2015. 'Did the Farmer Suicides Really Halve Last Year'. *Mint*, Delhi (Thursday, 23 July 2015). Accessed 28 January 2017. www.livemint.com/Politics/LE0II4GyknGBTdKnuO/The-number-of-farmer-suicides-halved-last-year-Really.html?facet=amp.

Best, Steven, and Douglas Kellner. 1991. *Post-modern Theory: Critical Interrogation*. New York:Guildford Publication.

Bharatiya, Rakesh. 1984. 'Itminan'. In *Pragatisheel Vasudha*, edited by Harishankar Parsai, 146–151. Bhopal:Pragatisheel Lekhak Sangha.

Bhattacharya, Subhash. 1977. 'The Indigo Revolt of Bengal'. *Social Scientist* 5(12) (July): 13–23. Accessed 18 January 2020. doi: jstor.org/stable/3516809.

Bihari, Vipin. 2000. 'Shadayantra' ('Conspiracy'). In *Pashyanti*, (July–September 2000), edited by Pranva Kumar Vandyopadhyay, 64–84. New Delhi:Pashyanti, B/9/ 6327, Vasant Kunj (Prakashan), New Delhi.

Chatterji, Parth. 1999. *Omnibus: Impossible India*. New Delhi: Oxford University Press.

Choudhary, Prabhas Kumar. 1991. ' "Pita" ("Father")'. In *Kosi Ke Us Paar* (*Across the River Kosi*), edited by Ramesh Neelkamal, 54–59. Patna: Sanjay Prakashan.

Curtis, Bruce. Autumn 2002. 'Foucault and Governmentality and Population: The Impossible Discovery'. The Canadian Journal of Sociology 27(4): 505–33.

Dabhi, Brendan. 2019. 'Female Farmer Commits Suicide Allegedly After Crop Fails'. Ahmedabad Mirror (4 November 2019, 01:56 IST). Accessed 17 March 2020. https://ahmedabadmirror.indiatimes.com/ahmedabad/crime/female-farmer-commits-suicide-allegedly-after-crop-fails/articleshow/71883425.cms.

Devi, Mahashweta. 1995. 'Pterodactyl, Puran Sahai, and Pirtha'. In *Imaginary Maps*. Translated by Gayatri Chakravorty Spivak, 95–196. New York: Routledge.

Dews, Peter. 2007. *The Idea of Evil*. Oxford: Oxford University Press.

Dhawan, Ashish. 2020. 'Inequality Begins at Five'. In *The Times of India*, 20. 14 February 2020.

Dikshit, Damodar. 2014. 'Under-Weighment'. In *Gaon ki Chuninda Kahaniyan*, 9–19. Allahabad: Sahitya Bhandar.

Dikshit, Damodar. 2014. 'Samay Samrajyavadi'. In *Gaon ki Chuninda Kahaniyan*. Allahabad: Sahitya Bhandar.

Dikshit, Damodar. 1986. *Agriculture, Irrigation and Horticulture in Ancient Sri Lanka: From Earliest Times to 1186 A.D*. Delhi: Bharatiya Vidya Prakashan.

Dikshit, Damodar. 2014. 'Darvaje vala Khet'. In *Gaon ki Chuninda Kahaniyan*, 20–30. Allahabad: Sahitya Bhandar.

Durantaye, Leland de la. 2009. *Giorgio Agamben: A Critical Introduction*. Stanford, California: Stanford UP.

Eagleton, Terry. 1992. "Ideological Strategies' in *Ideology*, 33–61. London: Verso.

Eagleton, Terry. 2010. Chapter 2, 'Obscene Enjoyment'. In *on evil*. P. 96, Yale University Press, 2010.

Edelman, Mark. 2021. 'What Is a Peasant? What Are Peasantries?' Accessed 12 June 2021. medelman@hunter.cuny.edu.

Edkins, Jenny. 2007. 'Whatever Politics'. In *Giorgio Agamben: Sovereignty and Life*, edited by Matthew Calarco and Steven De Caroli, 70–91. Stanford, California: Stanford UP.

Finance Express. 2017. FE Online. Updated: 7 January 2017 11:32 AM.

Foucault, Michel. 1998. *The History of Sexuality: The Will to Knowledge*. London: Penguin.

Gandhi, Mohandas K. 1962. *Village Swaraj*. Ahmedabad: Navjivan Trust.

Gandhi, Mohandas K. 2019. 'Hind Swaraj and Other Writings'. In *Cambridge Texts in Modern Politics*, edited by Anthony J. Parel. Cambridge: Cambridge University Press.

Ghosh, Amitav. 2008. *Sea of Poppies*. New Delhi: Penguin.

Giri, Rajiv Ranjan. 2004. 'Vidambanaon Se Sakshatkar. Interview with Shrilal Shukla'. *Samakalin Bharatiya Sahitya* 3(122): 242–44.

Giri, Rajiv Ranjan. 2004. 'Vidambanaon Se Sakshatkar'. [Confronting Ironies]: 'An Interview with Kamaleshwar'. *Samakalin Bharatiya Sahitya* 3(122): 236–38.

Giridhar, Subramaniyan. 2009. 'The Way Forward'. In *Sunday Magazine*, 11 (22 November 2009, 20:53 IST). Accessed 27 November 2019. www.thehindu.com/features/education/The-way-forward.../article16893597.ece.

Gorrepati, Narendranath. 2010. Narendranath,Gorrepati, *Dilemmas in Agriculture: A Personal History*, edited and supplemented by Uma Shankari, New Delhi: Vasudehev Kutumbakam.

Gotz, Norbert. 2015. 'Moral Economy, Its Conceptual History and Analytical Prospects'. *Journal of Global Ethics*. II(2): 147–62. doi: 10.10 80/17449626.2015.1054556. Accessed 29 July 2016.

REFERENCES

Guha, Ranajit. 1999. *Elementary Aspects of Peasant Insurgency in Colonial India*. Durham: Duke University Press.

Gupta, Akhil. 2005. 'Narrative of Corruption: Anthropological and Fictional Accounts of Indian State'. *Ethnography* 6(5): 5–34.

Harriss-White, Barbara. 2003. *India Working: Essays on Society and Economy*. Cambridge: Cambridge University Press.

Hickey, Sam, and Sarah Bracking. 2005. 'Exploring the Politics of Chronic Poverty: From Representation to Politics of Injustice'. *World Development* 33(6): 851–65.

Joshi, Rohina. Magnolia Cardona. et al. 2020. 'The Burden of Fatal and Non-Fatal Injury in Rural India'. In *Injury Prevention* (6 August 2008). Accessed 16 April 2020. https://www.researchgate.net/publication/23146091_The_burden_of_fatal_and_non-fatal_injury_in_rural_India#fullTextFileContent.

Joshi, P. C. 1986. 'Founders of Lucknow School and Their Legacy: Radhakamal Mukerjee and D P Mukerji: Some Reflections'. *Economic and Political Weekly* 21(33) (16 Aug):1455–69.

Joshi, P. C. 2009. 'The Subaltern in Indian Literature: Some Reflections on Premchand and *Godan*'. *Hindi Language Discourse*. Mahatma Gandhi International Hindi U (July-September): 138–54. Accessed 10 February 2010.

Kantak, Suresh. 2018. 'Kisan kya Kare'. In *Katha mei Kisan*, Part 1, edited by Amit Manoj, 179–91. Mumbai: Samvad Prakashan.

Kaur, Banjot. 2018. 'Sugar Farmer's Crisis: Bumper Harvest Turns Bane'. *Down to Earth*, 10 July. Accessed 7 January 2021. www.downtoearth.org.in/author/banjot-kaur-113591?page=15&amp%bamp%3bper-page=25&per-page=25.

Kriyansh, Omprakash. 2018. 'Pretchhaya'. In *Katha me Kisan*, Part 2, edited by Amit Manoj, 172–81. Mumbai and Meerut: Samvad Prakashan, 2018.

Kumar, Dushayanta. 2020. https://hindisamay.com/kavita/Dushyant%20kumar.htmAccessed 9 August 2022

Kynadi, Vinay James. 2020. 'Safed Mueseli Farmers Cry Foul as Company Breaks Promise'. 1 October 2005. Accessed 17 March 2020. //economictimes.indiatimes.com/articleshow/1248766.cms?from=mdr&utm_source=contentofinterest&utm_medium=text&utm_campaign=cppst.

La Capra, Dominique. 2001. '*History, Memory, Trauma*'. A Public Lecture (28 September 2001).

La Capra, Dominique. 1999. 'Trauma, Absence Loss'. *Critical Inquiry* 25(4) (Summer 1999): 696–727. JSTOR. Accessed 8 January 2020. www.jstor.org/stable/1344100.

Lal, Sham. 2001. 'A Bad Dream'. In *A Hundred Encounters*. New Delhi: Rupa.

Lal, Sham. 2001. 'Pathology of Globalization'. In *A Hundred Encounters*. New Delhi: Rupa.

Ludden, David. 1990. 'World Economy and Village India 1600–1900: Exploring the Agrarian History of Capitalism'. In *South Asia and World Capitalism*, edited by Sugata Bose, 159–77. New Delhi: Oxford University Press.

Mander, Harsh. 14 August, 2010. 'Naren's Last Testament'. *The Hindu* (Sunday Magazine).

Mani, Premkumar. 2018. 'Jugaad'. In *Katha me Kisan*, Part 1, edited by Amit Manoj, 155–64. Mumbai-Meerut-Samvad: Prakashan.

Manoj, Amit, ed. 2018. *Katha me Kisan*. Mumbai-Meerut: Samvad Prakashan.
Markandeya. 2002. 'Bhoodan'. *Markandeya ki Kahaniyan*, 268–70. Allahabad: Lokbharati.
Markandeya. 2002. 'Doune Ki Pattiyan'. *Markandeya ki Kahaniyan*, 199–204. Allahabad: Lokbharati.
Markovits, Claude. 2006. *The Un-Gandhian Gandhi*. New Delhi: Anthem Press.
Mehta, A.K., and Sourabh Ghosh. 2005. 'Globalisation, Loss of Livelihoods and Entry into Poverty'. *Alternative Economic Survey, India 2004–2005, Alternative Survey Group*. Delhi: Daanish Books (assisted by Ritu Elwadhi).
Mills, Sara. 2004. *Michel Foucault*. London: Routledge.
Mohan, Madan. 2018. 'Jahrili Roshniyon ke Beech'. In *Katha me Kisan*, Part 2, edited by Amit Manoj, 58–78. Mumbai: Samvad Prakashan.
Mohan, Madan. 2018. 'Jahrili Roshniyon ke Beech'. *Katha me Kisan*, Part 2, edited by Amit Manoj, 58–78. Mumbai: Samvad Prakashan.
Morton, Stephen. 2003. *Spivak: Ethics, Subalternity. Critiques of Postcolonial Reason*. New York: Routledge.
'MP Forest Department Wants to Allow Killing of Nilgai, Wild Boars Which Damage Crops'. *Economic Times* (30 January 2022). Accessed 13 February 2022. m.economictimes.com/news/inndia/mp-forest-department-wants-to-allow-killing-of-nilgai-wild-boars-which-damage-crops/articleshow/89217267.cms.
Nibber, Gurpreet Singh. 2018. '70% Workforce in Panjab Cities Is From Outside the State, Says Study'. *Hindustan Times* (15 October 2018). Accessed 8 January 2020. https://www.pressreader.com/india/hindustan-times-patiala/20181015/281599536465383
Nibber, Gurpreet Singh. 2020. 'Government Has No Plan to Tab: Migrant Labors Are Reaching Panjab Everyday'. 11 June 2020. Accessed 11 August 2020. www.hindustantimes.com, Chandigarh.
'Nilgai Buried Alive in Bihar, One Booked'. 2019. *The Indian Express* (6 September 2019). Accessed 13 February 2022. https://indianexpress.com>India
Nixon, Rob. 2011. *Slow Violence and the Environmentalism of the Poor*. https://southwarknotes.files.wordpress.com/2018/10/slow-violence-and-the-environmentalism-of-the-poor.pdf. Accessed 14 January 2021.
O'Farrell, Clare. 2011. Michel Foucault: Key Concepts. https://michel-foucault.com/2011/06/22/michel-foucault-key-concepts-2011/
Orsini, Francesca. 2009. *The Hindi Public Sphere 1920–1940: Language and Literature in the Age of Nationalism*. New Delhi: Oxford University Press.
Orwell, George. 1981. *A Collection of Essays*. New York: Harcourt.
Orwell, George. 1999. *Animal Farm*. Delhi: Jainco.
Orwell, George. 1999. *Nineteen Eighty-Four*. Delhi: Jainco.
Padmanabhan, Anil. 2013. 'Understanding Farmer Suicides'. *Live Mint* (24 May 2013, 01:05 AM IST). Accessed 30 September 2019. https://www.livemint.com/Opinion/zR8V3yKF7wENz14OYBdpMN/Understanding-farmer-suicides.html.
Palival, Suraj. 2005. 'Gram Katha Likhna Aaj Chunouti Hai'. *Aakar*, January-March.
Pande Manager. 2006. 'Foreword: The Album of Multicolored Pictures of the Village'. In *Katha Me Gaon*, edited by Kushvaha, Subhash, 5–14. Meerut: Samvad Prakashan.
Pandey, Ganesh. 1999. *Aathhaven Dashak ki kahaniyoyn me Gramin Jeevan*. New Delhi: Radha Prakashan.

Pandey, Ganesh. 1999. *Gramin Jeevan in Aathaven Dashakki Hindi Kayaniyan*. New Delhi: Radha Publications.
Pandikattu, Kuruvilla. 2001. 'Global Village vs. Gandhian Villages: A Viable Vision'. In *Gandhi: The Meaning of Mahatma for the Millennium*, edited by Kuruvilla Pandikattu, 180–89. Washington, DC: The Council for Research in Values and Philosophy.
Pant, Sumitranandan. 2017. 'Gram Chitra'. *Kavita Kosh*. Accessed 14 November 2017. Kavitakosh.org.
Phansalkar, Sanjiv. 2018. 'People with Disabilities Languish across Rural India: Neglected Lives'. *Village Square* (13 June 2018). Accessed 8 January 2020. www.villagesquare.in/people-with-disabilities-languish-across-rural-India-neglected-lives/.
Pinto, Marina R. 1992. 'Rural Development and Bureaucracy in India'. *The Indian Journal of Political Science* 53(3): 2279–96. Accessed 17 July 2020. http://www.jstor.com/stable/41855614.
Popova, Maria. 2020. 'Walter Benjamin on Information vs Wisdom & Storytelling, as the Antidote to Death by News'. *Brain Picking*. https://www.themarginalian.org/2015/03/09/walter-benjamin-illuminations-the-storyteller/
Prakash, Gyan. 1994. 'Subaltern Studies as Postcolonial Criticism'. *The American Historical Review* 99(5) (December): 1475–90.
Prasad, H. Pradhan. 1974. 'Reactionary Role of Usurer's Capital in Rural India'. *Economic and Political Weekly* 9(32/34, Special Number) (August 1974): 1305–08. Accessed 2 January 2019. https://www.jstor.org/stable/4363910.
Prasad, Rajendra. 2018. 'Indigo—The Crop that Created History and then Itself Became History'. *Indian Journal of History of Science* 53(3): 296–301.
Prashad, Vijay. 2020. 'Hunger Gnaws at the Edge of the World'. 15 May 2020. Accessed 16 June 2020. indiaculturalforum.in.
Prashad, Vijay. 2021. 'We Hug the Trees Because the Trees Have No Voice'. *Tricontinental* 22(3 June 2021). Accessed 1 October 2021. www.tricontinental.org/newsletterissue/22-environment/ .
Premchand, Munshi. 2021. 'The Shroud: ("Kafan")'. Translated by Frances W. Pritchett. Accessed 10 August 2021. http://scroll.in.
Premchand, Munshi. 1962. *Vividh Prasang*. Allahabad: Hansa Prakashan.
Premchand, Munshi. 1999. *Premashram* [The Abode of Love]. New Delhi: Prakashan Sansthan.
Premchand, Munshi. 2006. *Karmabhoomi* [The Land Where One Works]. Translated by Lalit M. Shrivastava. New Delhi: Oxford University Press.
Premchand, Munshi. 2007. 'Poos ki Raat' [Winter's Night]. In *A Winter's Night and Other Stories*. Translated by Rakshanda Jalil, 1–6. India: Penguin.
Premchand, Munshi. 2007. *Godan* [The Gift of a Cow]. Translated by Gordon C. Radarmen. New Delhi: Permanent Black.
Punter, David. 2000. *Postcolonial Imaginings: Fiction of a New World Order*. Edinburgh: Edinburgh University Press.
Rabinow, Paul, ed. 1984. *The Foucault Reader*. London: Penguin.
Ramesh, Neel Kamal. 1991. *Kosike Aar Paar* [Across Kosi]. Patna: Sanjay Prakashan.
Rawal, Ritesh. 2019. 'What Is Rural Education Scenario in India? How Can We Change It?' In *India Today* (5 August 2019). Accessed 25 September 2022 https://www.indiatoday.in/education-today/featurephilia/story/what-is-the-rural-education-scenario-in-india-and-how-can-we-change-it-1577444-2019-08-05

Rawls, John. 1971. *A Theory of Justice*. Harward University Press.
Reeck, Matt. 2020. Translator. 'Several Days in Umraonagar'. By Shrilal Shukla, *In Translation*, July 2020. Accessed 4 October 2021. https://intranslation.brooklynrail.org/hindi/several-days-in-umraonagar/
Sahai, Suman. 2008. 'Urgent Need to Monitor the Farm Loan Waiver'. https://sumansahai-blog.blogspot.com/2008/04/urgent-need-to-monitor-farm-loan-waiver.html
Sahai, Suman. 2011. 'Good Harvest Do Not Always translate into Money in the Bank'. *The Hindu*, 19 October.
Sainath, Palagummi. 1996. 'And Silent Trees Speak'. In *Everybody Loves a Good Drought*, 126–32. New Delhi: Penguin.
Sainath, Palagummi. 2018. 'Migrated Laborer in India'. *Firstpost* (18 May 2018). Accessed 20 January 2020. https://youtu.be/FpaI_r7q0io.
Sainath, Palagummi. 1996. 'The Trickle up and Down Theory'. In *Everybody Loves a Good Drought*. 23–44. New Delhi: Penguin.
Sainath, Palagummi. 1996. 'Whose Forest Is It Anyway?' In *Everybody Loves a Good Drought*, 397–400. New Delhi: Penguin.
Sainath, Palagummi. 1996. 'Despots, Distillers, Poets and Artists: Characters of the Countryside'. *Everybody Loves a Good Drought*, 271–314. New Delhi: Penguin.
Sainath, Palagummi. 1996. 'Lenders, Losers, Crooks and Credit'. *Everybody Loves a Good Draught*, 193–230. New Delhi: Penguin.
Sainath, Palagummi. 1996. *Everybody Loves a Good Drought*. New Delhi: Penguin.
Sainath, Palagummi. 1996. 'The Swelling Register of Death". 03 January 2006. https://indiatogether.org> register-op-ed. Accessed 21 November 2017.
Sainath, Palagummi. 2006. 'Largest Mass Migration in History Is Unfolding in India'. *Rediff* (19 October 2006, 11 October 2008). Accessed 20 January 2020. https://youtu.be/FpaI_r7q0io.
Sainath, Palagummi. 2010. 'Oliver Twist Seeks Food Security'. *The Hindu*, 11 August.
Sainath, Palagummi. 2020. 13 May 2020. Accessed 12 January 2021. https:// www. Firstpost.com/category/12.35:50 India.
Sainath, Palagummi. 1996. 'This Is the Way to Go to the School'. In *Everybody Loves A Good Drought: Stories from India's Poorest Districts*, 45–68. New Delhi: Penguin Books India Private Ltd.
Sanjeev. 2016. *Phaans*. Delhi: Vaani Prakashan.
Schouten, P. 2010. 'Theory Talk #38: James Scott on Agriculture as Politics, the Danger of Standardization and Not Being Governed'. *Theory Talks*, 15 May. Accessed 19 December 2019. http://www.theory- talks.org/2010/05/theory-talk-38.html.
Scott, James C. 1976. 'Implications for the Analysis of Exploitation: Reciprocity and Subsistence as Justice'. In *The Moral Economy of the Peasant Rebellion and Subsistence in Southeast Asia*. New Haven: Yale University Press.
Scott, James C. 1985. *Weapons of the Weak*. New Haven and London: Yale University Press.
Scott, James C. 1990. *Domination and the Art of Resistance: Hidden Transcripts*. New Haven and London: Yale University Press.
Scott, James C. 2010. 'Theory Talk # 38: James Scott on Agriculture as Politics: The Dangers of Standardization and Not Being Governed'. *Theory Talks*, Saturday, 12 May. Accessed 18 May 2020. www.theory-talks.org.
Shambhunath. 2003. 'Hindi Navagagaran ke Kisan Prashna'. [The Peasant Issue in Hindi Awakening]. Pahal 75 (September-November): 168–75.

Shambhunath. 2005. 'Rajaniti me Manushya ki Vapasi ek Sawapna Hai'. *Shrilal Shukla, Jeevan Hi Jeevan*, edited by Namvar Singh, Rekha Awasthi. New Delhi: Amrit Mahotsava Samiti.

Sharma, Devinder. 2017. 'Does the Banking System Really Want to Help Farmers?' *The Wire* (30 March 2017). Accessed 8 January 2020. wire.in/agriculture/banking-system-farmers-loans.

Sharma, Kalpana. 2009. 'Will Anything Change?' *The Hindu*, 27 December. Accessed 17 February 2021.

Sharma, Krishnavatar. 2017. 'India Has 139 Million Internal Migrants. They Must Not Be Forgotten'. 1 October 2017. Accessed 14 November 2019. https://www.weforum.org/agenda/2017/10/india-has-139-million-internal-migrants-we-must-not-forget-them/.

Sharma, Seth Yogima. 07 July, 2014. 'India Has 100 Million More Poor'. Accessed 4 February 2021. https://economictimes.indiatimes.com/...Indicators

Sharma, Subhash. 2018. 'Bhookh'. In *Katha me Kisan*, Part 2, edited by Amit Manoj, 183–96. Mumbai-Meerut: Samvad Prakashan.

Shivmurti. 2020. 'Kasaibara'. *Gadyakosh*, 5 April. Accessed12 January 2021. http://gadyakosh.org/gk/

Shrivastava, Archana. 2010. 'Bhookh Ki Bhayavah Hoti Aag'. [The Frightening Fire of Hunger] Yojana (October): 30–35.

Shrivastava, Harishchandra, and Kumar, Manjit. 1980. 'Gramin Samaj me Parajeevita'. In *Samajika, Khand-1*, Allahabad.

Shukla, Amandeep. 2019. 'One out of every four Class 8 students from rural India cannot read a simple text' (16 January 2019). Accessed 31 December 2019. www.hindustantimes.com.

Shukla, Girija Gaurav. 2020. 'Drop outs in rural children areas are already high: Post lockdown they may go up further'. 13 June 2020, Updated, 17 August 2002. Gaonconnection.com.

Shukla, Shrilal. 2004. 'Unnis Sau Chaurasi', *Jahalat Ke Pachchas Saal*, 55–61. New Delhi: Rajkamal Prakashan.

Shukla, Shrilal. 2005. 'Is Uhapoh ka Koi Anta Nahin' (There is no end to the Predicament). In *Shrilal Shukla, Jeevan Hi Jeevan: Amrit Mahotsava*, edited by Namvar Singh, and Rekha Awasthi, 520–29. New Delhi: Navchetan Printers.

Shukla, Shrilal. 1996. 'Umraonagar me Kuchch Din'. In *Jahalat ke Pachas Saal*, 1986, 407–22. New Delhi: Rajkamal Prakashan.

Shukla, Shrilal. 1980. *Bisrampur ka Sant*. New Delhi: Rajkamal Prakashan.

Shukla, Shrilal. 2004. 'Gram Varsha'. *Jahalat Ke Pachchas Saal*, 5–8. New Delhi: Rajkamal Prakashan.

Shukla, Shrilal. 2004. 'Hori aur Unnis Sau Chourasi'. [Hori and 1984]. In *Jahalat Ke Pachchas Saal*, 55–61. New Delhi: Rajkamal Prakashan.

Shukla, Shrilal. 2004. 'Pahali Chook'. *Jahalat Ke Pachchas Saal*, 123–25. New Delhi: Rajkamal Prakashan.

Shukla, Shrilal. 2008. *Raag Darbari*, 1968. New Delhi: Rajkamal Prakashan.

Shukla, Shrilal. 2019. *Raag Darbari*, 1968. New Delhi: Rajkamal Prakashan.

Shukla, Shrilal. 2012. *Raag Darbari*, 1968. Translated by Gillian Wright. India: Penguin.

Shukla, Shrilal. 'Is Uhapoh ka koi Ant Nahin' In *Shrilal Shukla: Jeevan hi Jeevan, Amrit Mahotsava*, edited by Namvar Singh and Rekha Awasthi, 520–529. New Delhi: Amrit Mahotsava Samiti Prakashan.

Singh, Anant Kumar. 2018. 'Bhookh'. In *Katha me Kisan*, Part 1, edited by Amit Manoj, 193–208. Mumbai-Meerut: Samvad Prakashan.

Singh, Charan. 1978. *India's Economic Policy*. Delhi: Vikas.

Singh, Jaivir. 2018. 'Why Rural India Still Has Poor Access to Quality Education?' *Financial Express* (26 November 2018). Accessed 8 January 2020. www.financialexpress.com/education-2/why-rural-india-still-has-poor-access-to-quality-education/1393555/.

Singh, Punni. 2006. 'Mansa Badai'. In *Katha me Gaon*, edited by Subhash Kushvaha, 178–84. Mumbai: Samvad Prakashan.

Singh, Punni. 2018. 'Mukti'. In *Katha me Kisan*, Part 2, edited by Amit Manoj, 29–40. Mumbai-Meerut: Samvad Prakashan.

Sudhakar, Salil. 2018. 'Khari ke Gavon ki Kishtiyan'. In *Katha me Kisan*, Part 2, edited by Manoj Amit, 221–43. Mumbai-Meerut: Samvad Prakashan.

Talwar, Veer Bharat. 1990. *Kisan Rashtriya Andolan aurPremchand*. New Delhi: Northern Book Centre.

Tharoor, Shashi. 1998. *India from Midnight to the Millennium*. New Delhi: Penguin Books.

Thompson, E.P. 1993. 'The Moral Economy Reviewed'. In *Customs in Common: Studies in Traditional Popular Culture*, edited by E.P. Thompson, 76–136. London: Penguin.

Times News Network. 2019. 'Safed Muesli Farmers Cry Foul as Company Breaks Promise' (1 October 2005). Accessed 13 October 2019. //economictimes.indiatimes.com/articleshow/1248766.cms?from=mdr&utm_source=contentofinterest&utm_medium=text&utm_campaign=cppst.

Tongia, Rahul. 2019. 'India's Biggest Challenge: The Future of Farming'. *The India Forum* (4 October 2019). Accessed 8 January 2020 https//www.theindiaforum.in/.

Tumbe, Chinmay. 2018. *India Moving: A History of Migration*. Delhi, Penguin Random House India Private Limited.

Tumbe, Chinmay. 2019. 'A Million Migrations: Journey in Search of Jobs' (16 January 2019). Accessed 19 March 2019. https://www.justicenews.co.in/a-million-migrations-journeys-in-search-of-jobs/.

Upadhyay, Shashi Bhushan. 2010. 'Premchand and the Moral Economy of Peasantry in Colonial North India'. *Modern Asian Studies* 45(5) (29 June): 1–34.

Van Nooten, B.A. Van. 2006. 'Introduction'. In *Ramayana*, edited by William Buck, ix–xxii. Delhi: Motilal Banarasidas.

Vanashree, trans. 2012. 'Shrilal Shukla: "Hori and 1984"'. In *Indian Literature*. Vol. 56.2, March–April, edited by A. J. Joseph, 268–73. New Delhi: Sahitya Akademi.

Vanavasi, Kailash. 2018. 'Prakop'. In *Katha me Kisan*, Part 2, edited by Amit Manoj, 259–74. Mumbai-Meerut: Samvad Prakashan.

Venkatsubramanian, K. 2012. 'Land Reforms Remain an Unfinished Business'. 23 August. Accessed 23 August 2012. http://www.nrcddp.org.

Webster, Roger. 1996. *Studying Literary Theory*. Bloomsbury.

Webster, Neil and Lars Engberg-Pedersen 2002. 'Political Agencies and Spaces'. In *The Name of the Poor: Contesting Political Space for Poverty Reduction*, Ed. Lars Engberg-Pedersen and Neil Webster 255–71. London: Zed Books Ltd.

Worster, Donald. 1993. *The Wealth of Nature: Environmental History and the Ecological Imagination*. Oxford UP.

Index

For the benefit of digital users, indexed terms that span two pages (e.g., 52-53) may, on occasion, appear on only one of those pages.

abject misery of hunger 144
absence of permanent doctor 181
acute food insecurity 154
a deceitful confidential deal 151-52
a dissolute arena of roguery, violence, selfishness 16, 102
Agamben, Giorgio 165, 173
Agents of microfinancing programme inveigle the gullible 33-34
    exorbitant rates of interest imposed upon destitute borrower 35
    Microfinance scheme of the Gramin(rural) bank dedicated to profit making 35
agrarian crisis 1-3, 4-5, 7-8, 21, 129
agricultural history of India 4-5
agricultural transformations in Post-colonial India 66-67
alternative modes of subsistence 158-60
amaran anshan (fast unto death) 94
Anand, Shailendra 133
    'Uttha Puttar' (Wake up son) 133
analysis of rural development 189
ancestral work crumbling 131
'Anchalikata ke Bahane' (In the pretext of regionalism) 23n.4
anganwadi 106, 123, 152-53, 156n.14
ancient forest almost belonging to the hoary past of *Treta yug* 189-90
Angrej sahib 15, 55-56
Annapurna yojana 151
annual status of education report 118
an underhand method that guarantees great success 187-88
apathy of the school system to the poor 106
appropriation of land 184-85

armed struggle against the rich land owners 57
Assistance Programmes of Nationalized Banks 33-34
Atreya, Ram Kumar 160
    'Tractor aur Suhaga' (Tractor and the Icing) 160, 166-69
avenues of loot, complicity in corruption 179-80
Awadh movement of peasants 1920-22, 6-7
'a way of life ebbs away' 18, 127

backwardness and poverty in rural India 105
Bakhtin, Michael 22
Balani, Khushbu 107
banks and registered micro-finance institutes 157-58
battered by adversities 19-20, 157
Baviskar, Amita. 7-8
Benama 92
    benami holdings (holding without endorsed legal papers) 59-60
benefits of mortgaging 89-90
Benjamin, Walter 1-2
Bhagalpur sheets, no longer in demand 137
Bhojpuri belt of eastern UP and western Bihar 136
Bhudan committee 53, 54
Bhudan functionaries 53, 54
Bhudan (land gift) 8-9, 15, 52-53, 57
bias against the tribal and the Dalits 116
Bihari, Vipin 107, 109-10, 116
    'Shadayantra' (conspiracy) 107, 109-10, 118, 122
bio-power 38
black market 194-95

208 INDEX

blazing heat scorches many saplings 171–72
bloody clashes 133
bodily decrepitude 144–45
Brechtian 110, 121–22
buffalo with three teats 27–50, 131
burden of debt 136, 157

Cane Cooperative Committee 74
Cane purchase Centre 72
'Can studies make a crow sprout peacock's wings' 113–15
Capra, La 172–73
  condition of incomprehensible pain 102
  traumatized soul 135
Cardona, M. 145–46, 177n.23
carrying the burden of family 195
caste configurations 110
Caste Identity, Branding and Expletives 112–13
caste of Power 42–43
casual Cruelty to Inhuman Punishment 113–15
casual leave slips ready and updated 116
chakbandi (land ceiling or land consolidating act) 8–9, 15, 38, 39, 52–53, 59–60, 61, 63–66
chakbandi courts 65–66
chakbandi hurt the small peasants 59–66
chamaroti (locality of Chamars) 54
Champaran and Kheda 6
changing equations in a village family 162
chaos of plans and programmes 178
Charles Dickens' repressive school scenario 109–10
Chemicals depleted the natural fertilizer of the soil 9–10
children from the subaltern groups 109–10
Choudhury, Prabhas Kumar 107–9
  'Pita' (Father) 107–9
circular migration 128–29
class/caste-elite relationship to the poor 105
closure of village cottage industries 130
coercive revenue collectors 4–5
collapse of peasant utopia 46
colonialism to elite nationalism 28–29
colourful charts and figures 170
complex universe of agrarian lives 21

compromised by financial entanglement 162–63
continued drought condition 133
cooperative shops or agencies withholding the grain, 156n.13
corruption and litigations 59–60
corruption and the politics and economics of development 188–89
corruption at many levels punches holes in the relief 153
counter claims on the lands of small landowners 59–60
corruption made development possible 188
Covid 19, 18, 106, 127
crop gets fatally pest infested 164
crops set on auction 32
cultivation of cane and paddy 70–71
curse of dowery and caste system 95

dabangs (lathi wielding goons, gun trotting musclemen) 59–60
dalit 144–45
dal-roti 143
daughter's *gouna* 87–88
daughter's wedding 167
death by starving or cardiac arrest 76
death from alcohol poisoning 43–44
'death row' 157–77
decaying tradition of indigenous industries 137
deficient infrastructure facilities and resources 110
deficient nutrition 144–45
deforestation 179, 184, 193, 194–95, 196n.4, 197n.13
  business of contract logging, auctioneering 183
  chaos of plans and programmes of development 178
  habitually regulated by a few principal players 180
  harmful impact of deforestation on air and water 192–93
  'Land Utilization Act', by the end of 1948 192
  mammoth-scale operations in logging 179

INDEX

'Money Grows on Trees' 20–21, 178–97
   timber smuggling 190–91
   lands we converted into money 192
delays and non-payment 15–16, 70–71
denied the red card on the pretext –old age, limping body 152–53
destiny of an ancient forest 187–88
development programmes 65–66
development projects 28, 178, 183–84
Devi, Mahasweta 118
dharma of a usurer 14–15
difficult to seek hearing, Sahib speaks English 79–81
digital classroom measures are unavailable 106
dignity of proper names –not be assigned to them 112
Dikshit, Damodar Dutta 39, 59–60, 61, 63, 70, 71–72, 73, 74, 80–81, 197n.10
   'Darwaje vala khet', (The Farm at the Door) 52–53, 59–60, 64
   'Under- weighment' 70, 71–72, 80–81
directionless life of the village youth 158
disabled in rural areas 145–46
disabled, aged, accident victims or afflicted with severe health issues 18
dismantling rural resources 127
disruption of self- contained rural resources 6
doctrines of Sarvodaya 8–9
documents of dubious ownership 59–60
doublethink in a welfare state 35–37
dowery demands 33
down to Earth 1, 81–82n.6
drift into criminal route 136–37
drought relief measures, a huge scam site 156n.13
drought, debt, daughter, disease 160–63
drowned in suffering 165
Durantaye, Leland de la 172–73
dysfunctional medical care 14–15

Eagleton Terry
   On Evil 102
early education of quality 106
earning outcomes are lowest in ailing states 107

Edelman, Marc 22–23n.3
elected women members of panchayat 83
elegiac obituary 107–8
embezzlement, smuggling 179
emigration to the gulf 136
environmental degradation 51–52
erratic rainfall, unseasonal hailstorm 159, 167
every day delay bleeds the farmer 74–75
every individual becomes a predator 186–87
eviction notices 51–52
exchange of manual labour for edibles 36
experts and intermediaries 35–37
extinction of both animals and trees 191

families headed by women 84–85
family battled with prolonged drought 145
family structure however strong-seemed let down 174
famine -poured from the sky 167
famine relief and the intermediaries 151–53
farmers have been committing suicide since ages 159–60
farmers of India, drowned in debt 4–5
farmers post- liberalization 168
farming households and weavers descending into poverty 137–38
farming of indigo 55
farming on lease 163–64
farming once an employment hub 129
Fasal Bima Yojana 2016 (Crops Insurance Plan) 10, 159–60
fault lines in the claims of development 178–79
Faustian bargain 53, 57
fear of losing-small landholding 80–81
   fear of the biggies 94–95
   fear of their dishonour' 99
   fear of police and the MLA 92–93
feel the cash in hand—distancing of youth from farming 93–94
feed of propaganda and toddy 30–32
   new land sharks in the form of on-sight managers 184
financial crunch forces 107
First five- year plan 59–60

210 INDEX

Five-year plan of the government of
    India 57–58
flash report: second highest teacher
    absenteeism 123n.4
flouting of moral economy 5, 76
folk custom of rural India 112
folk customs of appeasing rain gods 163
folk narratives of lands at stake 51–52
for *pardes* (foreign land) 133–35
forced to take loans 158–59
forcible auction of cash crops 5
foreign companies lure farmers 169
forest timber from the forestry
    department 184–85
forests made the playground of
    rogues 194–95
Foucault 59
four deaths made a news 152
fractured land, holding 1
frantic indulgence in echo-sadism 189
frenzied thrashing 113–14
funds allocated for the schools 109
fungus disease 164

Gandhi 4–5, 6, 24n.9
Gandhian principles 7–8
Gangetic belt 70–71
Gangetic belt-rich harvest 70–71
girl like the blossom of Gular 83, 96
global firms, spurious seeds and pesticides by
    private agents 169, 170
Good harvest do not always translate into
    money 70–71
government bank officials bring police for
    loan recovery 166–67
governmentality 14–15, 69n.20, 196n.8
government paddy centre 70–71
government relief 18–19, 143
gram panchayat 44
gram swaraj, a farce 11–12
grievous injury – a caste specific task, as a
    chamar 146–47
grossly inept education 158
guns and goons in the village scenario 133

hailstorm 167
'Hanka' 65–66

hardened wood took the shape and texture of
    ashta dhatu 189–90
Harris, White Barbara 37–38, 64–65
Hathras and Unnao 99
heavy downpour, many more saplings
    die 171–72
hidden transcript 68n.12
Hindi and Bhojpuri belt 127
Hindi belts of UP and Bihar 8–9
Hindi heartland 3
*Hindi Public Sphere 1920-1940: Language and
    Literature in the Age of Nationalism* 6–
    7, 25n.16
Hindu household perform varied
    ceremonies 33
historic times of 1980s and 1990s 109–10
historical and structural conditions of a rural
    township 1
huge population of non-cultivators 129
hunger and an injured disabled
    body 146–48
heavy downpour or drought
    conditions, the labourers are laid off
    indefinitely 145
indignity of hunger: the joys of a great
    feast 143–45
No job no money to buy food 145
rural life is difficult and really accident
    prone 145–46
the world's hungry people, farmers 143

idyllic serenity of rural life 28
If they study, they'll become *Bhasmasur* 116
illegal country liquor (tharra) 181–82
ill-fated stories 159
illiteracy 105
Illiteracy the biggest killer
    disease 123n.3, 123n.4
illiterate-trained to parrot
    statement 84–85
literate offenders defend their crimes 100
incursion of globalization 130
indefinitely shelved development
    programmes 158
India is progressing–a truism 83
India's farmer suicide narrative 157–58,
    162, 165

INDEX

Indian diaspora abroad 127
indifferent, heteromorphous subjectless that controls 59
Indira Gandhi, Garib Makan Yojana 89–90
inducement to the handlers 78
injustice becomes an accomplishment to be admired 102
insecurities threatening the farmers 70–71
in the service of augmenting mercenary designs 178–79
in the wake of lockdown 127
investment required for a successful crop 159

'Jahrili Bijlion ke Beech' (In the Midst of Poisonous Lights) 16–17, 83, 92
jamakhori (hoarding) 156n.13
Jaykaran, a scapegoat 152
Joshi, R. 145–46, 177n.23
'Jugaad' 61, 145, 153–55
   Pairavi and Jugaad 115–16
jurisdictionally acquired prerogative 187–88

Kamaleshwar 35–36
Kantak, Suresh,
   'Kisan kya Kare' (What can a farmer do) 70–71, 78–79, 80–81
Katha me Gaon 142n.8
Katha me Kisan 1–26, 160
Kaur, Banjot 81–82n.6
'Khadi me *Gaon* ki *Kashtiyan*' (Village Boats in the Gulf) 136
Kisan Credit Scheme 89–90
Kosi ke Us Par 142n.10
Krityansh, Omprakash 160
   'Pretchhaya' 160
Kumar, Dushyant 157
Kumar, Manjit and Shrivastava, Harishchandra 101

labyrinthine network of village politics 85–86
lack of toilet facilities 119–20
'Land Grab: The Dispossessed in the Spectacles of Jugaad' 70
land mafia 51–52
land profiteering 16–17

land reforms 8–9
land remains a covert, but contentious Issue 85–86
Land Utilization Act of 1947–49 192, 197n.12
land, declared *benami* 92–93
lands for public purposes 51–52
larger populace of the rural region, sickly, living in filth 180
largest diaspora in the history of Asia 127
legend of Chelik 55
Lekhpal (village accountant, munshi) 62–63, 86, 87–88, 89
'Let us depart for good' 157
lingering effect of trauma 162–63
literate offenders defend their crime 100
lives hostage to anonymity 139–40
living wages for the agriculture workers 154–55
local arrangers and state appointed agencies 70–71
logging in the forest village 20–21
logical heir to elite nationalism, the progeny of messy policies 35–36
losing land to money lender–the oldest story 51–52
Ludden, David 39–40, 141n.3
   late nineteenth century transition to capitalism 141n.3

mahadalit musahar 145, 149, 156n.7
Maiku's travails of wait 72–73
Maila Aanchal (Soiled Border) 27–28
male-centric rural mores 84
Mandal Commission report was constitutionally endorsed 109–10
mango kernel and field rats 150–51
Mani, Prem Kumar 153–55
   'Jugaad' 153–55
manipulate school inspection 115–16
manipulating provisions of law 61–63
Manoj, Amit 26n.25
   '*Bhumika*' (A short Introduction to *Katha me Kisan*, Part 1) 26n.25
manual for cultivating the white muesli 171–72
margin of subsistence 128–29

212 INDEX

Markandeya 39, 52–53, 57
   'Bhudan' (Land Gift) 52–53, 57
   'Doune ki Pattiyan' (the Leaf Plate) 52–53
marker of rural urban divide 122
Markovits, Claude 4–5
mass diversion of government funds 28
mass unrest of peasantry 6
mass wedding of girls from poor families 94–96
meal of mice and the dead cow 143–56
measures of land reforms 59–60
measures to empower women 83
mechanics of Panchayat body 85
messy legal battles 59–60
methods of conventional agriculture 129
methods of extortion 32
middlemen, grocers and dealers 78–79
middle poor and middle- middle class 178
migrant subculture in the cities 128–29
migration is the only option 129
   circular migration 128–29
   margin of subsistence 128–29
   non-cultivators, associated with farming, buckled under pressure 129
mind boggling world of multinationals—tall tales of profit 172–73
minimum support price—never paid 80–81
MLA (Member of Legislative Assembly) 88, 89, 91, 92
mob lynching 148
Mohan, Madan 16–17, 100–1
moneylenders –closing in 164
money-not paid in due instalment 166–67
moral economy 5, 51, 53, 55–56, 66–67
mother sister abuses and brutal thrashing 32, 112
much applauded globalization 174
mukti (deliverance) 160, 169
multinational company 170, 171
Murari's unkempt, sweaty attire 80

narratives dealing with peasantry 1, 3
nationalistic and patriotic slogans 36–37
Naxal 57, 99, 121–22
Naxal militia 119
neither rural nor urban 178

nepotism, cut/commission 179–80
new class of rich: progenies of parasitism 100–2
parasitism 84, 100–2, 104n.14
Nibber, Gurupreet Singh 136
Nixon, Rob 194–95
non-cultivators, associated with farming, buckled under pressure 129
none even gives to crying openly 132
nonpayment strengthens the stranglehold of usurers 80–81
nonviolent Gandhian struggle for injustice 94
nothing wrong in eating a dead cow 147–48
notices to defaulting householders for recovery 34
not programmed to deal with subsistence issues 158

one in four farmers driven to suicide has been under 30, 177n.19
opium addiction 160–61, 176n.10
ordeal grows multiple -when marketing the produce 70–71
Orsini, Francesca 6–7
   Hindi Magazines 6–7
   Journalistic Writings of 1920s and 1930s 6–7
Orwell 14–15, 27–28, 29–30, 31–32, 35–37, 43–44, 45–46, 106
   Orwell's *1984* 31–32, 46, 106
   Squealer in *Animal Farm* 36–37
outbreak of famine 163
ownership is the basic need 51

paddy sale centre 78, 80
Pairavi, jugaad 115–16
panchayat and Pradhan 124n.10
   display of clout and deal-making 84–85
   illiterate people are trained to parrot statements 84–85
   panchayat as the hub of corruption and political hobnobbing 85
Pandey, Ganesh 65–66, 101, 123n.3
   Aathhaven Dashak ki Kahaniyon me Gramin Jeevan (Rural life in the stories of the 1980s) 83–104, 123n.3

INDEX 213

Panjab, to join the work as a labourer 142n.13
passengers in the company of goats and hens 180
patta (lawfully valid papers of land ownership) 100
pawned the jewelry of Janaki 164
paying the burden of father's debts 160–61
peasant lives matter 172–73
peasant's resistance 55–56
peasants, targets of the indignity of vasectomy 29–39
pending court hearings 65–66
people with disabilities languish across rural India 145–46
perform a *murga* 114
performing devotional rituals 165
performing ritual of obedience 55
period of Emergency (1975- 1977) 38–39, 48–49n.22
persuasive tactics of marketing and profiteering 169
pesticides for paddy farming 167
pesticides and insecticides for self- poisoning, readily available method of suicide 22, 177n.19
Phansalkar, Sanjiv 145–46
   'People with Disabilities (PWD) Languish across Rural India: Neglected Lives' 145–46
planning commission 2012 59–60
plans initiated by the ministries, experts and the outsourced 179
plough and oxen–now rendered useless 131
plunder in the name of development 179
plundering the government funds 88
poaching timber with the connivance of forest officials and the stakeholders 189
police action 79
police extortion 165–66
policies of rate fixing and unfixing 71–72
politically strategic means of absolving the perpetrators 86
politician pushed forward the example 182–83
poor access to health care services 128–29

poor peasants, target of the indignity of vasectomy S 27–50
poor, aged and disabled 143–44
popular slogans and programmes 109
population dependent on *anganwadi* network-for pre-primary education 106
post independent rural India 7–9
post-mandal 119
Pradhan 84–85, 86, 88, 89, 91, 92–93, 94
Pradhanji 94–99
Prakash Gyan 109
Prashad, Vijay 154
Precarious world of migrant labourers 133–35
predators of drought 163–64
prejudice against physically challenged 148
Premchand 4–7, 45–46, 128–29, 143–45
   Godan 4–5, 6, 7–8, 29–30, 31, 32, 33–34, 38, 39–40, 41, 42–43, 46, 127–42
   'Kafan' 143–45
   Karmabhoomi 4–5
   'Poos ki Raat' (Winters' night) 30–31, 41, 72
   Premashram 4–5, 24n.13, 36
Premchand to Shrilal Shukla 29–30
Premchand's Hori 27–28, 29–30, 71–72
Premchand's journalistic analysis 6
primary and middle level schools in Bihar and Uttar Pradesh 110
probe report 120–21
probe study, 48 percent of government schools have no teaching activity 114–15
process of going wrong –catalyzed since the 1970s 109
procurement price 1
produce from the harvest 133
profiteering 59–60
project of canal building 57–58
prolefeed 31–32, 33–34, 43–44, 45–46
proles are natural inferiors 105
promise of quick money 157–77
Punarvasu, Purva, Hathiya 133n.12

rabi, kharif 1
Rai, Viveki 52–53, 65–66
   'Tarikhen' (Dates) 65–66

INDEX

Ramlila 36
rampant agrarian crisis 4–5
Rawls, John 102
reasons of failing education mission 107
recurring crop failure 159
red card was withheld 151–53
red flag instigated, but failed to help 149–50
red flag party 149–50
refashioning the art of money laundering 190–91
regions of Hindi belt 83
regulations sanctioned by the colonial governance 4–5
relief announced, but on the paper 164
relief camp—outrageous joke 167
relying for subsistence on farming 159
remote sounds of *dhol, majira* 132
Renu, Phanishwar Nath 27–28
    Maila Aanchal (Soiled Border) 27–28
reservation 109
reserved category 49n.26
resistance to Indigo Planting 55–57
    disguised resistance 55–56
rich remittances 136
Right to education act 107, 109
Right to Education Act will merely guarantee schooling, not education 118
Rise of Hindi 3
rise of Ranveer Sena (1994-2000) 119
rising cost of fertilizers, irrigation and seeds 87–88
ritual of punishment 148
role of a fixer, facilitator 36–37
romantic view of village 28
rural boys led stray 140
rural economic conditions 4–5
rural economy 178–79
rural health care 28
rural indebtedness 1, 10–11
rural India was let down by the newly independent democratic state 107–8
rural labour market 144–45
rural landless 143, 144–45
rural life, accident prone 145–46
rural poor continue to remain poor and uneducated 105–26
rural schools in Hindi belt 122
rural-urban 178–79
rural-urban politics 179
rural women 16–17

Sahai, Suman 70–71, 74–75, 77–78
'Sahib has no patience for nonsense' 63–64
Sainath P. 13–14, 31–32, 33, 37–38, 43–44, 51–52, 66–67, 105, 110–11, 127, 152–53, 157, 178, 179, 181, 190–91, 193
    Everybody loves a good drought 106, 152–53
    'Here we go to the school' 105–26
    'And Silent Trees Speak' 195n.1
    'Swelling register of deaths' 157
    teesra fasl (third crop) 153
Sant Vinoba 54, 57
sarkar (state) in Hori's world 35–36
scheduled caste and tribe 111
school dropouts in rural areas are high 106
school master cum aspiring leader 94–95, 97–98
Scott C. James 2–3, 4–5, 51, 55–56, 61, 66–67
SDM (Subdivisional Magistrate) 63
seasonal migrants 128–29
seed capital and more network 190–91
several hundred crores on training teachers 113
severe deficit of guidance 106
severe indictment of marketing and profiteering 169
sexual expletives 96–98
shadow state for the accumulative projects of local capitalist cases 64–65
shadow state 37–38, 64–65
Sharma, Subhash 144–45, 149, 153, 154
    'Bhookh' (Hunger) 144–45, 149, 153, 154–55
shift from traditional farming to the farming of high yielding commercial crops 169
shishya of the Swami 181–82
Shivmurti 83, 94, 95–96, 97, 98
    Kasaibada' (Butcher house) 16–17, 83, 99
    underbelly of rural life in '*Kasaibada*' 94–96
Shukla, Girija Gaurav 106
Shukla, Shrilal 8–9, 27–28, 31–32, 33–34, 39–40, 45–46, 70–82

INDEX

Bisrampur ka Sant 8–9
'Hori aur 1984' (Hori and 1984) 14–15, 29–30, 38, 39–40
Hori, the iconic small peasant 14–15
Jahalat ke Pachas Saal (Fifty Years of Stupidity) 20–21, 27–28, 29, 37–38, 178, 182–83
Jeevan hi Jeevan 191–92
1984 14–15, 27–28, 33–34, 35–36
'Pahali Chook' (First Mistake) 27–28, 29
Raag Darbari 14–15, 17–18, 39–40, 102, 129
'Swarna Varsha' (Golden Rain) 27–28
'Umraonagar me Kuchch Din' (Several days in Umraonagar) 20–21, 178–79, 193–94, 195
sikmi land 68n.9
Singh, Anant 144–45, 146, 147–48
'Bhookh' (Hunger) 144–45, 146, 148, 153, 154–55
Singh, Punni 130, 132, 133, 160, 169
'Mansa Badai' (Mansa Carpenter) 130
'Mukti' 160, 163, 169, 170
siphoning of millions of pounds of aid for education, under *Sarva Shikhsha Abhiyan* 107
slighting and bullying 113
slow violence, calamities—slow but long lasting 194–95
small peasantry 4–5, 15, 27–28, 43
small, middle level, landless peasants 1
snare of moneylending 33
special connect with the police 98–99
specialist in fire-arms 132
spectrum of cultural and political information 83
speedier destruction of environment 179
speeding buses and trucks kill with impunity 149
spirit of mother India in the rural world 6–7
starving in parched Fields 149
state education in UP and Bihar 107
state of indebted peasant 32
state of private buses 180
state run storage; the grain was rotting 152
stealing and skimming 188
story of development 93–94

story of rice pounding woman and her son 134–35
straddling country and the city 130–31
stupidity allowed the fraudulent medical practices to make money 180
subalternity of Indian rural population 6–7
Subramanian, Giridhar 105–26
subsistence of peasantry 4–5
suburban forest village 179
Sudhakar, Salil 136, 137, 138, 139–40
'Khari mein Gaon ki Kashtiyan' (Village Boats in the Gulf) 136
Sugar mill owners owe more than Rs. 23270 crores to the farmers 70–82
suicidal thoughts 169
Sukumar, Surendra 52–53
'Hanka' 65–66
surplus land in phony names 61

technology of tube well and tractors 131
Thakur Sahib and Iqbal Miya –the champions of development 185
the bowl of sugarcane farming 71–72
there was no toilet 111
Thompson E.P 24n.13, 68n.9
Thompson Reuter Foundation News 155n.1
threat of displacement 51–52
thumbprint acquired with stamp 89–90
tolerance of high level of inequality 27–28
topography of a village in UP 87
touts and fixers 33–34
trafficking of young brides 94–95
transaction of cane and paddy, dittoed the colonial system 71
transition from colonialism to elite nationalism 30
Tumbe, Chinmay 127–28, 153
Families from Bhojpuri belt of Bihar 136
'Migration and Development' 141n.4
two traditionally rioting communities, Hindu and Muslim 182–83

Umraonagar, a scarred victim of slow violence 194–95
ancient forest almost belonging to the hoary past of *Treta Yug* 189–90, 197n.9
princely state, Umraonagar 184

unable to quit farming 157
unchecked serial violence 29
underhand connection 71–72
unequal education 105
unorganized sector, the mechanism of surplus appropriation 45
unpaid debt 133
unseasonal heavy downpour 144
UP and Bihar 3, 7–9, 11–12, 18–19, 104n.10, 104n.18, 112, 128–29, 197n.10
    1960-1980 in UP, India 178–79
usury renders them refugees in their own lands 32, 33

vagaries of weather 18, 145, 163–64, 174
Vanavasi, Kailash 160
    'Prakop'(calamity) 160, 163–64
    'Van Samitis and Vanishing Trees' 196n.4
Vijaykant 52–53, 57
    armed struggle against the rich land owners 57
    'Beech ka Samar' (War in the Middle) 57
village administration 77–78
village *sahukar* (grocer) allotted the charge of government grocery 151
village school in debris 110–11
villages as romantic or revolutionary 102
vocabulary of knowledge 37–38

warped circle of share 134
Wedding of daughters 4–5
wedding, death of a near one, or of cattle 159
who wants to learn and to teach 125n.14

women and the village administration 84–85
    female illiteracy–exacerbating their crisis 84
women's land rights 85–86
Women in Peasantry 83
    customary law assigns property rights to men 85–86
    incredible violence perpetrated upon the soul of women 102
    No FIR at the Police station 96–98
    rapes and murders of *dalit* women 83–84
    trafficked into prostitution 86
    triple jeopardy, being *Dalit*, uneducated, and poor 83–84
    'a woman is fasting to retrieve her land' 92–93
    worst casualties in caste- clashes, sexual assaults, human trafficking 83–84
women under the precincts of ashram 179–80
working in MNREGA (Mahatma Gandhi, National Rural Employment Act) 87–88
work is seasonal but hunger is not 143
Worster, Donald 195
worthlessness in the village youth 137
wrongs since the foundation of New India 107–10

yearly battle with crops 1

Zamindar 5, 47, 101, 192

The manufacturer's authorised representative in the EU for product safety is
Oxford University Press España S.A. of el Parque Empresarial San Fernando de
Henares, Avenida de Castilla, 2 – 28830 Madrid (www.oup.es/en or product.
safety@oup.com). OUP España S.A. also acts as importer into Spain of products
made by the manufacturer.

www.ingramcontent.com/pod-product-compliance
Lightning Source LLC
Chambersburg PA
CBHW071833290825
31867CB00003B/121